Literature-Based Activities for Integrating Mathematics with Other Content Areas, Grades 3–5

Robin A. Ward

RICE UNIVERSITY

Boston New York San Francisco
Mexico City Montreal Toronto London Madrid Munich Paris
Hong Kong Singapore Tokyo Cape Town Sydney

Series Editor: Kelly Villella Canton
Series Editorial Assistant: Christine Pratt Swayne
Marketing Manager: Danae April
Production Editor: Paula Carroll
Editorial Production Service: Kathy Smith Editorial Production
Composition Buyer: Linda Cox
Manufacturing Buyer: Linda Morris
Interior Design and Composition Services: Schneck-DePippo Graphics
Cover Administrator: Linda Knowles
Cover Designer: Elena Sidorova
Director of Professional Development: Alison Maloney

For related titles and support materials, visit our online catalog at www.ablongman.com.

Between the time website information is gathered and then published, it is not unusual for some sites to have closed. Also, the transcription of URLs can result in typographical errors. The publisher would appreciate notification where these errors occur so that they may be corrected in subsequent editions.

Cataloging in Publication Data on file at the Library of Congress

ISBN–13:   978-0-205-51409-0
ISBN–10:   0-205-51409-X

Printed in the United States of America

10 9 8 7 6 5 4 3 2 1   11 10 09 08

Allyn & Bacon
is an imprint of

PEARSON   www.pearsonhighered.com

Contents

CHAPTER

2

Literature-Based Mathematics and Social Studies Activities   69

CHAPTER **3**

Literature-Based Mathematics and Visual Arts Activities *133*

About the Author

After earning a Bachelor's degree in math/physics from Immaculata College and a Master's of Arts degree in mathematics from Villanova University, Robin worked as an aerospace engineer and systems programmer. Prompted by a growing interest in teaching mathematics she pursued a PhD in mathematics education from the University of Virginia. Since graduating with her doctorate, Robin has spent ten years working as a professor of mathematics education at California Polytechnic State University and the University of Arizona. A devoted mathematics teacher educator, she sought and received numerous grants from NASA, NSF, and the U.S. Department of Education, all geared toward improving K–12 teachers' mathematical and pedagogical knowledge. A two-time recipient of a Stanford-ASEE fellowship, she partnered with the NASA Dryden Flight Research Center to develop web-based materials for K–12 teachers that showcase the work of NASA scientists. In 2005, the University of Arizona's College of Education bestowed upon her the Outstanding Teaching Award. Robin has written numerous articles and has presented many professional development workshops and talks at national conferences on improving mathematics pedagogy and using children's literature to enhance the teaching and learning of K–8 mathematics.

Robin lives in Houston with her husband, Chris DelConte, and two young daughters, Sienna and Sophia Arabella. There she pursues her passion for improving K–12 teachers' mathematical and pedagogical knowledge as the Associate Director of Curriculum Integration at the Rice University School Mathematics Project. In addition, she gives professional development workshops for local teachers and integrated mathematics-art classes for Pre-Kindergarten–Grade 8 students.

Acknowledgments

I would like to thank the many elementary and middle school teachers whose ideas served as the basis for many of the integrated activities included in this book. I also thank my former students who allowed me to use the classroom as a laboratory for my ideas on how to integrate children's literature into the teaching and learning of mathematics. Their active participation in literature-based classroom activities and their candid responses shared in their reflections assisted me in formulating and fine-tuning many of the ideas presented in this book.

Also, I'd like to acknowledge and thank Dawn Corso, my dear friend and colleague, for her insight and spirited efforts during the initial design phases of this book.

I am also grateful for the thoughtful comments and feedback on this book series from the reviewers lined up by Allyn and Bacon: Tammy Brown, Denver Public Schools; Karen Caldwell, John Early Paideia Middle School; Linda Cole, Barrie School; Bethany Dannelly, Hampton Roads Academy; Amanda Guinn, Monroe County Community Schools-University School; Cheri Howard, Fairbanks North Star Borough School District; Tim Linnet, Maywood Middle School; Kris O'Clair, Denver Public Schools; Lorel Preston, Westminster College; E. Elaine Rafferty, Charleston County School District; Ellen Szecsy, Math Consultant; Alexandra Thompson, Devon Elementary School; Karen Ward, Centennial Middle School.

Thank you to my other friends and colleagues spread far and wide, who supported me in a variety of immeasurable ways during this book endeavor and who continue to inspire me, namely, Gina Bernitt, Michelle Bickman, Andy Chan, Elaine Chin, Winnie Doyle, Shirley Fisher, Gassia Gerges, Mary

Beth Gilbert, Therese Grahn, my friends at JMH, Cynthia Johnson, Ingrid Johnson, the Kinerk family, Lori Levitt, the Livengood family, Michelle Lozano, Nicole O'Fiesh, Sheryl O'Neill, Diana Perdue, Patricia Reedy-Deserio, Gazala Siddiqui, Sheila Tobias, and Fred and Nancy Utter.

Finally, a huge thank you to my husband, parents, family, and two daughters. Sienna and Sophia Arabella, Mommy is all done!

Literature-Based Activities for Integrating Mathematics with Other Content Areas, Grades 3–5

Introduction

Reading in the mathematics classrooms? Absolutely! Integrating children's literature into the teaching and learning of mathematics, however, is more than just reading a book to students. By exploring picture books and reading works of fiction, nonfiction, and poetry, students can engage in worthwhile and stimulating mathematical activities that encourage them to communicate their ideas verbally or through drawing or writing. In short, mathematics can be viewed as "a vehicle for thinking, a medium for creating, and a language for communicating" (Kleiman, 1991, p. 48). In addition, using children's literature requires students to listen and comprehend—two vital skills needed for academic success. Thus, the goal of integrating children's literature into the teaching and learning of mathematics is to improve the overall literacy of students.

Using Children's Literature to Teach Mathematics

Integrating children's literature into the teaching and learning of mathematics is gaining momentum. In fact, a growing body of research and anecdotal evidence documents the potential and power of using children's literature in mathematics classrooms (Avery & Avery, 2001; Burns, 1995; Burns & Sheffield, 2004; Capraro & Capraro, 2006; Carr, Buchanan, Wentz, Weiss, & Brant, 2001; Draper, 2002; Hellwig, Monroe, & Jacobs, 2000; Hunsader, 2004; Johnson & Giorgis, 2001; Leitze, 1997; Leu, Castek, Henry, Coiro, & McMullan, 2004; MacGregor & Price, 1999; Monroe & Livingston, 2002; Moyer, 2000; Schiro,

1997; Ward, 2003, 2004a, 2004b, 2004c, 2005, 2006a, 2006b; Ward & Muller, 2006; Whitin & Whitin, 1996, 2004; Whitin & Wilde, 1992, 1995; Young, 2001). Because many mathematical ideas and concepts are abstract or symbolic in nature, children's literature offers teachers the opportunity to present and discuss these ideas and concepts within the context of a story, using illustrations, prose, and more informal, familiar language. This, in turn, can make the learning of mathematics less intimidating and more engaging, especially for students whose first language is not English. Further, using children's literature to teach mathematics provides students with additional opportunities, encouragement, and support for speaking, writing, reading, and listening in mathematics classes.

Johnson & Giorgis (2001) posit that interacting with children's literature "encourages delight, nurtures curiosity and wonderment, and invites readers to discover things never experienced before" (p. 204). Additionally, shapes can be more readily understood through clear visuals in picture books, while number relationships can spark new interests when the facts are incorporated into fiction, poetry, and visually enticing illustrations. Because children's literature can be used to initiate a discussion on a social issue, introduce a theme, trigger a round of creative writing, or strengthen an appreciation for poetry, even secondary teachers are discovering the therapeutic and instructional value of this genre (Avery & Avery, 2001). In fact, it has been noted that picture books used in the mathematics and science curricula that relate content to the real world are beneficial for students' understanding of specific concepts and may encourage them to seek a career in the sciences (Carr et al., 2001). Additionally, many pieces of children's literature can be appreciated at different grade levels and can provide strategic opportunities for students to engage in problem solving.

Many national educational organizations, such as the National Council of Teachers of Mathematics (NCTM), the National Council of Teachers of English (NCTE), and the International Reading Association (IRA) also advocate that preK–8 mathematics teachers regularly integrate children's literature into their teaching because of its many benefits. For example, in its *Principles and Standards for School Mathematics* (NCTM, 2000), NCTM asserts that "students who have opportunities, encouragement, and support for speaking, writing, reading, and listening in mathematics classes reap dual benefits: they communicate to learn mathematics, and they learn to communicate mathematically" (p. 60). NCTE (1996), noted for its history of commitment to the teaching of literature in connection with the teaching of reading and English/language arts, advocates the extensive use of children's and adolescent's literature throughout the reading and writing curriculum and as a valuable source in content-area studies. The NCTE further endorses preparing and certifying teachers with strong content and pedagogical knowledge of children's and/or adolescent's literature. Finally, in its position statement, IRA (2006) recognizes excellent reading teachers as those who are familiar with children's literature and who include a wide variety of fiction and nonfiction genres (such as storybooks, novels, and biographies) in their teaching.

Teaching Using an Integrated Approach

Gaining equal momentum is the movement by preK–8 teachers to integrate their teaching across content areas with the goal of building connections between and among the various subject matters taught in school. Organizations such as NCTM, the National Council for the Social Studies (NCSS), the National Research Council (NRC), and the Music Educators National Conference (MENC) support an integrated approach to teaching. For example, in its *Curriculum Standards for the Social Studies,* NCSS (1994) states that "a social studies perspective is academically sound, multidisciplinary, and integrative" (pp. xvii–xviii). The *National Science Education Standards* (NRC, 1996) offer that "school science and mathematics programs should be coordinated so that students learn the necessary mathematical skills and concepts before and during their use in the science program" (p. 214). Similarly, MENC (1994) has identified as its goal for the *National Standards for Arts Education* to "help students make connections between concepts and across subjects," as the learning tasks defined by these standards serve as "bridges among the arts disciplines, and finally as gateways from the arts to other areas of study" (p. 13). NCTM (2000) echoes these same sentiments and advocates that students' mathematical experiences at all levels include opportunities for connections to other subject areas and disciplines, especially because mathematics permeates music and art content, and is used in science, the social studies, and other fields of study. Finally, the National Middle School Association (NMSA, 1995) argues that the school curriculum needs to be integrative in order to help young adolescents make sense out of their life experiences and connect school experiences to their daily lives outside of the classroom.

The benefits of an integrated curriculum, which recognizes that the subjects within the curriculum are connected to each other and to the real world, have been noted by several educational philosophers, curriculum theorists, and others (Beane, 1993, 1995, 1997; Bruner, 1977; Dewey, 1924, 1933; Drake & Burns, 2004; Gelineau, 2003; Howey, 1996; Jacobs, 1989; Kim, Andrews, & Carr, 2004; McDonald & Fisher, 2006; Schwartz & Pollishuke, 2005; Vars, 1997; Wortham, 1996). Beane (1997) notes that for many students, the separate subject approach offers a "disconnected and incoherent assortment of facts and skills. There is no unity, no real sense to it all" (p. 42). Gardner (1997) also recognizes that students need to explicitly see connections and nonconnections between domains of knowledge, or else generalization and transfer will not occur. Beane (1993, 1995, 1997) as well as others (Jacobs, 1989; Vars, 1997) advocate for integrated curriculum models because they center on the problems and interests of young adolescent learners and serve as a valuable lens for understanding student thinking (Perkins, 1989). According to Wortham (1996), "An integrated curriculum crosses subject areas. . . . [T]he intent is to construct meaningful bridges to show connections in development and learning" (p. 330). Thus, curriculum integration is often achieved through the design of integrated thematic units or through the study of a topic.

A growing body of literature continues to document the effectiveness of integrated curriculum on student achievement (Arhar, 1997; Cornett, 2003; Davies, 1992; Drake, 1998; Drake & Burns, 2004; National Association for Core Curriculum, 2000; Vars 1996, 1997; Vars & Beane, 2000; Watts, 2004) and its ability to increase student motivation, elicit higher order thinking, and build stronger interpersonal skills (Vars, 1997). Several scholars argue that an integrated curriculum is warranted, as a truly integrated curriculum enables teachers and their students to make connections between real life and their classroom learning experiences (Bailey, 2000; Caskey, 2001; Caskey & Johnston, 1986). Further, an integrated curriculum engages teachers, stimulates students, and energizes classroom learning environments (Meinbach, Fredericks, & Rothlein, 2000).

Using Children's Literature Combined with an Integrated Approach to Teaching

Given that more and more teachers are turning to children's literature as a means to enliven and demystify the study of mathematics, and given that teachers are striving to build rich connections for students by using an integrated approach to teaching, this book was written to address these two merging efforts. This book series is divided into three volumes for the following grade bands: K–2, 3–5, and 6–8. Within each of these grade-specific volumes are three chapters of classroom-tested activities. The first chapter in each series articulates literature-based activities that integrate mathematics and science; Chapter 2 contains literature-based activities that integrate mathematics and the social studies; and Chapter 3 describes literature-based activities that integrate mathematics and the visual arts.

Each of the chapters opens with a brief overview, articulating the connection between mathematics and the specific content area (whether it be science, social studies, or the visual arts), followed by a list of the concepts and skills featured in the literature-based activities. A matrix follows, which lists each piece of children's literature used in that chapter's integrated activities, and which identifies other relevant cross-curricular concepts and skills. The collection of literature-based activities follows next.

Featured in many of the literature-based activities in this book are book pairs and, in some cases, book trios: that is, two or three pieces of children's literature that work powerfully together when teaching an integrated lesson. Also, several biographies are featured as well as works of nonfiction and poetry.

The format of each activity is as follows:

Book title (along with the name(s) of the author(s), publisher, and ISBN number)

Overview of Book (brief overview of the story line of each book or poem featured in the activities)

Mathematical Concepts and Skills (list of the mathematical concepts and skills serving as the focus of the activities)

Content-Area Concepts and Skills (list of the content-area concepts and skills serving as the focus of the activities)

Overview of Activities (brief description of the activities to follow)

National Mathematics Standards (mathematical expectations of students as defined by NCTM)

National Standards for the Content Area (content-area expectations of students as defined by NRC, NCSS, or MENC)

Materials (list of necessary materials)

Description of Activities (step-by-step procedure describing how to implement the literature-based activities)

Assessment (considerations and questions to ask when assessing student understanding of the concepts and skills presented in activities; see the appendix for more assessment ideas and rubrics)

Activity Extensions (description of potential follow-up activities)

Cross-Curricular Connections (brief description of related, follow-up activities for other content areas)

Related Children's Literature (list of other pieces of children's literature that feature the same or similar concepts and skills presented in the activities)

Related Instructional Resources (list of resources useful to the teacher)

Related Websites (list of websites pertinent to the concepts and skills presented in the activities)

Worksheets/Handouts (if applicable)

Located at the end of the book is an extensive bibliography of over three hundred pieces of children's literature cited throughout this book as well as over one hundred citations of instructional resources that will support the teacher. Additionally, an appendix includes several assessment tools and rubrics useful in evaluating students' performance, skills, and abilities as they engage in the literature-based activities.

Finally, a word of advice: Prior to implementing the integrated, literature-based explorations articulated in this book, read through the entire activity *before* class to assess whether you need to modify or delete any steps in the activities due to student accommodations, lack or substitution of materials, limited resources or space, prior preparation of materials, or other reasons. Do not feel as though these activities are scripted! Use your judgment and pedagogical ingenuity to take tangents as deemed appropriate and to capitalize on those teachable moments. The ultimate goal is to maximize student understanding and to make the teaching and learning of mathematics and the other content areas come to life.

The author hopes that the interdisciplinary, literature-based activities presented in this book will provide readers with the information, resources, and confidence to make the teaching and exploration of mathematics, science, social studies, and the visual arts more meaningful, cohesive, interactive, and exciting to learners.

Helpful Hints

For teachers who are incorporating children's literature into their teaching for the first time, consider these suggestions:

- Situate your audience so that all students can clearly hear you and easily see the pages and illustrations during the read-aloud of each book.

- Take time to stop and allow students to ask questions about the text or illustrations in the book. Take advantage of those teachable moments when insightful questions are asked!

- Read each piece of children's literature in its entirety *prior* to implementing the accompanying activities so that you are familiar with the story line and so you can anticipate questions from students.

- In some of the activities featured in this book, the author suggests that only excerpts from a piece of children's literature be read. If, depending on your audience, you deem it appropriate to read the book in its entirety, then do so. You know your students best.

- Maintain each piece of children's literature that you use in the classroom library, allowing students access to the book should they want to view it later.

Regarding Assessment

Toward the end of each activity in this book, several questions are included under the heading, Assessment. Consider posing these questions as a means to assess students' understanding of the concepts and mastery of the skills presented in each of the literature-based activities. NCTM (1989, 2000) advocates that student assessment be integral to instruction, that teachers use multiple means of assessment, and that all aspects of mathematical knowledge (e.g., confidence, attitude, problem-solving abilities) be assessed. Examples of multiple means of assessment include observations, interviews and questions, student journal entries, portfolios, student self-evaluations, and peer evaluations.

Included in the appendix are several assessment tools and rubrics a teacher might employ as a means to better assess students as they engage in the literature-based activities. Other helpful assessment resources are included at the end of this book in the Assessment Resources section.

1

Literature-Based Mathematics and Science Activities

The Mathematics-Science Connection

Science encompasses many domains including life science, physical science, and earth and space science. It can be described as the study and exploration of our world, our universe, our environment, and other phenomena. In studying science, students should not memorize facts but, instead, be encouraged to think, observe, hypothesize, reason, communicate, and problem-solve, activities NCTM (1989, 2000) and NRC (1996) strongly advocate. Recognizing the interplay between mathematics and science, the German mathematician Carl Gauss once stated that "mathematics is the Queen of the Sciences." Given the strong interconnectedness between mathematics and science, a mounting movement continues to support the integration of mathematics and science in the classroom curriculum (Basista & Mathews, 2002; Cobb, 2000;

Johnson & Giorgis, 2001, Kaser, 2001; Moyer, 2000; Putnam & Borko, 2000; Roth & McGinn, 1998). One of the best ways for young learners to increase their knowledge and understanding of their world to make sense out of nature's sometimes complicated phenomena and today's advanced technological society is to integrate children's literature into the study of science and mathematics.

This chapter articulates a variety of literature-based activities that integrate concepts and skills used and learned in the study of mathematics with those in science. While engaged in these activities, students will discover and gain practice with such mathematics concepts and skills as integers, addition of positive and negative numbers, fractions, decimals, ratio, proportional reasoning (Number and Operations Standard); pattern recognition (Algebra Standard); symmetry, shapes (Geometry Standard); size, scale, proportion (Measurement Standard); and sorting, classification, data collection and interpretation, graphing, Venn diagrams, bar graphs, pie charts, line graphs (Data Analysis and Probability Standard).

> "Children's literature can help young learners make sense out of nature and today's advanced technological society."

Science concepts and skills featured in this chapter include scientific inquiry (Science as Inquiry, Content Standard A); electricity, light, positive and negative charges, wind, weather, aerodynamics of flight (Physical Science, Content Standard B); life cycles and characteristics of organisms, animal habitats, animal classification (Life Science, Content Standard C); the moon, moon phases, movement of the moon in the sky, relative size of the planets, the solar system (Earth and Space Science, Content Standard D); understanding about science and technology (Science and Technology, Content Standard E); personal health, food pyramid, nutrients, food groups (Science in Personal and Social Perspectives, Content Standard F); and science as a human endeavor (History and Nature of Science, Content Standard G).

The integrated literature-based activities also provide students with many opportunities to predict, estimate, problem-solve, and reason (Problem Solving and Reasoning and Proof Standards) as well as communicate and use various representations to organize, record, model, and interpret mathematical ideas (Communication and Representation Standards). Further, students will discover and explore real-life applications of mathematics and science and careers in mathematics and science (Connections Standard).

Remember to check the appendix for ideas and samples of assessment ideas and rubrics.

Matrix of Mathematics and Science Activities

BOOK TITLE	MATHEMATICAL CONCEPTS AND SKILLS	SCIENCE CONCEPTS AND SKILLS	SOCIAL STUDIES CONCEPTS AND SKILLS	VISUAL ARTS CONCEPTS AND SKILLS
"Zebra Question" (a poem in *A Light in the Attic*); *My Light*	number line, positive and negative numbers, integers, addition of positive and negative numbers	electricity, light, positive and negative charges	alternate sources of power, exploration of a biographical piece	artists' renditions of light and electricity, positive and negative images
"The Planet of Mars" (a poem in *Where the Sidewalk Ends*); *The Planets in Our Solar System*	fractions, decimals, measurement, ratio, size and scale, estimation	relative size of the planets, planets in the solar system	exploration of a biographical piece	artists' renditions of the night sky, space, or solar system
Wild Fibonacci: Nature's Secret Code Revealed	patterns, pattern recognition, prediction	characteristics of organisms, scientific inquiry	exploration of a biographical piece, patterns in population growth	golden mean in architecture, artists who have used the golden mean
"Strange Wind" (a poem in *A Light in the Attic*); *Let's Fly a Kite*	line symmetry attributes of quadrilaterals (kites)	wind, aerodynamics of flight	cultural history of kites, exploration of a biographical piece, fallout and implications of historic hurricanes and tornadoes	artists' renditions of windy scenes
"Me and My Giant" (a poem in *Where the Sidewalk Ends*); *Beanstalk: The Measure of a Giant*	measurement, ratio, proportional reasoning, data collection and interpretation, line graphs, estimation	life cycles of organisms, scientific inquiry	mapping of grasslands, jungles, rain forests; exploration of a biographical piece on Johnny Appleseed	van Gogh's renditions of trees
If You Hopped Like a Frog	measurement, size and scale, ratio, proportional reasoning, estimation	characteristics of organisms	expanding populations' and industry's impact on animal habitats; interplay between geography, climate, and habitat	collage of animals

BOOK TITLE	MATHEMATICAL CONCEPTS AND SKILLS	SCIENCE CONCEPTS AND SKILLS	SOCIAL STUDIES CONCEPTS AND SKILLS	VISUAL ARTS CONCEPTS AND SKILLS
"A Closet Full of Shoes" (a poem in *Falling Up*); *Zoo-ology*	sorting, classification, Venn diagrams, sets, subsets	characteristics of organisms, animal classification, animal habitats	expanding populations' and industry's impact on animal habitats	artwork of various wildlife artists, coloring and patterning in animal skin
Good Enough to Eat: A Kid's Guide to Food and Nutrition	data collection and interpretation, tallying, bar graphs, pie charts	personal health, food pyramid, nutrients, food groups	malnourished and obese populations, food traditions in other countries	Floris van Dijck's *Breakfast Still Life*
The Moon Seems to Change	data collection and interpretation, bar graphs	moon phases, movement of the moon in the sky	exploration of a biographical piece, history of the Apollo missions	artists' renditions of the moon
My First Book of Biographies	real-life applications of mathematics, careers in mathematics	real-life applications of science; careers in science, science and technology	importance of working independently and cooperatively to accomplish goals	mathematics used by artists, collage of career images

"Zebra Question" (a poem in A Light in the Attic) (1981)

by Shel Silverstein

HarperCollins, ISBN #0060256737

My Light (2005)

by Molly Bang

Scholastic, ISBN #0439751160

Overview of Poem and Book: Learn about opposites in Silverstein's humorous "Zebra Question." Then, discover everything you wanted to know about light and how it is transformed into the energy we use in our homes by exploring the captivating fact-filled book *My Light*.

Mathematical Concepts and Skills: number line, positive and negative numbers, integers, addition of positive and negative numbers

Science Concepts and Skills: electricity, light, positive and negative charges

Overview of Activities: Students explore characteristics of static electricity, a real-life example of combining positive and negative values. Students also gain practice with understanding and identifying negative numbers and adding positive and negative numbers.

National Mathematics Standards (2000):

Students in grades 3 through 5 should "explore numbers less than zero by extending the number line and through familiar applications" (Number and Operations Standard) (p. 392).

National Science Standards (1996):

Students in grades K–4 should "develop an understanding of light, heat, electricity, and magnetism" (p. 123). "By experimenting with light, heat, electricity, magnetism, and sound, students begin to understand that phenomena can be observed, measured, and controlled in various ways" (Physical Science, Content Standard B) (p. 126). Also, as a result of activities, students should "develop abilities necessary to do scientific inquiry" and "develop understanding about scientific inquiry" (Science as Inquiry, Content Standard A) (p. 121).

Materials: tile spacers, scissors, balloons, black marker or pen, string, tape, salt, pepper, combs

Description of Activities:

1. Read the short poem "Zebra Question" by Shel Silverstein to set the stage for the upcoming activity involving numbers of opposite signs.

2. To provide a rationale and to excite students about the upcoming exploration of positive and negative numbers, introduce the book *My Light* and read the brief paragraph about lightning located at the end of the book. Students will learn that lightning is a form of electricity that occurs due to an exchange of positive and negative energy.

3. Prior to class, purchase enough tile spacers for each student to have at least ten. A tile spacer looks like a plus sign. Manipulate the tile spacer to resemble a minus sign by cutting off its top and bottom tip. Distribute to students five tile spacers that look like plus signs and five tile spacers manipulated to look like minus signs.

4. Begin a discussion about negative numbers by challenging students to think of real-life examples of negative numbers (e.g., below-zero temperatures, being in debt, below sea level, negative charges, below par in golf, etc.).

5. Show students on a number line where negative numbers reside and also the symbolic notation of a minus sign used to represent a negative number.

6. Model several problems involving integers using the tile spacers. For example, to help students make sense of the problem $3 + (-1)$, ask students to place in a row three of the plus signs (i.e., three uncut tile spacers) and to place one minus sign underneath in a separate row. Remind students how a positive plus a negative sums to zero. (Consider putting this into a more meaningful and familiar context by pointing out if you have two pencils and someone takes two away, then you have none.) Remove the one vertical pair of positive and negative signs since they add to zero, and notice that two plus signs are left over. Thus, $3 + (-1) = 2$. Model this same problem using the number line. Next, model $-3 + 1$ by placing three minus signs in a row and one plus sign underneath. Since a positive and a negative sum to zero, remove the one vertical pair of the positive and negative sign, leaving two minus signs. Thus, $-3 + 1 = -2$. Model this same problem again using the number line.

7. Challenge students to solve word problems involving positive and negative numbers using the tile spacers as concrete manipulatives to assist them in their computations. The word problems should place negative numbers into a real-life context (e.g., The temperature was 5 degrees below zero. By noon, the temperature had risen 4 degrees. How cold was it?; I was in debt $3 and then I found a $5 bill. How much money do I have now?, etc.).

8. Challenge students to create their own word problems involving negative numbers and let a classmate model and solve it.

9. Remind students that lightning is a form of electricity that results from an exchange of positive and negative energy. Read all or excerpts from *My Light* and let students enjoy and discover the many forms of light energy.

10. Ask students to define electricity. Students might brainstorm first and then share their collaborative ideas and definitions. Discuss the importance of electricity in one's life. Students give examples of how electricity is used for light (lamps), sound (radio), heat (oven), and movement (fan).

11. Discuss static electricity, which is the buildup of electric charges on an object. When two objects are rubbed, both become charged and unlike charges attract. To demonstrate static electricity, engage students in the following activities where they first make predictions as to what might happen and then record their observations of what occurred:

    a. Give pairs of students an inflated balloon. Mark a large X on one side of the balloon. Students tie a string to one end and tape the balloon so that it hangs freely off of a desk. Students hold the balloon with one hand, rub the X several times with the other hand, and let it hang freely again. Take the hand that rubbed the balloon and hold it close to the balloon. Students will see the X side of the balloon move toward their hand. This movement occurs because the rubbing resulted in a buildup of positive charges on the hand and negative charges on the balloon. Since opposite charges attract, the balloon moved closer to the hand.

    b. Students rub a balloon several times against their head. When the balloon is placed near, but not touching their head again, their hair will rise and stick to the balloon. This movement occurs because the rubbing resulted in a buildup of positive charges on the hand and negative charges on the balloon. Since opposite charges attract, the balloon pulled hair toward it.

    c. Students take two balloons and mark an X on both. Attach a string to both and tape them to a desk so they hang freely, close to each other but not touching. Students rub the X side of both balloons on their shirts and then let the balloons hang freely again. Students will notice the balloons repel, or move away from one another, because they have the same charge.

    d. Pour a teaspoon of salt onto a piece of paper. Sprinkle pepper on top of the salt pile. Students rub a comb several times through their hair and then hold it over the salt and pepper mixture. Students will see the pepper rise and stick to the comb. This happens because unlike charges attract and the pepper is lighter than the salt.

12. Students share their predictions and observations.

13. Revisit portions of *My Light*, reminding students how integral light and electricity are to our daily lives. Students write a paragraph or short essay entitled "A Day without Light (or Electricity)." Students share their creative writing samples.

Assessment:

- Did students locate positive and negative numbers on a number line?

- Did students correctly compute problems involving positive and negative numbers?

- Did students create meaningful word problems that involved negative numbers?

- Did students provide a reasonable definition for electricity?

- Did students record reasonable predictions for each experiment?

- Did students record accurate observations of each experiment?

- Did students develop a creative essay or paragraph about light and electricity?

Activity Extensions:

- Explore a biography of the sixteenth-century Italian mathematician, Rafael Bombelli, who is noted to be the first to express how to operate on negative numbers. Or explore a biography of sixteenth-century French mathematician, Francois Viete, who was the first to use a minus sign to indicate a negative number. Or explore biographies of other mathematicians who encountered and/or attempted to explain negative numbers in their work (e.g., Giolarmo Cardano, Frances Maseres, Fibonacci, Leonhard Euler, etc.).

- Explore and/or engage in activities that investigate photosynthesis and other topics in Bang's book.

- Using the Weather Channel and Where Lightning Strikes websites listed below, students explore frequency and location of lightning strikes. Students then create bar graphs or pictographs depicting lightning strikes data.

- Enjoy poetry about the sun authored by Shel Silverstein (e.g., "A Battle in the Sky" in *Falling Up* [1996]).

- Enjoy poetry about the concept of negative authored by Jack Prelutsky (e.g., "I'm Drifting through Negative Space" in *A Pizza the Size of the Sun* [1996]).

Cross-Curricular Connections:

Visual Arts

- Explore artists' renditions of light and electricity (e.g., Theodore Gericault's *Horse Frightened by Lightning*, Joseph Beuys's *Lightning with Stag in Its Glare*).

- Explore positive and negative images in art by taking a square piece of colored paper, folding it in half, and then cutting out some shape (e.g., a lightning bolt, triangle, heart, etc.) from the middle. The resulting two pieces of paper are the positive and negative representation of that shape (i.e., the positive representation is the shape you cut out; the negative representation is the outline of the shape that results from cutting). Glue the positive and negative representations of the shape onto contrasting colored paper squares.

Social Studies

- Research alternate sources of power (fossil fuels, solar power, hydroelectricity).

- Explore a biographical piece of a scientist who experimented with light and electricity (Thomas Edison, Ben Franklin, Albert Einstein, etc.).

Related Children's Literature

Bang, M. (2005). *My light*. New York: Scholastic.

Barasch, L. (2005). *Ask Albert Einstein*. New York: Frances Foster Books.

Barretta, G. (2006). *Now and Ben: The modern inventions of Ben Franklin*. New York: Holt.

Branley, F. (1999). *Flash, crash, rumble, and roll*. New York: HarperCollins.

Brown, D. (2004). *Odd boy out: Young Albert Einstein*. Boston: Houghton Mifflin.

Claybourne, A. (2006). *The shocking story of electricity*. Tulsa, OK: EDC.

DeMauro, L. (2002). *Thomas Edison: A brilliant inventor* (Time for kids series). New York: HarperCollins.

Fradin, D. (2002). *Who was Ben Franklin?* New York: Penguin Young Readers.

Frith, M. (2005). *Who was Thomas Alva Edison?* New York: Penguin Young Readers.

Fritz, J. (1996). *What's the big idea, Ben Franklin?* New York: Penguin Young Readers.

Marzollo, J. (1994). *My first book of biographies: Great men and women every child should know*. New York: Scholastic.

Mayes, S. (2006). *Where does electricity come from?* Tulsa, OK: EDC.

Murphy, S. (2003). *Less than zero*. New York: HarperCollins.

Parker, S. (2005). *Electricity* (Eyewitness book series). New York: Dorling Kindersley.

Prelutsky, J. (1996). *A pizza the size of the sun*. New York: Scholastic.

Satterfield, K. (2005). *Benjamin Franklin: A man of many talents* (Time for kids series). New York: HarperCollins.

Scieszka, J., & Smith, L. (1995). *Math curse*. New York: Penguin Books.

Scieszka, J., & Smith, L. (2004). *Science verse*. New York: Penguin Books.

Silverstein, S. (1981). *A light in the attic*. New York: HarperCollins.

Silverstein, S. (1996). *Falling up*. New York: HarperCollins.

Related Instructional Resources

Burnie, D. (2000). *Light* (Eyewitness book series). New York: Dorling Kindersley.

Lauw, D. (2001). *Electricity*. New York: Crabtree.

Levine, S., & Johnstone, L. (2005). *First science experiments: Nature, senses, weather, & machines*. New York: Sterling.

Schwartz, D. (2001). *Q is for quark: A science alphabet*. Berkeley, CA: Ten Speed Press.

Stillinger, D. (2003). *Battery science: Make widgets that work and gadgets that go*. Palo Alto, CA: Klutz.

VanCleave, J. (2006). *Energy for every kid*. Hoboken, NJ: Wiley.

Related Websites

Albert Einstein Biography
http://www-history.mcs.st-and.ac.uk/history/Biographies/Einstein.html

Benjamin Franklin
http://www.fi.edu/franklin/

Electricity and Magnetism Lesson Plans
http://www.galaxy.net/~k12/electric/index.shtml

Francois Viete Biography
http://www-history.mcs.st-and.ac.uk/history/Biographies/Viete.html

Index of Biographies on Mathematicians
http://www-history.mcs.st-and.ac.uk/history/BiogIndex.html

Joseph Beuys: Lightning with Stag in Its Glare
http://www.massmoca.org/visual_arts/visual_arts.html
http://www.guggenheimcollection.org/site/artist_work_md_17_3.html

Light Activities
http://www.fi.edu/fellows/fellow7/mar99/light/index.shtml

Lightning Images
http://www.photolib.noaa.gov/nssl/lightning1.html

Rafael Bombelli Biography
http://www-history.mcs.st-and.ac.uk/history/Biographies/Bombelli.html

Static Electricity Activities
http://www.sciencemadesimple.com/static.html

Symbols for Plus and Minus
http://www.roma.unisa.edu.au/07305/symbols.htm#Plus

Theodore Gericault
http://www.allaboutart.com

Thomas Edison
http://www.fi.edu/franklin/inventor/edison.html

Weather Channel
http://www.weather.com

Where Lightning Strikes
http://science.nasa.gov/headlines/y2001/ast05dec_1.htm

"The Planet of Mars" (a poem in Where the Sidewalk Ends) (2004)

by Shel Silverstein

HarperCollins, ISBN #0060572345

The Planets in Our Solar System (1998)

by Franklyn M. Branley

HarperCollins, ISBN #006445178X

Overview of Poem and Book:	Learn what a Martian might dress like as compared to us in Silverstein's short poem. Then, readers will discover interesting facts about the planets in *The Planets in Our Solar System*.
Mathematical Concepts and Skills:	fractions, decimals, measurement, ratio, size and scale, estimation
Science Concepts and Skills:	relative size of the planets, planets in the solar system
Overview of Activities:	Students explore the relative size and scale of the planets in our solar system using Playdoh as a concrete model.

National Mathematics Standards (2000):

Students in grades 3 through 5 should "develop and use strategies to estimate computations involving fractions and decimals in situations relevant to students' experiences" (Number and Operations Standard) (p. 392). Students should also "understand such attributes as length, area, weight, volume, and size of angle and select the appropriate type of unit for measuring each attribute." Finally, students "select and use benchmarks to estimate measurements" (Measurement Standard) (p. 398).

National Science Standards (1996):

Students in grades K–4 should "develop an understanding of objects in the sky" (p. 130) and "Earth in the solar system" (Earth and Space Science, Content Standard D) (p. 158). Also, as a result of activities, students should "develop abilities necessary to do scientific inquiry" and "develop understanding about scientific inquiry" (Science as Inquiry, Content Standard A) (p. 121).

Materials: at least five pounds of Playdoh, plastic knife, nine pieces of paper (each one labeled with the name of a planet)

Description of Activities:

1. Read the short poem "The Planet of Mars" by Shel Silverstein to set the stage for the upcoming activities.

2. In small groups, students develop and record in their journals a list of all of the planets in our solar system from biggest to smallest.

3. Ask some groups to share their predictions and to describe their ordering strategies.

4. As a whole class, discuss, agree on, and record on the board a class consensus of the ordering of the planets from biggest to smallest.

5. Inform students that they are going to develop a scaled model of the planets in our solar system by engaging them in an activity where they take a large mound of Playdoh (which represents the volume of all the nine planets combined), continually divide it into fractional pieces, and then shape the Playdoh into balls, forming planets. The teacher can implement this activity as a whole-class demonstration or divide the class in half and allow each group to carry out the activity. (This activity is a modified version of the Worlds in Comparison activity created by Project Astro. See the Project Astro website listed below.)

    a. Prior to the activity, print the name of each planet on a piece of paper. Place all nine pieces of paper on a long table.

    b. Roll five pounds of Playdoh into a log shape. (It is acceptable if the Playdoh is different colors since planets are multicolored.)

    c. Cut the Playdoh into ten equal pieces. Take six pieces and place them on the sheet of paper labeled *Jupiter*. Place three pieces on the paper labeled *Saturn*.

    d. Take the remaining one piece and roll it into a log and cut it again into ten equal pieces. Place five pieces on the paper labeled *Saturn*. Place two pieces on the paper labeled *Neptune*. Put two pieces on the paper labeled *Uranus*.

    e. Take the remaining one piece and cut it into four equal pieces. Take three pieces and place them on the paper labeled *Saturn*.

    f. Cut the remaining one piece into ten equal pieces. Place two on the paper labeled *Earth*. Place two pieces on the paper labeled *Venus*. Place four pieces on the paper labeled *Uranus*.

    g. Roll the remaining two pieces into a log and cut into ten equal pieces. Place one piece on the paper labeled *Mars*. Place four pieces on the paper labeled *Neptune*. Place four pieces on the paper labeled *Uranus*.

h. Cut the remaining one piece into ten equal pieces. Place seven on the paper labeled *Mercury*. Place two pieces on the paper labeled *Uranus*.

i. Cut the remaining one piece into ten equal pieces. Place nine on the paper labeled *Uranus*. Place one on the paper labeled *Pluto*.

j. For each planet, roll all of the pieces of Playdoh into a ball, forming nine individual planets.

6. Slide the labeled pieces of paper around on the table and order the planets from biggest to smallest in terms of the sizes of the balls of Playdoh. Compare this ordering to students' original predictions. How accurate were their predictions? Which planet is biggest? Smallest? About equal size? Are students surprised at how many times larger Jupiter is, for example, as compared to Earth? To Mercury?, etc.

7. Students check the accuracy of their size ordering of the planets by viewing the website, Order of Planets from Biggest to Smallest.

8. Ask students to look at their Playdoh planets and to visually estimate and then record in their journals how many times larger one planet is relative to another (e.g., Earth looks almost three times larger than Mercury). Students compare their estimations to the planets' actual sizes using the Planet Size Comparison website or the Relative Sizes of the Planets in the Solar System website.

9. Share all or excerpts from *The Planets in Our Solar System*, allowing students to learn more facts about the planets in our solar system.

10. Students record in their journals the three most interesting facts learned today about the planets in our solar system.

Assessment:
- Did students make accurate predictions about the relative sizes of planets?
- Did students make good visual estimations of the comparative sizes of planets?

Activity Extensions:
- Challenge students to predict how many times bigger the sun is as compared to Earth and how many times smaller the moon is as compared to Earth. Students then view the Planet Size Comparison website to check their predictions. Were they surprised to learn how massive the sun is as compared to Earth? Were their predictions accurate regarding how many times larger Earth is as compared to the moon?

- Students create another scaled model of the universe, but this time exploring planets' distances from the sun. Visit the Toilet Paper—Planets' Distances from the Sun website for an excellent activity.

- Implement the useful teaching activities appearing at the end of *The Planets in Our Solar System*.

- Read and enjoy the poem "An Irritating Creature" (Prelutsky, 1984).

Cross-Curricular Connections:

Visual Arts

- Explore and imitate artists' renditions of the night sky, space, or solar system (e.g., van Gogh's *Starry Night*).

Social Studies

- Explore biographies of astronauts (Buzz Aldrin, Neil Armstrong, Sally Ride, etc.) or scientists and astronomers who studied the moon, planets, or our solar system (Copernicus, Galileo, Johannes Kepler, Edwin Hubble, Carl Sagan, etc.), and place the individuals' lives in a larger historical context.

Related Children's Literature

Branley, F. (1981). *The sky is full of stars*. New York: HarperCollins.

Branley, F. (1987). *The moon seems to change*. New York: HarperCollins.

Branley, F. (1998). *The planets in our solar system*. New York: HarperCollins.

Gibbons, G. (1997). *The moon book*. New York: Holiday House.

Gibbons, G. (2005). *Planets*. New York: Holiday House.

Goldsmith, M. (2001). *Galileo Galilei* (Scientists who made history series). New York: Raintree Steck-Vaughn.

Levy, D. (2003). *Stars and planets* (Discoveries series). New York: Barnes & Noble Books.

Prelutsky, J. (1984). *The new kid on the block*. New York: Scholastic.

Scieszka, J., & Smith, L. (1995). *Math curse*. New York: Penguin Books.

Scieszka, J., & Smith, L. (2004). *Science verse*. New York: Penguin Books.

Silverstein, S. (2004). *Where the sidewalk ends*. New York: HarperCollins.

Sis, P. (1996). *Starry messenger*. New York: Farrar Straus Giroux.

Sweeney, J. (1999). *Me and my place in space*. New York: Dragonfly Books.

Related Instructional Resources

Dickinson, T. (1995). *Other worlds: A beginner's guide to planets and moons*. Tonawanda, NY: Firefly.

Holland, S. (2001). *Space* (Eye wonder series). New York: Dorling Kindersley.

Schwartz, D. (2001). *Q is for quark: A science alphabet*. Berkeley, CA: Ten Speed Press.

Simon, S. (1992). *Our solar system, vol. 1*. New York: HarperCollins.

Simon, S. (1995). *The solar system: Facts and exploration*. New York: Holt.

Twist, C. (2004). *Our solar system: A first introduction to space and the planets*. Hauppauge, NY: Barron's Educational Series.

Related Websites

Family Astro
> http://www.astrosociety.org/education/family.html

Hands-On Astronomy Activities
> http://www.astrosociety.org/education/activities/handson.html
> http://www.astrosociety.org/education/activities/astroacts.html

Order of Planets from Biggest to Smallest
> http://coolcosmos.ipac.caltech.edu/cosmic_kids/AskKids/planet_sizes.shtml

Planet Size Comparison
> http://www.sciencenetlinks.com/interactives/messenger/psc/PlanetSize.html

Planets
> http://www.nineplanets.org/
> http://solarsystem.jpl.nasa.gov/planets/profile.cfm?Object=SolarSys&Display=Overview

Playdoh Recipe
> http://www.kinderplanet.com/playdo.htm

Project Astro
> http://www.astrosociety.org/education/astro/project_astro.html

Relative Sizes of the Planets in the Solar System
> http://www.solarviews.com/raw/misc/ss.gif

Surfing the Solar System: A Treasure Hunt Game and Puzzle
> http://www.astrosociety.org/education/surf.html

Toilet Paper—Planets' Distances from the Sun
> http://www.astrosociety.org/education/activities/handson.html

Views of the Solar System
> http://www.solarviews.com/eng/homepage.htm

Women in Astronomy
> http://www.astrosociety.org/education/resources/womenast_bib.html

Your Age on Other Worlds
> http://www.exploratorium.edu/ronh/age/

Your Weight on Other Planets
> http://www.exploratorium.edu/ronh/weight/

Activities Featuring Algebra

Wild Fibonacci: Nature's Secret Code Revealed (2005)

by Joy N. Hulme

Tricycle Press, ISBN #1582461546

Overview of Book:	Discover how the Fibonacci sequence works and how Fibonacci numbers permeate nature and our world.
Mathematical Concepts and Skills:	patterns, pattern recognition, prediction
Science Concepts and Skills:	characteristics of organisms, scientific inquiry
Overview of Activities:	Students discover the pattern in the Fibonacci numbers and explore how the Fibonacci numbers appear in nature. Students create their own patterns and challenge their classmates to identify and continue the patterns.
National Mathematics Standards (2000):	Students in grades 3 through 5 should "describe, extend, and make generalizations about geometric and numeric patterns." They should also "represent and analyze patterns and functions, using words, tables, and graphs" (Algebra Standard) (p. 394).
National Science Standards (1996):	Students in grades K–4 should "develop understanding of the characteristics of organisms, life cycles of organisms, and organisms and environments" (p. 127). Students should understand that "each plant or animal has different structures that serve different functions in growth, survival, and reproduction" and that "many characteristics of an organism . . . result from an individual's interactions with the environment," while inherited characteristics of organisms "include the color of flowers and the number of limbs of an animal" (Life Science, Content Standard C) (p. 129). Also, as a result of activities, students should "develop abilities necessary to do scientific inquiry" (Science as Inquiry, Content Standard A) (p. 121).
Materials:	images of (or actual) flowers and pine cones

Description of Activities:

1. Read *Wild Fibonacci: Nature's Secret Code Revealed*. As the story unfolds, list the numbers on the board (appearing on the bottom right of the right-hand pages) that comprise the Fibonacci sequence. After listing several numbers, ask students to predict what number comes next and to explain the rule (the next number in the sequence is the sum of the preceding two numbers). Once students recognize the pattern, let students guess what number comes next as you continue to read the book.

2. Students explore the Annenberg *Numbers in Nature* website and dynamically see how the Fibonacci numbers apply to the geometric spiral of a seashell.

3. Explore the Fibonacci's Rabbits website and discover how Fibonacci numbers appear in population growth.

4. Explore the Fibonacci's Numbers in the Petals on Flowers, Pinecones, or Leaf Arrangements website and discover how the Fibonacci numbers appear in nature. The two introductory pages in *Wild Fibonacci* also detail the many places in nature that students might find Fibonacci numbers. Students locate and bring to class flowers, pinecones, or leaf arrangements and determine if the Fibonacci numbers are apparent.

5. Challenge students to think of a pattern (comprised of numbers, letters, or symbols). Students list the first three or four entries in the pattern. Students challenge their classmates to identify the pattern and list the next three entries in the pattern.

Assessment:

- Did students notice the numeric pattern in the Fibonacci sequence?
- Did students correctly continue the Fibonacci sequence?
- Did students locate and recognize Fibonacci numbers in nature?
- Did students correctly determine the next entry in various patterns?

Activity Extensions:

- Using calculators, ask students to take each Fibonacci number and divide it by the previous Fibonacci number. Students will see that the ratios approach a number called Phi (1.618 . . .). Introduce the golden mean (also known as the golden ratio or the golden section), which is represented by the Greek letter Phi.
- Challenge students to discover the pattern in other number and geometric sequences by viewing the Virtual Manipulatives websites listed below.

Cross-Curricular Connections:

Visual Arts

- Research the golden mean and how it is evident in architecture (e.g., Acropolis, Parthenon, etc.).

- Research and report on artists who have used the golden mean in their works (e.g., Albrecht Durer, Leonardo Da Vinci, etc.).

Social Studies

- Students explore the life and accomplishments of Leonardo of Pisa (also known as Fibonacci).

- Research geometric and numeric patterns in population growth.

Related Children's Literature

Hulme, J. (2005). *Wild Fibonacci: Nature's secret code revealed*. Berkeley, CA: Tricycle Press.

Raboff, E. (1988). *Albrecht Durer*. New York: HarperCollins.

Scieszka, J., & Smith, L. (1995). *Math curse*. New York: Penguin Books.

Scieszka, J., & Smith, L. (2004). *Science verse*. New York: Penguin Books.

Venezia, M. (1989). *Da Vinci* (Getting to know the world's greatest artists series). Chicago: Children's Press.

Venezia, M. (1992). *Michelangelo* (Getting to know the world's greatest artists series). Chicago: Children's Press.

Related Instructional Resources

Dorling Kindersley. (1998). *DK nature encyclopedia*. London: Dorling Kindersley.

Krull, K. (1995). *Lives of the artists: Masterpieces, messes*. San Diego: Harcourt Brace.

Renshaw, A., & Ruggi, G. (2005*). The art book for children*. New York: Phaidon Press.

Schwartz, D. (2001). *Q is for quark: A science alphabet*. Berkeley, CA: Ten Speed Press.

Scieszka, J., & Smith, L. (2005). *Seen art?* New York: Viking Press.

Williams, D. (1995). *Teaching mathematics through children's art*. Portsmouth, NH: Heinemann.

Related Websites

Annenberg *Numbers in Nature*—Spiral of a Seashell
  http://www.learner.org/exhibits/renaissance/fibonacci/shell.html

Fibonacci Series
  http://www.sciencenetlinks.com/lessons.cfm?BenchmarkID=2&DocID=134

Fibonacci Numbers in Art, Architecture, and Music
  http://www.mcs.surrey.ac.uk/Personal/R.Knott/Fibonacci/fibInArt.html

Fibonacci Numbers in the Leaf Arrangements
  http://www.mcs.surrey.ac.uk/Personal/R.Knott/Fibonacci/fibnat.html#leaf

Fibonacci Numbers in the Petals on Flowers
  http://www.mcs.surrey.ac.uk/Personal/R.Knott/Fibonacci/fibnat.html#petals

Fibonacci Numbers in the Pinecones
  http://www.mcs.surrey.ac.uk/Personal/R.Knott/Fibonacci/fibnat.html#pinecones

Fibonacci's Rabbits
  http://www.mcs.surrey.ac.uk/Personal/R.Knott/Fibonacci/fibnat.html#Rabbits

Golden Section in Architecture
  http://www.mcs.surrey.ac.uk/Personal/R.Knott/Fibonacci/fibInArt.html#arch

Virtual Manipulatives—Color Patterns
  http://nlvm.usu.edu/en/nav/frames_asid_184_g_2_t_1.html

Virtual Manipulatives—Fibonacci Sequence
  http://nlvm.usu.edu/en/nav/frames_asid_315_g_3_t_1.html

Virtual Manipulatives—Golden Rectangle
  http://nlvm.usu.edu/en/nav/frames_asid_133_g_2_t_3.html?open=instructions

Virtual Manipulatives—Number Patterns
  http://nlvm.usu.edu/en/nav/frames_asid_185_g_2_t_1.html

Virtual Manipulatives—Patterns in the Sieve of Erastosthenes
  http://nlvm.usu.edu/en/nav/frames_asid_158_g_2_t_1.html?open=instructions

Activities Featuring Geometry

"Strange Wind" (a poem in A Light in the Attic) (1981)

by Shel Silverstein

HarperCollins, ISBN #0060256737

Let's Fly a Kite (2000)

by Stuart Murphy

HarperCollins, ISBN #0064467377

Overview of Poem and Books:	Enjoy the silliness of Silverstein's poem about the wind. Then, explore the concept of symmetry in *Let's Fly a Kite*, as a family builds a kite and heads to the beach, only to encounter many other examples of line symmetry.
Mathematical Concepts and Skills:	kites, attributes of quadrilaterals, line symmetry
Science Concepts and Skills:	wind, aerodynamics of flight
Overview of Activities:	Students define, sketch, and explore the attributes of a kite, in particular its symmetry. After seeing examples of objects with line symmetry, students create a symmetry collage containing images of symmetrical objects. Then, students explore and discover where wind comes from and engage in various kite-related activities.
National Mathematics Standards (2000): π	Students in grades 3 through 5 should "identify and describe line and rotational symmetry in two- and three-dimensional shapes." They should "identify, compare, and analyze attributes of two- and three-dimensional shapes and develop vocabulary to describe the attributes." They should also "recognize geometric ideas and relationships and apply them to other disciplines" (Geometry Standard) (p. 396).

National Science Standards (1996):

Students in grades K–4 should "develop an understanding of position and motion of objects" (p. 123). Students should "describe and manipulate objects by pushing, pulling, throwing, dropping, and rolling" and therefore "begin to focus on the position and movement of objects: describing location as up, down, in front, or behind, and discovering the various kinds of motion and forces required to control it" (Physical Science, Content Standard B) (p. 126). Also, as a result of activities, students should "develop abilities necessary to do scientific inquiry" and "develop understanding about scientific inquiry" (Science as Inquiry, Content Standard A) (p. 121).

Materials:

magazines, 9" × 12" piece of posterboard, rulers, scissors, gluesticks, black markers, rulers, paper plate, hanger, string, lamp

Description of Activities:

1. Read "Strange Wind" to set the stage for the upcoming activity dealing with kites.

2. While most students are familiar with a kite as an object one might fly on a windy day, a kite, like a square or rectangle, is a member of the quadrilateral family and has a specific definition. Ask students to make a sketch of a kite in their notebooks and to work collaboratively in small groups to develop an accurate mathematical definition of a kite. Discuss students' working definitions and then provide the definition and a sketch of a kite, which is a quadrilateral with two distinct pairs of equal adjacent sides.

3. Show the inside cover page of *Let's Fly a Kite* to students. Ask students to study the picture and to notice what the kites have in common. Students should notice that all of the kites are symmetric. Ask students to describe what symmetry is and to articulate the symmetry they see in the illustrations of the kites. Explain how a kite has line symmetry; that is, one can fold a kite down the middle and create a mirror image on each side of the fold, or line of reflection (or line of symmetry).

4. Read *Let's Fly a Kite*. Challenge students to look for and identify other examples of symmetric objects in the illustrations, noting their line(s) of symmetry.

5. Students work in small groups to create a symmetry collage (described on page 33 in *Let's Fly a Kite*) whereby they cut images of symmetrical objects from a magazine. Students paste the images onto a 9" × 12" piece of posterboard and use a ruler and black marker to mark the line (or lines) of symmetry.

6. Hang all of the individual collages in a rectangular formation, creating a symmetry mural for all students to observe.

7. Reread page 20 in *Let's Fly a Kite,* which describes how kites depend on wind to fly. Students work in small groups and discuss and define what wind is, where it comes from, why it is important, how it can be destructive, etc. Students share their responses with the class.

8. Prior to class, cut a large spiral out of a paper plate. Make a hole in the center of the spiral and thread a piece of string through it, knotting it at one end. Tie the other end of the string to a hanger.

9. With students gathered around, hold the hanger steady and just above a light source (e.g., a lamp without a lampshade). Ask students to first predict what will happen and then observe what happens. Students will see the spiral move because as the heat generated from the light source rose, it pushed against the spiral, making it spin. Explain to students that this upward movement of air causes wind. Wind is moving air caused by differences in air pressure. As the warm air rose, the heavier, cooler air rushed to takes its place, creating wind.

10. Students can now engage in a variety of activities where they might:

    a. create and decorate kites (see the Virtual Kite Zoo Catalog website or Kite Making website) and reinforce the concept of symmetry.

    b. discover and discuss the aerodynamic forces that act on a kite in motion (see websites listed at end of activity).

    c. explore the Energy Kid's Page website listed below, where students learn about wind, wind machines, and how wind is converted into energy. Students then report and share their findings with the class.

    d. visit the Make a Tornado website and allow students to create a tornado using simple materials and then research and discuss what tornados are, how a tornado forms, where and why they occur, etc.

Assessment:

- Did students notice that a kite has line symmetry?

- Did students provide accurate descriptions and definitions of what a kite is and what wind is?

- Did students correctly identify objects with line symmetry?

- Did students make reasonable predictions regarding what might happen in the spiral/lamp experiment?

- Did students actively participate in the kite-related activities?

Activity Extensions:

- Students discover the rule for area of a kite, which is one-half times the product of the length of the two diagonals (the horizontal and vertical lines).

- Students take a symmetry walk on the school campus and locate objects with line symmetry.

- Read *Feel the Wind* (Dorrus, 1990) and share with students other facts and information about wind.

- Enjoy poetry about reflections including "Reflection" (Silverstein, 1981), "Mirror" (Lewis, 1998), or "egamI rorriM ruoY mA I" (Prelutsky, 1996).

Cross-Curricular Connections:

Visual Arts

- Explore and discuss the work of artists who captured windy scenes (e.g., Vincent van Gogh's *Wheat Fields under Threatening Skies,* Winslow Homer's *The Coming Storm,* etc.).

Social Studies

- Research the cultural history of kites (e.g., Korea, China, Japan, etc.).

- Explore biographies of scientists and other historical figures who experimented with kites (e.g., Benjamin Franklin, the Wright Brothers, Paul Garber, etc.).

- Research the fallout and implications of historic hurricanes and tornadoes.

Related Children's Literature

Birmingham, D. (1988). *M is for mirror*. Norfolk, UK: Tarquin.

Birmingham, D. (1991). *Look twice!*. Norfolk, UK: Tarquin.

Chorao, K. (2001). *Shadow night*. New York: Dutton Children's Books.

Cutts, D. (1998). *Thunder and lightning* (I can read about series). New York: Scholastic.

Demi. (2000). *Kites: Magic wishes that fly up to the sky*. New York: Dragonfly Books.

DeWitt, L. (1991). *What will the weather be?* New York: HarperCollins.

Dorros, A. (1990). *Feel the wind*. New York: HarperCollins.

Gibbons, G. (1989). *Monarch butterfly*. New York: Scholastic.

Higham, C. (2004). *Snowflakes for all seasons*. Layto, UT: Gibbs Smith.

Jonas, A. (1987). *Reflections*. New York: Greenwillow Books.

Lasky, K. (1995). *The gates of the wind*. New York: Harcourt Children's Books.

Lewis, J. (1998). *Doodle dandies: Poems that take shape*. New York: Aladdin.

Martin, J. (1998). *Snowflake Bentley*. Boston: Houghton Mifflin.

Murphy, J. (2000). *Blizzard!: The storm that changed America*. New York: Scholastic.

Murphy, S. (2000). *Let's fly a kite*. New York: HarperCollins.

Prelutsky, J. (1996). *A pizza the size of the sun*. New York: Scholastic.

Scieszka, J., & Smith, L. (1995). *Math curse*. New York: Penguin Books.

Scieszka, J., & Smith, L. (2004). *Science verse*. New York: Penguin Books.

Silverstein, S. (1981). *A light in the attic*. New York: HarperCollins.

Simon, S. (2006). *Weather*. New York: HarperCollins.

Sitomer, M., & Sitomer, H. (1970). *What is symmetry?* New York: Crowell.

Supraner, R. (1997). *Weather* (I can read about series). New York: Scholastic.

Yolen, J. (1987). *The girl who loved the wind*. New York: HarperCollins.

Yolen, J. (1998). *The emperor and the kite*. New York: Putnam Books.

Related Instructional Resources

Guerra, R. (2004). *The kite making handbook*. Devon, UK: David & Charles.

Honqxun, W. (1989). *Chinese kites: Traditional Chinese arts and culture*. San Francisco: China Books and Periodicals.

Hunt, L. (1971). *25 kites that fly*. Mineola, NY: Dover.

Levine, S., & Johnstone, L. (2003). *First science experiments: Wonderful weather*. New York: Sterling.

Mack, L. (2004). *Weather* (Eye wonder series). New York: Dorling Kindersley.

Pelham, D. (2000). *Kites*. New York: Overlook TP.

Schwartz, D. (2001). *Q is for quark: A science alphabet*. Berkeley, CA: Ten Speed Press.

Related Websites

Children's Books on Wind

http://sln.fi.edu//tfi/units/energy/booklist.html

Energy Kid's Page

http://www.eia.doe.gov/kids/energyfacts/sources/renewable/wind.html

EPA Kids Site

http://epa.gov/climatechange/kids/index.html

Kites—Aerodynamics

http://www.grc.nasa.gov/WWW/K-12/airplane/kite1.html

http://www.gombergkites.com/nkm/why.html

Kite History

http://www.nationalkitemonth.org/history/

http://www.gombergkites.com/nkm/hist2.html

Kite Making

http://www.aka.org.au/kites_in_the_classroom/plans.htm

http://kckiteclub.org/DaveEllis/TOC.htm

http://www.gombergkites.com/nkm/plan3.html

http://kckiteclub.org/DaveEllis/TetKite.htm

Kite Resources for Teachers

http://www.nationalkitemonth.org/teachers/

http://www.gombergkites.com/nkm/index.html

http://classroom.kitingusa.com/resources.htm

http://sln.fi.edu//tfi/units/energy/blustery.html

Make a Tornado

http://www.weatherwizkids.com/tornado1.htm

Symmetry

http://www.emints.org/ethemes/resources/S00000202.shtml

http://www.hbschool.com/activity/show_me/e673.htm

http://regentsprep.org/Regents/math/symmetry/Photos.htm

http://www.bbc.co.uk/schools/gcsebitesize/maths/shape/symmetryrev2.shtml

Virtual Kite Zoo Catalog

http://www.kites.org/zoo/catframe.html

Virtual Manipulatives Library—Reflections

http://nlvm.usu.edu/en/nav/frames_asid_206_g_1_t_3.html?open=activities

Weather Facts and Events (Tornadoes, Hurricanes, Monsoons)

http://www.pbs.org/wgbh/imax/weather.html

"Me and My Giant" (a poem in Where the Sidewalk Ends) (2004)

by Shel Silverstein

HarperCollins, ISBN #0060572345

Beanstalk: The Measure of a Giant (2005)

by Ann McCallum

Charlesbridge, ISBN #1570918945

Overview of Poem and Book: Learn about a child's giant friend in Silverstein's "Me and My Giant." Then, in *Beanstalk: The Measure of a Giant, a* mathematical spin on the original *Jack and the Beanstalk,* Jack awakes to a beanstalk outside of his window, so he climbs it and meets his new giant friend, Ray. Discover the mathematical challenges small Jack and his giant friend, Ray, encounter as they try to play basketball and checkers, encountering "*ray*-tios" along the way.

Mathematical Concepts and Skills: measurement, ratio, proportional reasoning, data collection and interpretation, line graphs, estimation

Science Concepts and Skills: life cycles of organisms, scientific inquiry

Overview of Activities: Students explore ratios by measuring their height and comparing it to the measure of certain parts of their body. Then students predict and observe the growth of plants, all growing under varying conditions, and plot the plants' growth.

National Mathematics Standards (2000):

Students in grades 3 through 5 should "understand such attributes as length, area, weight, volume, and size of angle and select the appropriate type of unit for measuring each attribute." Students should also "carry out simple unit conversions" and "understand that measurements are approximations" (Measurement Standard) (p. 398). Students in grades 3 through 5 should "collect data using observations, surveys, and experiments." Students should "represent data using tables and graphs such as line plots, bar graphs, and line graphs," and they should "propose and justify conclusions and predictions that are based on data" (Data Analysis and Probability Standard) (p. 400). Students should also "develop fluency in adding, subtracting, multiplying, and dividing whole numbers" and "select appropriate methods and tools for computing with whole numbers from among mental computation, estimation, calculators, and paper and pencil, according to the context and nature of the computation" (Number and Operations Standard) (p. 392).

National Science Standards (1996):

Students in grades K–4 should develop understandings that "organisms have basic needs (. . . plants require air, water, nutrients, and light)," and "organisms can survive only in environments in which their needs can be met" (p. 129). Students should develop understandings that "plants and animals have life cycles that include being born, developing into adults, reproducing, and eventually dying" (Life Science, Content Standard C) (p. 129). Also, as a result of activities, students should "develop abilities necessary to do scientific inquiry" and "develop understanding about scientific inquiry" (Science as Inquiry, Content Standard A) (p. 121).

Materials:

measuring tapes, *Beanstalk* worksheet, 9" × 12" white construction paper, calculators, half-pint milk cartons (or small containers), potting soil, fast-growing seeds (rye grass, bean, etc.), rulers, graph paper, four colored pencils

Description of Activities:

1. Read the short poem "Me and My Giant" by Shel Silverstein to set the stage for the upcoming activities.

2. Read *Beanstalk* to students. Pause at specific points when measurement and ratio situations arise. For example, on pages 12–13, Jack realizes that the basketball hoop's height is three times Ray's height. Challenge students to determine the height of a basketball hoop if it were three times their height.

3. With the help of a classmate, students measure their height and record it on the *Beanstalk* worksheet. (Students need to convert their height from feet and inches into inches only.)

4. Students complete the second column labeled "My Prediction" on the *Beanstalk* worksheet, where they make and record predictions about the measure of various parts of their body. Students work in pairs to record the actual measurements (in the third column) and then compute and record the ratio of their height to these various parts (in the fourth column). Students may use calculators to assist them in computing ratios.

5. Students compare their data to the actual ratios:

   - Ratio of height to circumference of head (3:1)
   - Ratio of height to hand span (pinky to thumb on a fully stretched-out hand) (8.5:1)
   - Ratio of height to arm span (1:1)
   - Ratio of height to circumference of wrist (6:1)
   - Ratio of height to ulna (bone connecting wrist to elbow) (7:1)
   - Ratio of height to femur length (thigh bone) (4:1)
   - Ratio of height to foot (6:1)
   - Ratio of circumference of neck to circumference of wrist (2:1)
   - Ratio of circumference of wrist to thumb (2:1)

6. How accurate were their predictions? Their recorded measurements and ratios? Why might some ratios not match their body ratios exactly? For certain ratios to match better, how might their height need to be modified? Is there no relationship between height and certain body parts (e.g., length of nose to one's height, etc.)? Facilitate a discussion.

7. Revisit the first few pages (pp. 3–5) of the story, *Beanstalk*, where a young boy awakens to a gigantic beanstalk growing outside of his window. Generate a discussion about what plants need to grow (e.g., soil, light, water, air, etc.).

8. Break students into four groups. Each group will grow a plant under one of the following four conditions:

   a. Condition #1: soil, water, air, no light (These plants will be placed in a cardboard box.)

   b. Condition #2: soil, water, no air, light (These plants will be placed in a sealed plastic bag.)

   c. Condition #3: soil, no water, air, light (These plants will not receive any water.)

   d. Condition #4: soil, water, air, light

   Students plant their seeds and label the milk cartons with SWA (soil, water, air—Condition #1), SWL (soil, water, light—Condition #2), SAL (soil, air, light—Condition #3), and SWAL (soil, water, air, light—Condition #4).

9. Students record in their journals predictions about the growth of their plant. For example, do they predict it will flourish? Die? Not grow at all?, etc.

10. Students record regular observations of their group's plant in terms of its appearance. Using rulers, students also measure and record the plant's growth daily.

11. Each group shares their growth data. Students graph the change in height over time of each plant on one line graph using a different color pencil to distinguish the data. Students compare and discuss the data. For example, which condition(s) allowed the plants to grow? To not grow? Which condition resulted in the tallest plant? The shortest? What factor seemed most crucial in allowing a plant to grow? In what ways are a plant's growth and needs similar to those of humans and animals? Generate a discussion.

Assessment:
- Did students make and record accurately body part measurements?
- Did students offer reasonable explanations for why their body ratios did not match the actual ratios?
- Did students identify needs of a plant?
- Did students successfully grow plants under the various conditions?
- Did students make and record accurate observations of their plants?
- Did students accurately graph and interpret their data?

Activity Extensions:
- Students develop a short essay entitled "If I Were Only 1 Foot Tall" (or "If I Were 20 Feet Tall"), complete with computations and illustrations, in which they describe what one day would look like if they awoke and found they measured only 12 inches (or 20 feet) tall. Students describe how their world would need to change, in terms of the dimensions of objects, to live that day comfortably. Or, write an essay about a day in the life of an ant, beetle, or ladybug through the insect's eyes.
- Enjoy the poem "One Inch Tall" by Shel Silverstein (2004) and the poem "Spaghetti Seeds" by Jack Prelutsky (1996).
- The Greeks and Romans believed the "ideal man" was 7 heads tall. Students measure their heads (i.e., vertical length from the top of one's head to the chin), multiply this number by 7, and compare this product to their height. Are they "ideal"?

- Discuss how changing environmental conditions (floods, draughts, heat, dehydration, famines, etc.) can impact plants and other living organisms.

- Demonstrate the importance of sunlight for plants by creating a maze using a cardboard box and cardboard for dividers. Punch holes in the dividers. Place an already-growing, small bean plant at one end of the maze. Shield the maze from light by covering all of it, except for one hole at the opposite end of the box from where the plant is located. Water the plant, perhaps in a dark room to keep light out. Over time, the plant will grow toward the light hole at the end of the maze.

Cross-Curricular Connections:

Visual Arts

- Explore the paintings of trees created by Vincent van Gogh (e.g., *Olive Trees with Yellow Sky and Sun, Cypresses, Orchard with Blossoming Plum Trees*, etc.).

Social Studies

- Locate on a map such areas including grasslands, jungles, and rain forests.

- Explore a biography of Johnny Appleseed.

Related Children's Literature

Aliki. (1963). *The story of Johnny Appleseed*. New York: Aladdin.

Charman, A. (2003). *I wonder why trees have leaves and other questions about plants*. Boston: Houghton Mifflin.

Cronin, D. (2003). *Diary of a worm*. New York: Scholastic.

Leedy, L. (1997). *Measuring Penny*. New York: Holt.

Lionni, L. (1960). *Inch by inch*. New York: HarperCollins.

McCallum, A. (2005). *Beanstalk: The measure of a giant*. Watertown, MA: Charlesbridge.

Myller, R. (1990). *How big is a foot?* New York: Dell Yearling.

Prelutsky, J. (1996). *A pizza the size of the sun*. New York: Scholastic.

Schwartz, D. (2003). *Millions to measure*. New York: HarperCollins.

Scieszka, J., & Smith, L. (1995). *Math curse*. New York: Penguin Books.

Scieszka, J., & Smith, L. (2004). *Science verse*. New York: Penguin Books.

Shipton, J. (1999). *What If?* New York: Dial Books for Young Readers.

Silverstein, S. (2004). *Where the sidewalk ends*. New York: HarperCollins.

Sweeney, J. (2001). *Me and the measure of things*. New York: Dell Dragonfly Books.

Wyatt, V. (2000). *Wacky plant cycles*. New York: Mondo.

Related Instructional Resources

Burnie, D. (2004). *Plant* (Eyewitness books series). London: Dorling Kindersley.

Levine, S., & Johnstone, L. (2005). *First science experiments: Nature, senses, weather, & machines*. New York: Sterling.

Schwartz, D. (2001). *Q is for quark: A science alphabet*. Berkeley, CA: Ten Speed Press.

Spilsbury, L. (2002). *Plant parts* (Life of plants series). Portsmouth, NH: Heinemann.

Unwin, M. (1993). *Science with plants* (Science activities series). Tulsa, OK: EDC.

Related Websites

Body Ratios and the Golden Ratio
   http://www.markwahl.com/golden-ratio.htm

Johnny Appleseed
   http://www.appleseed.org/johnny.html
   http://www.enchantedlearning.com/school/usa/people/Appleseedindex.shtml

Plant Activities for the Classroom
   http://www.proteacher.com/110013.shtml

Recipe for an Ecosphere
   http://spaceplace.nasa.gov/en/kids/earth/wordfind/

Beanstalk Worksheet
Exploring Ratio and Measurement

My height is _____ inches.

	My prediction (inches)	Measurement of body part (inches)	Ratio of height to body part (inches)
Circumference of head			
Circumference of neck			
Face (top of head to chin)			
Nose			
Ear			
Circumference of wrist			
Thumb			
Hand span			
Arm span			
Ulna (wrist to elbow)			
Femur (thigh bone)			
Foot			

If You Hopped Like a Frog (1999)

by David Schwartz

Scholastic, ISBN #0590098578

Overview of Book: In *If You Hopped Like a Frog,* readers will delight in learning what they could do if they possessed the same animal abilities as the ones mentioned in the book. Readers will also enjoy the humorous illustrations that accompany the many fascinating animal facts. The closing pages will assist the reader in understanding the calculations used throughout the story.

Mathematical Concepts and Skills: measurement (length, height, weight, capacity), size and scale, ratio, proportional reasoning, estimation

Science Concepts and Skills: characteristics of organisms

Overview of Activities: Students explore the classes and characteristics of animals while gaining practice with measurement, ratios, and proportions.

National Mathematics Standards (2000): Students in grades 3 through 5 should "understand such attributes as length, area, weight, volume, and size of angle and select the appropriate type of unit for measuring each attribute." Students should also "carry out simple unit conversions" and "understand that measurements are approximations" (Measurement Standard) (p. 398). Students in grades 3 through 5 should "develop fluency in adding, subtracting, multiplying, and dividing whole numbers" (Number and Operations Standard) (p. 392).

National Science Standards (1996): Students in grades K–4 should "develop understanding of the characteristics of organisms, life cycles of organisms, and organisms and environments" (p. 127). Students should understand that "each plant or animal has different structures that serve different functions in growth, survival, and reproduction" (p. 129). Students should understand that "many characteristics of an organism . . . result from an individual's interactions with the environment" (Life Science, Content Standard C) (p. 129).

Materials: measuring tapes, 9" × 12" posterboard, crayons, markers, calculators, almanac or Internet

Description of Activities:

1. Introduce the title of the book, *If You Hopped Like a Frog,* to students and ask them to estimate how far they think a frog can leap. Read the first two pages of the book allowing students to discover just how far a frog can leap. Continue reading the book, allowing students to make predictions about each animal. Students should explain their reasoning before reading the answers.

2. List the following amazing animal facts on the board (that appeared in *If You Hopped Like a Frog*):

   • A snake can swallow something twice the width of its mouth.

   • A crane's neck is one-third the length of its body.

   • An ant can lift fifty times its weight.

   • A spider can travel 33 times the length of its body in one second.

3. Students work in pairs, take measurements of each other, and relate each of the animal facts to themselves (e.g., If I could swallow like a snake, I could swallow an object as big as . . .).

4. Using an animal almanac, Internet resources, or other pieces of children's literature cited below, students work in pairs to locate an amazing animal statistic and apply it to themselves. Using 9" × 12" posterboard and markers, students create an exaggerated and humorous illustration of their findings, in the spirit of Schwartz's book, and include written text and calculations explaining their work. Students share their work with the class. Which animal is the most amazing?

Assessment:

• Did students make accurate measurements?

• Did students correctly compute problems involving proportional reasoning?

• Did students make an exaggerated animal illustration and explain their calculations and reasoning clearly?

Activity Extensions:

• Read the poem "The Tongue Sticker-Outer" (Silverstein, 1996) and challenge students to determine how long their tongue must be in order to touch the stars.

• Explore books authored by Steve Jenkins allowing students to learn more animal statistics and to gain practice with measuring and using their proportional reasoning skills.

Cross-Curricular Connections:

Visual Arts

- Create a collage of amazing animals. Students attach an essay articulating why the featured animals are amazing.

Social Studies

- Research how expanding populations and industry are impacting animal habitats and animal populations.

- Explore in which continents and in which countries various species of animals live. Research why the geography and climate of the land lends itself to be an ideal habitat for these animals.

Related Children's Literature

Arnold, T. (2000). *Parts*. New York: Puffin Books.

Arnold, T. (2005). *More parts*. New York: Puffin Books.

Arnold, T. (2007). *Even more parts*. New York: Puffin Books.

Bergen, D. (2004). *Life-size dinosaurs*. New York: Sterling.

Florian, D. (2001). *Lizards, frogs, and polliwogs*. Orlando, FL: Voyager Books.

Harris, N. (2004). *How big?* Oxfordshire, UK: Orpheus Books.

Jenkins, S. (1995). *Biggest, strongest, fastest*. Boston: Houghton Mifflin.

Jenkins, S. (2004). *Actual size*. Boston: Houghton Mifflin.

Jenkins, S. (2005). *Prehistoric actual size*. Boston: Houghton Mifflin.

Jenkins, S. (2006). *Almost gone: The world's rarest animals*. New York: Scholastic.

Jenkins, S., & Page, R. (2003). *What do you do with a tail like this?* Boston: Houghton Mifflin.

Most, B. (1994). *How big were the dinosaurs?* Orlando, FL: Harcourt Brace.

O'Brien, P. (1999). *Gigantic! How big were the dinosaurs?* New York: Holt.

Schwartz, D. (1999). *If you hopped like a frog*. New York: Scholastic.

Schwartz, D. (2003). *Millions to measure*. New York: HarperCollins.

Schwartz, D. (2005). *If dogs were dinosaurs*. New York: Scholastic.

Scieszka, J., & Smith, L. (1995). *Math curse*. New York: Penguin Books.

Scieszka, J., & Smith, L. (2004). *Science verse*. New York: Penguin Books.

Silverstein, S. (1996). *Falling up*. New York: HarperCollins.

Wells, R. (1993). *Is a blue whale the biggest thing there is?* Morton Grove, IL: Whitman.

Wells, R. (1995). *What's smaller than a pygmy shrew?* Morton Grove, IL: Whitman.

Related Instructional Resources

Berger, M., & Berger, G. (1998). *Why don't haircuts hurt? Questions and answers about the human body*. New York: Scholastic.

Dorling Kindersley. (1998). *DK nature encyclopedia*. London: Dorling Kindersley.

Farndon, J. (2002). *1000 facts on human body*. New York: Barnes & Noble Books.

Hare, T. (2005). *Animal fact file: Head-to-tail profiles of more than 90 mammals*. New York: Checkmark Books.

National Geographic Society. (2000). *National Geographic animal encyclopedia*. Hanover, PA: National Geographic Children's Books.

Parsons, J. (2000). *Children's illustrated encyclopedia*. London: Dorling Kindersley.

Schwartz, D. (2001). *Q is for quark: A science alphabet*. Berkeley, CA: Ten Speed Press.

Twist, C. (2005). *Reptiles and amphibians dictionary: An A to Z of cold-blooded creatures*. New York: Scholastic.

Related Websites

Animal Facts and Statistics

http://www.indianchild.com/amazing_facts.htm
http://www.bbc.co.uk/education/mathsfile/shockwave/games/animal.html
http://lsb.syr.edu/projects/cyberzoo/a_list.html
http://www.factmonster.com/ipka/A0768508.html
http://sunsite.berkeley.edu/KidsClick!/midanim.html
http://www.kidsplanet.org/factsheets/map.html
http://www.sandiegozoo.org/animalbytes/index.html
http://www.worldalmanacforkids.com/explore/animals.html

"A Closet Full of Shoes" (a poem in Falling Up) (1996)

by Shel Silverstein

HarperCollins, ISBN #0060248025

Zoo-ology (2002)

by Joelle Jolivet

Roaring Brook Press, ISBN #0761318941

Overview of Poem and Book: Learn about the zillions of shoes in a certain closet in Silverstein's "A Closet Full of Shoes." Then, in the 2-foot high oversized book *Zoo-ology*, readers encounter all kinds of animals categorized into eclectic groups such as black and white, underground, and spots and stripes. The closing pages reveal fascinating secrets about each of the animals appearing in the colorfully illustrated book.

Mathematical Concepts and Skills: sorting, classification, Venn diagrams, sets, subsets

Science Concepts and Skills: characteristics of organisms, animal classification, animal habitats

Overview of Activities: Students explore the classes and characteristics of animals while gaining practice with sorting, classification, and Venn diagrams.

National Mathematics Standards (2000):

Students in grades 3 through 5 should "collect data using observations" and "represent data using tables and graphs." Students should also "propose and justify conclusions and predictions that are based on data" (Data Analysis and Probability Standard) (p. 400).

National Science Standards (1996):

Students in grades K–4 should "develop understanding of the characteristics of organisms, life cycles of organisms, and organisms and environments" (p. 127). Students should understand that "each plant or animal has different structures that serve different functions in growth, survival, and reproduction" and that "many characteristics of an organism . . . result from an individual's interactions with the environment," while inherited characteristics of organisms "include the color of flowers and the number of limbs of an animal. Other features, such as the ability to ride a bicycle are learned through interactions with the environment and cannot be passed on to the next generation" (Life Science, Content Standard C) (p. 129).

Materials: blank Venn diagrams for each student (see website below), posterboard, markers or crayons

Description of Activities:

1. Ask students to name different types of footwear (e.g., sneakers, sandals, spikes, roller skates, slippers, flippers, boots, ballet shoes, bare feet, etc.). Encourage them to be creative in their thinking. Record their responses on the board.

2. Ask students to think of ways to categorize the footwear listed on the board (e.g., those with laces, those used in sports, etc.).

3. Read "A Closet Full of Shoes," setting the stage for the upcoming classification activity.

4. Prior to class, using a sticky note, cover up the category labeled "Cold" on page 9 of *Zoo-ology*. Allow students to view the animals appearing on pages 8 and 9 and to guess how they are categorized by looking for commonalities. Students should explain their reasoning and mention the attributes they noticed about the various animals that helped them determine their classification scheme. After students have offered some possibilities for how the animals are sorted, reveal that the category name is "Cold." Ask what other animals might belong (e.g., Siberian tiger) or not belong (e.g., camel) to this group.

5. Ask students to continue viewing pages 8 and 9 and to think of other ways to classify the "Cold" animals into smaller groups, or subsets; for example, those with (or without) fur, those with (or without) horns, those found in the ocean, etc.

6. Draw two large overlapping circles on the board. Describe how you will use a Venn diagram (i.e., the two overlapping circles) to categorize the "Cold" animals into subgroups. Label one circle, "Animals with Four Feet" and the other circle, "Animals of One Color." Call out the names of various animals listed on pages 8 and 9 and ask students to indicate where the name should appear in the Venn diagram. Assist students in understanding that animals appearing in the overlapping portion of the Venn diagram have four feet *and* are of one color.

7. Let students view another page in *Zoo-ology* (e.g., the "Hot" animals appearing on pages 6 and 7) and determine how these animals are classified. (Remember to cover up the category's name appearing at the bottom of the page.) Students should explain their reasoning. After students have offered some possibilities for how the animals are classified, reveal the category name. Share some of the animal facts about the animals found at the end of *Zoo-ology*.

8. Using the Blank Venn diagram website listed below, give students blank Venn diagrams (with either two loops or three loops) and ask them to think of a way to classify the "Hot" animals into smaller subsets (e.g., those with no feet, mammals vs. reptiles, poisonous vs. nonpoisonous, etc.). Students place the names of various animals in their appropriate locations on their Venn diagrams, but do *not* label the loops. Each student passes his or her Venn diagram to a classmate, challenging the second student to determine how each loop on the Venn diagram should be labeled.

9. Students choose any animal appearing in *Zoo-ology*. In pairs, students research the animal and create a poster displaying the following: the animal's name, classification (e.g., mammal, bird, reptile, etc.), and a description of its habitat. Students also record at least three interesting animal facts about their animal. Students share their findings in small groups or with the whole class.

Assessment:
- Did students discern attributes of animals and identify categories?
- Did students identify subsets of a larger set?
- Did students correctly construct, label, and interpret a Venn diagram?
- Did students provide accurate information about their animal and articulately present their posters to the class?

Activity Extensions:
- Students choose an animal and write a poem or short story from the animal's point of view.
- Locate ten interesting animal facts appearing at the end of *Zoo-ology* and list them on a sheet of paper along with ten animal names. Students match the name of the animal to the animal fact.

Cross-Curricular Connections:

Visual Arts
- Explore the artwork of various wildlife artists including John James Audubon.
- Explore and identify coloring and patterning in animal skin.

Social Studies
- Research how expanding populations and industry are impacting animal habitats.

Related Children's Literature

Florian, D. (2001). *Lizards, frogs, and polliwogs*. Orlando, FL: Voyager Books.

Goldsmith, M. (2001). *Galileo Galilei* (Scientists who made history series). New York: Raintree Steck-Vaughn.

Jenkins, S. (1995). *Biggest strongest fastest*. Boston: Houghton Mifflin.

Jenkins, S. (2004). *Actual size*. Boston: Houghton Mifflin.

Jenkins, S. (2005). *Prehistoric actual size*. Boston: Houghton Mifflin.

Jenkins, S. (2006). *Almost gone: The world's rarest animals*. New York: Scholastic.

Jenkins, S., & Page, R. (2003). *What do you do with a tail like this?* Boston: Houghton Mifflin.

Jolivet, J. (2002). *Zoo-ology*. Brookfield, CT: Roaring Brook Press.

Jolivet, J. (2005). *Almost everything*. Brookfield, CT: Roaring Brook Press.

Otto, C. (1996). *What color is camouflage?* New York: HarperCollins.

Pallotta, J. (2006). *Snakes: Long longer longest*. New York: Scholastic.

Schwartz, D. (1999*). If you hopped like a frog*. New York: Scholastic.

Scieszka, J., & Smith, L. (1995). *Math curse*. New York: Penguin Books.

Scieszka, J., & Smith, L. (2004). *Science verse*. New York: Penguin Books.

Silverstein, S. (1996). *Falling up*. New York: HarperCollins.

Wells, R. (1995). *What's smaller than a pygmy shrew?* Morton Grove, IL: Whitman.

Related Instructional Resources

Dorling Kindersley. (1998). *DK nature encyclopedia*. London: Dorling Kindersley.

Hare, T. (2005). *Animal fact file: Head-to-tail profiles of more than 90 mammals*. New York: Checkmark Books.

National Geographic Society. (2000). *National Geographic animal encyclopedia*. Hanover, PA: National Geographic Children's Books.

Parsons, J. (2000). *Children's illustrated encyclopedia*. London: Dorling Kindersley.

Schwartz, D. (2001). *Q is for quark: A science alphabet*. Berkeley, CA: Ten Speed Press.

Twist, C. (2005). *Reptiles and amphibians dictionary: An A to Z of cold-blooded creatures*. New York: Scholastic.

Related Websites

Animal Facts

http://www.indianchild.com/amazing_facts.htm

http://www.quia.com/cm/1000.html

http://www.bbc.co.uk/education/mathsfile/shockwave/games/animal.html

http://lsb.syr.edu/projects/cyberzoo/a_list.html

http://www.factmonster.com/ipka/A0768508.html

http://sunsite.berkeley.edu/KidsClick!/midanim.html

http://www.kidsplanet.org/factsheets/map.html

http://www.wildlifeart.org/ArtTales/index.html

http://www.sandiegozoo.org/animalbytes/index.html

http://www.worldalmanacforkids.com/explore/animals.html

Blank Venn Diagram

http://home.att.net/%7Eteaching/graphorg/venn.pdf

John James Audubon

http://www.audubon.org/bird/boa/BOA_index.html

Venn Diagram

http://www.readwritethink.org/lessons/lesson_view.asp?id=378

Virtual Manipulatives—Venn diagram

http://nlvm.usu.edu/en/nav/frames_asid_153_g_2_t_1.html?open=instructions

http://nlvm.usu.edu/en/nav/frames_asid_187_g_2_t_1.html?open=instructions

http://nlvm.usu.edu/en/nav/frames_asid_269_g_1_t_1.html?open=instructions

Good Enough to Eat: A Kid's Guide to Food and Nutrition (1999)

by Lizzy Rockwell

Scholastic, ISBN #0439819776

Overview of Book:	Learn about the food pyramid and eating healthy and wise by exploring the various nutrients present in food (carbohydrates, protein, fat, water, vitamins, and minerals), their functions, and how the body digests food and burns calories.
Mathematical Concepts and Skills:	data collection and interpretation, bar graphs, pie charts, tallying
Science Concepts and Skills:	personal health, food pyramid, nutrients, food groups
Overview of Activities:	Students explore the food pyramid and engage in graphing activities that prompt students to reflect on what they eat and whether they are eating in healthy ways. Students then plan a delicious and balanced menu that reflects the USDA Food Pyramid Guide.
National Mathematics Standards (2000):	Students in grades 3 through 5 should "collect data using observations, surveys, and experiments." Students should "represent data using tables and graphs such as line plots, bar graphs, and line graphs," and they should "propose and justify conclusions and predictions that are based on data" (Data Analysis and Probability Standard) (p. 400).
National Science Standards (1996):	Students in grades K–4 should "develop an understanding of personal health" (p. 138). Students should "understand how the body uses food and how various foods contribute to health." They should be aware of "recommendations for good nutrition including eating a variety of foods, eating less sugar, and eating less fat" (Science in Personal and Social Perspectives, Content Standard F) (p. 140).
Materials:	copy of the most recent USDA Food Pyramid
Description of Activities:	1. Record the following headings on the board: ALL OF THE TIME, MOST OF THE TIME, SOME OF THE TIME, RARELY. Using these headings, tally students' response to the question, "I eat in healthy ways . . ." Demonstrate how to tally. Total the responses for each category and circle the response that had the highest frequency. (This data will be used later in Step #5.)

2. Begin reading *Good Enough to Eat*. Pause at page 5 and generate verbal responses to the prompt, "Food makes you able to . . ." See how well students' responses match those in the book.

3. Continue reading, where students learn about the nutrients in food needed by our bodies. List the six nutrients on the board (carbohydrates, protein, fat, water, vitamins and minerals) and their functions.

4. Continue reading *Good Enough to Eat* and, when arriving at the page on which the Food Guide Pyramid is illustrated, give students a hardcopy of the food pyramid using one of the Food Pyramid websites below. (Make sure students are viewing the most recent guide.) Spend time discussing the number of servings of different foods we should eat to acquire all the nutrients and fiber our body needs.

5. Now that students are aware of the various types and amounts of food our body needs, ask students to respond to the same question posed in step #1 (i.e., "I eat in healthy ways . . .") and tally their responses. Compare the totals for each response category to those in step #1. Did the total count for each response category change? Now that they know more about nutrients and food groups, did the students indicate that they eat in healthy ways most of the time? Some of the time? Rarely? What are the implications and long-term effects of not eating in healthy ways? Of eating in healthy ways?

6. Finish reading *Good Enough to Eat*.

7. In their journals, students create a list of the various foods they ate the previous day and tally how many foods fall into the pyramid's subcategories (bread, cereal, rice, and pasta; vegetables; fruits; milk, yogurt, and cheese; meat, poultry, fish, dry beans, eggs, and nuts; fats, oils, and sweets).

8. Students create a bar graph (older students might create a pie chart) depicting the number of servings they ate from each food group. Students make observations of their data and graphs. From which food group did they eat the most? The least?

9. Students compare their serving totals to the number of servings prescribed by the USDA in their Food Guide Pyramid. Students decide whether they did or did not have a healthy diet yesterday, offering how they could improve their diet by eating more or less of different food groups.

10. Students design a menu for themselves, choosing delicious but healthy foods for each meal that would support the recommendations of the USDA. To help students choose foods, share with students the two introductory pages of *Good Enough to Eat* where they can view various types of foods in various food groups.

Assessment:

- Did students correctly tally, total, graph, and interpret their data?

- Did students make accurate observations about their diet relative to USDA recommendations?

- Did students create a healthy menu that would be advocated by the USDA?

Activity Extensions:

- Using pictures from magazines, students create collages of healthy foods showing foods from each food group.

- Discuss the importance of activity and exercise in maintaining a healthy lifestyle. Research how many calories are burned during various activities (bike riding, walking, jump rope, etc.). Students compute problems determining how many calories are burned when engaged in various activities.

- Read poetry about food and healthy eating in Shel Silverstein's *Where the Sidewalk Ends* (2004) (e.g., "I Must Remember," "Recipe for a Hippopotamus Sandwich," and "Hungry Mungry").

Cross-Curricular Connections:

Visual Arts

- Examine the seventeenth-century Dutch painter Floris van Dijck's painting entitled *Breakfast Still Life*. Would the USDA approve of this breakfast?

Social Studies

- Research and discuss which countries have the highest rates of malnourished populations and/or obesity. Why do these conditions exist? What are the implications? How can we ameliorate such circumstances?

- Research and discuss food traditions in other countries.

Related Children's Literature

Cole, J. (2000). *The magic school bus gets baked in a cake: A book about kitchen chemistry.* New York: Scholastic.

Gibbons, G. (2007). *The vegetables we eat.* New York: Holiday House.

Hoberman, M. (2000). *The seven silly eaters.* New York: Scholastic.

Leedy, L. (2001). *The edible pyramid: Good eating everyday.* New York: Holiday House.

Murphy, S. (2004). *Tally O'Malley.* New York: HarperCollins.

Needham, K. (1993). *Why do people eat?* Tulsa, OK: EDC.

Rabe, T. (2001). *Oh, the things that you can do that are good for you! All about staying healthy.* New York: Random House.

Rockwell, L. (1999). *Good enough to eat: A kid's guide to food and nutrition.* New York: Scholastic.

Royston, A. (2005). *Why do we need to eat?* Portsmouth, NH: Heinemann.

Scieszka, J., & Smith, L. (1995). *Math curse.* New York: Penguin Books.

Scieszka, J., & Smith, L. (2004). *Science verse.* New York: Penguin Books.

Sharmat, M. (1989). *Gregory, the terrible eater.* New York: Scholastic.

Silverstein, S. (2004). *Where the sidewalk ends.* New York: HarperCollins.

Silverstein, A., Silverstein, V., & Nunn, L. (2000). *Eat your vegetables! Drink your milk!* New York: Scholastic.

Related Instructional Resources

Dorling Kindersley. (2005). Food (DK eyewitness book series). New York: Dorling Kindersley.

Schlosser, E., & Wilson, C. (2006). *Chew on this: Everything you don't want to know about fast food.* Boston: Houghton Mifflin.

Schwartz, D. (2001). *Q is for quark: A science alphabet.* Berkeley, CA: Ten Speed Press.

Related Websites

Create a Graph
   http://nces.ed.gov/nceskids/createagraph/

Floris van Dijck—Dutch Painter of Still Life
   http://www.artcyclopedia.com/artists/dijck_floris_van.html

Food Pyramid
   www.usda.gov/cnpp/Pubs/Pyramid/fdgdpyr1.pdf
   http://www.nalusda.gov/fnic/Fpyr/pyramid.gif
   http://kidshealth.org/kid/stay_healthy/food/pyramid.html

The Moon Seems to Change (1987)

by Franklyn M. Branley

HarperCollins, ISBN #0064450651

Overview of Book: Readers will discover the various phases of the moon, what they look like, and why the moon changes its appearance as it revolves around the earth.

Mathematical Concepts and Skills: data collection and interpretation, bar graphs

Science Concepts and Skills: moon phases, movement of the moon in the sky

Overview of Activities: Students learn about and create the phases of the moon in an interactive experiment. Students then predict, collect class data, and graph which phase of the moon occurs on their next birthday.

National Mathematics Standards (2000): Students in grades 3 through 5 should "collect data using observations, surveys, and experiments." Students should "represent data using tables and graphs such as line plots, bar graphs, and line graphs." Students should also "propose and justify conclusions and predictions that are based on data" (Data Analysis and Probability Standard) (p. 400).

National Science Standards (1996): Students in grades K–4 should "develop an understanding of objects in the sky and changes in Earth and sky." Students should "identify sequences of changes" and "look for patterns by observing the day and night sky." Students should "draw the moon's shape for each evening on a calendar and then determine the pattern in the shapes over several weeks" (Earth and Space Science, Content Standard D) (p. 130). Also, as a result of activities, students should "develop abilities necessary to do scientific inquiry" and "develop understanding about scientific inquiry" (Science as Inquiry, Content Standard A) (p. 121).

Materials: pencils, oranges, flashlights, Internet, 4" × 6" index cards

Description of Activities:

1. Ask students to describe the various ways the moon might appear when they view it at night (e.g., full, crescent, not visible, etc.). Ask students to explain why they think the moon changes its appearance. Is the moon moving? The earth? Which body revolves around the other?, etc.

2. Begin reading *The Moon Seems to Change*. At the end of page 19, define and discuss the various phases of the moon and how and when they occur. Visit one of the Interactive Moon Phases websites so that students can watch the phases of the moon occur dynamically.

3. Engage students in the activity described on page 20, where students work in pairs to create the phases of the moon (using a pencil, orange, and flashlight). Make the classroom as dark as possible and let only two or three pairs work at one time so that the light from the flashlights does not interfere with each pairs' experiment.

4. Finish reading *The Moon Seems to Change*.

5. Using the What Will the Moon Look Like Tonight? website, students enter their birthdays and, on 4" × 6" index cards, make sketches of what the moon will look like on the night of their upcoming birthdays. Students label the bottoms of their sketches with the names of the moon phases. On the back of the cards, students should record their names and birthdays.

6. List the eight phases of the moon on the board in a vertical column. Students create a classroom horizontal bar graph by placing their index cards in the row that corresponds to their birthday's moon phase. Students make observations about the graph: What moon phase corresponded to the most birthdays? The least? Did two or more phases occur with the same frequency? Is there another way to graph our data?

Assessment:

- Did students accurately describe the appearance of the moon in terms of its phases?

- Did students create and identify the phases of the moon in their experiments?

- Did students make correct sketches of their birthday moons?

- Did students make accurate observations about the bar graph?

Activity Extensions:

- Explore which other planets in our solar system have moons.

- Explore the positioning of the sun, moon, and Earth in a solar and lunar eclipse by viewing the Eclipse Info websites listed below.

- Students view and record the phases of the moon on several past and present birthdays. Is the phase always the same?

- Visit the Plaque on Moon website and view the plaque Apollo 11 astronauts left on the moon. If you were to leave a plaque on the moon, what would it read?

- Enjoy poetry about the moon authored by Shel Silverstein (e.g., "Moon-Catchin' Net" [1981] and "A Battle in the Sky" [1996]).

Cross-Curricular Connections:

Visual Arts

- Explore and imitate artists' renditions of the moon (Vincent van Gogh's *Landscape with Couple Walking and Crescent Moon*, Alexander Calder's *Blue Moon over the Steeple,* Robert DeLaunay's *Simultaneous Contrast: Sun and Moon*, etc.).

Social Studies

- Explore biographies of astronauts who visited the moon or research the various Apollo missions.

Related Children's Literature

Branley, F. (1986). *What makes day and night*. New York: HarperCollins.

Branley, F. (1987). *The moon seems to change*. New York: HarperCollins.

Branley, F. (1998). *The planets in our solar system*. New York: HarperCollins.

Folwer, A. (1992). *So that's how the moon changes shape*! New York: Scholastic.

Gibbons, G. (1996). *The reasons for the seasons*. New York: Holiday House.

Gibbons, G. (1997). *The moon book*. New York: Holiday House.

Gibbons, G. (2005). *Planets*. New York: Holiday House.

Scieszka, J., & Smith, L. (1995). *Math curse*. New York: Penguin Books.

Scieszka, J., & Smith, L. (2004). *Science verse*. New York: Penguin Books.

Silverstein, S. (1981). *A light in the attic*. New York: HarperCollins.

Silverstein, S. (1996). *Falling up*. New York: HarperCollins.

Sis, P. (1996). *Starry messenger*. New York: Farrar Straus Giroux.

Sweeney, J. (1999). *Me and my place in space*. New York: Dragonfly Books.

Related Instructional Resources

Dickinson, T. (1995). *Other worlds: A beginner's guide to planets and moons*. Tonawanda, NY: Firefly.

Schwartz, D. (2001). *Q is for quark: A science alphabet*. Berkeley, CA: Ten Speed Press.

Simon, S. (1992). *Our solar system, vol. 1*. New York: HarperCollins.

Simon, S. (1995). *The solar system: Facts and exploration*. New York: Holt.

Twist, C. (2004). *Our solar system: A first introduction to space and the planets*. Hauppauge, NY: Barron's Educational Series.

Related Websites

Eclipse Info

http://sunearth.gsfc.nasa.gov/eclipse/lunar.html

http://www.factmonster.com/ipka/A0933255.html

http://www.kidseclipse.com/pages/a1b3c1d0.htm

Interactive Moon Phases

http://www.spaceday.org/conmgmt/index.php?option=displaypage&Itemid=156&op=page&SubMenu

http://www.harcourtschool.com/activity/moon_phases/

Moon Facts

http://solarsystem.jpl.nasa.gov/planets/profile.cfm?Object=Moon&Display=Kids

Moon Phases

http://www.kidsastronomy.com/astroskymap/lunar.htm

http://www.factmonster.com/ipka/A0875447.html

http://tycho.usno.navy.mil/vphase.html

Plaque on Moon

http://starchild.gsfc.nasa.gov/docs/StarChild/space_level2/apollo11_plaque.html

StarDate Moon Phases

http://stardate.org/nightsky/moon/

What Will the Moon Look Like Tonight?

http://www.nasa.gov/audience/forkids/home/CS_What_Will_Moon_Look_Like.html

Activities Featuring Connections

My First Book of Biographies (1994)

by Jean Marzollo

Scholastic, ISBN #0590450158

Overview of Book:	Discover the accomplishments and historical significance of forty-five famous individuals from various time periods, cultures, and backgrounds. Biographies include those on astronauts, U.S. presidents, artists, scientists, world leaders, athletes, etc.
Mathematical Concepts and Skills:	real-life applications of mathematics, careers in mathematics
Science Concepts and Skills:	real-life applications of science, careers in science, science and technology
Overview of Activities:	Students select, research, and share a biography of someone who has contributed to the fields of mathematics and/or the sciences. Students design a stamp honoring this individual.
National Mathematics Standards (2000):	Students in grades 3 through 5 should "recognize and apply mathematics in contexts outside of mathematics" (Connections Standard) (p. 402). Students should also "communicate their mathematical thinking coherently and clearly to peers, teachers, and others" (Communication Standard) (p. 402).
National Science Standards (1996):	Students in grades K–4 should "develop understanding of science as a human endeavor" and that "many people choose science as a career and devote their entire lives to studying it." Students should understand that "men and women have made a variety of contributions throughout the history of science and technology," but that "much more remains to be understood" (History and Nature of Science, Content Standard G) (p. 141). Students should also "develop an understanding about science and technology" and understand that "people have always had questions about their world. Science is one way of answering questions and explaining the natural world." Students should understand that people have "invented tools and techniques to solve problems" and to "make better observations, measurements, and equipment for investigations."

Students should understand that "women and men of all ages, backgrounds, and groups engage in a variety of scientific and technological work" (Science and Technology, Content Standard E) (p. 138).

Materials: Internet (or almanac or library resources), 8.5" × 11" white paper, crayons or markers

Description of Activities:

1. Read the introduction page appearing in *My First Book of Biographies* to set the stage for students' research project.

2. Read the short sentence appearing underneath each name entry in Marzollo's book, giving students a brief idea of what the person accomplished or is best known for.

3. Students are charged with selecting an individual to appear on an upcoming stamp. Students choose one individual from Marzollo's book (or someone else who contributed to the fields of mathematics and/or the sciences using the resources and websites listed below) and write a short biography on that person defending why he or she should be chosen. Students also design the stamp using 8.5" × 11" white paper (placed portrait style). Students share their stamps and biographies with the class and vote which individuals are responsible for the most remarkable accomplishments.

Assessment:
- Did students clearly articulate how their chosen individual contributed to the fields of mathematics and/or the sciences?

Activity Extensions:
- Visit the Birthplaces of Famous Mathematicians website and learn about mathematicians that may have been born in your ancestors' birthplaces.

- Discover the ingenious inventions of females in books authored by Catherine Thimmesh (2000, 2002).

Cross-Curricular Connections:

Visual Arts
- Research artists who used mathematics in their works (Leonardo da Vinci, Albrecht Durer, M. C. Escher, Henri Matisse, etc.).

- Create a collage depicting various careers in which people use math or science (e.g., medical doctor, computer technician, astronaut, etc.).

Social Studies
- Discuss the importance of working independently and cooperatively to accomplish goals.

Related Children's Literature

Barasch, L. (2005). *Ask Albert Einstein*. New York: Foster Books.

Barretta, G. (2006). *Now and Ben: The modern inventions of Ben Franklin*. New York: Holt.

Borden, L., & Kroeger, M. (2004). *Fly high! The story of Bessie Coleman*. New York: Aladdin Books.

Brown, D. (2004). *Odd boy out: Young Albert Einstein*. Boston: Houghton Mifflin.

DeMauro, L. (2002). *Thomas Edison: A brilliant inventor* (Time for kids series). New York: HarperCollins.

Fradin, D. (2002). *Who was Ben Franklin?* New York: Penguin Young Readers.

Frith, M. (2005). *Who was Thomas Alva Edison?* New York: Penguin Young Readers.

Fritz, J. (1996). *What's the big idea, Ben Franklin?* New York: Penguin Young Readers.

Goldsmith, M. (2001). *Galileo Galilei* (Scientists who made history series). New York: Raintree Steck-Vaughn.

Hulme, J. (2005). *Wild Fibonacci: Nature's secret code revealed*. Berkeley, CA: Tricycle Press.

Kupchella, R. (2004). *Girls Can! Make it happen*. Golden Valley, MN: Tristan.

Lasky, K. (1994). *The librarian who measured the earth*. Boston: Little, Brown.

Marzollo, J. (1994). *My first book of biographies: Great men and women every child should know*. New York: Scholastic.

Moss, M. (2001). *Brave Harriet: The first woman to fly the English Channel*. Orlando, FL: Harcourt.

Reimer, L., & Reimer, W. (1995). *Mathematicians are people, too*. Palo Alto, CA: Dale Seymour.

Ryan, P. (1999). *Amelia and Eleanor go for a ride*. New York: Scholastic.

Satterfield, K. (2005). *Benjamin Franklin: A man of many talents* (Time for kids series). New York: HarperCollins.

Saunders, H. (1988). *When are we ever gonna have to use this?* Palo Alto, CA: Dale Seymour.

Scieszka, J., & Smith, L. (1995). *Math curse*. New York: Penguin Books.

Scieszka, J., & Smith, L. (2004). *Science verse*. New York: Penguin Books.

Sis, P. (1996). *Starry messenger*. New York: Farrar Straus Giroux.

Thimmesh, C. (2000). *Girls think of everything: Stories of ingenious inventions by women*. Boston: Houghton Mifflin.

Thimmesh, C. (2002). *The sky's the limit: Stories of discovery by women and girls*. Boston: Houghton Mifflin.

Related Instructional Resources

Childhood of Famous Americans Series (Aladdin)

Giants of Science Series (Penguin Young Readers)

History Maker Bio Series (Lerner Publishing)

Time for Kids Series (HarperCollins)

Krull, K. (1993). *Lives of the musicians: Good times, bad times (and what the neighbors thought)*. San Diego: Harcourt.

Krull, K. (1995). *Lives of the artists: Masterpieces, messes*. San Diego: Harcourt.

Schwartz, D. (2001). *Q is for quark: A science alphabet*. Berkeley, CA: Ten Speed Press.

VanCleave, J. (2004). *Scientists through the ages*. Hoboken, NJ: Wiley.

Related Websites

Biographies of Scientists
> http://www.blupete.com/Literature/Biographies/Science/Scients.htm
> http://www.infoplease.com/spot/scibio8.html
> http://www.maths.tcd.ie/pub/HistMath/Links/SciBiog.html

Biographies of Women Mathematicians
> http://www.awm-math.org/biographies.html
> http://www-groups.dcs.st-and.ac.uk/~history/Indexes/Women.html

Biographies of Women in Science
> http://www.awm-math.org/biographies.html#sciencebios

Birthplaces of Famous Mathematicians
> http://www-groups.dcs.st-and.ac.uk/~history/BiogIndex.html

Literature-Based Mathematics and Social Studies Activities

2

The Mathematics–Social Studies Connection

Social studies encompasses many disciplines including anthropology, archaeology, economics, geography, history, law, philosophy, political science, psychology, religion, and sociology. Social studies also draws on "appropriate content from the humanities, mathematics, and natural sciences" (NCSS, 1994, p. vii). According to the National Council for the Social Studies (1994), the primary purpose of teaching social studies is to enable learners to become informed consumers and skilled decision makers working toward the public good in a culturally diverse, democratic society coexisting in an interdependent world. Further, exemplary social studies programs prepare students to acquire, organize, interpret, and communicate information; process data and draw conclusions; and generate and assess alternative approaches to problem solving and making decisions (NCSS, 1994). These same skills of thinking, observing, hypothesizing, reasoning, communicating, and problem solving are skills the National Council of Teachers of Mathematics advocates in its *Principles and Standards for School Mathematics* (NCTM, 2000).

A growing body of research and anecdotal evidence documents the power of teaching social studies and mathematics in an integrated fashion, in particular by using children's literature (Butzow & Butzow, 2006; Donoghue, 2001; Fredericks, 1991, 2000; Gallavan, 2001; Martinez & McGee, 2000; McCoy, 2003; Moss, 2003; Rose, 2000; Thompson & Holyoke, 2000; Ward, 2004b; Whitin & Whitin, 2004). Further, works of fiction and nonfiction offer a lens for students to see, understand, and experience their world. By integrating children's literature into one's teaching, students can explore the many themes of social studies (such as culture, economics, and geography) while learning the mathematics and statistics that support and define these themes.

> "Children's literature enables students to explore the many themes of social studies while learning about mathematics and statistics."

This chapter articulates a variety of literature-based activities that integrate concepts and skills used and learned in the study of mathematics with those in social studies. While engaged in these activities, students will discover and gain practice with such mathematics concepts and skills as money, computation with money, ratio, multiplication, division, percentages (Number and Operations Standard); writing number sentences, patterns, functions (Algebra Standard); two- and three-dimensional shapes, attributes of shapes, classification of polygons and polyhedra, coordinate graphing (Geometry Standard); time (Measurement Standard); and sorting, classification, combinations, chance, data collection and interpretation, graphing, pie charts, histograms, stem-and-leaf plots (Data Analysis and Probability Standard).

Social studies concepts and skills featured in this chapter include individuals' wants and needs, role of money in everyday life, currencies of different countries, voting, history of voting, voting as a right and responsibility of citizens, electoral college, purpose of government, how government provides or does not provide for peoples' needs, characteristics of governments, map features, plotting latitude and longitude, exploration and comparison of the various types of maps, geography, world population distributions, literacy and hunger rates, religions and languages in the world, distribution of money and access to resources in the world, tourism and industry in states, state facts, Egyptian culture, Egyptian architecture, geography of Egypt, pyramids, Navajo people and their culture, aspects of the Chinese New Year, creation and interpretation of timelines, comparing and contrasting different stories or accounts about events, history of transportation, modes of transportation, identification of scientific and technological advances, and promoting the common good through civic action.

The integrated literature-based activities also provide students with many opportunities to predict, estimate, problem-solve, and reason (Problem Solving and Reasoning and Proof Standards) as well as communicate and use various representations to organize, record, model, and interpret mathematical ideas (Communication and Representation Standards). Further, students will discover and explore real-life applications of mathematics and social studies and careers in mathematics and social studies (Connections Standard).

Remember to check the appendix for ideas and samples of assessment rubrics.

Matrix of Mathematics and Social Studies Activities

BOOK TITLE	MATHEMATICAL CONCEPTS AND SKILLS	SOCIAL STUDIES CONCEPTS AND SKILLS	SCIENCE CONCEPTS AND SKILLS	VISUAL ARTS CONCEPTS AND SKILLS
Sam and the Lucky Money	money, computation with money, ratio, multiplication	individuals' wants and needs, role of money in everyday life, currencies of different countries, aspects of the Chinese New Year	history and development of the Chinese calendar and other calendars	create Chinese lanterns or paper dragons, artwork of foreign currencies
The Great Divide	division, writing number sentences, patterns, problem solving	history of transportation, modes of transportation, creation of timelines	transportation and pollution	artists' renditions of transportation
One Grain of Rice	patterns, functions, estimation	purpose of government, how government provides or does not provide for peoples' needs, characteristics of governments	importance of nutrition, impact of malnutrition and famine, rice, Indian animals	geometric patterns in Indian artwork
"Safe?" (a poem in *Falling Up*); *Maps and Globes*	coordinate graphing, ordered pairs, plotting points, moving directionally	map features (equator, lines of latitude and longitude, hemispheres), determining latitude and longitude	characteristics and habitats of organisms in various environments, geographical facts	creation of state or international flags, artists' renditions of maps
Mummy Math: An Adventure in Geometry; Mummies, Pyramids, and Pharaohs: A Book about Ancient Egypt	two- and three-dimensional shapes, polyhedra, prisms, pyramids, cones, cylinders, spheres, sorting, classification	Egyptian culture, architecture, geography, pyramids, maps	mummification	drawing three-dimensional shapes, three-dimensional shapes in works of arts, art in Mayan and Aztec pyramids
How Do You Know What Time It Is?; Alice Yazzie's Year	measurement of time, estimation, prediction	comparing and contrasting different stories or accounts about events, Navajo people and culture	passage of time and changes in temperature in Alaska, create and read sundials, early civilizations' observations of the moon	create southwestern illustrations, Navajo artists, Native American artwork and crafts, geometry in Navajo and Native American quilts, Salvador Dali's "melting clocks"

BOOK TITLE	MATHEMATICAL CONCEPTS AND SKILLS	SOCIAL STUDIES CONCEPTS AND SKILLS	SCIENCE CONCEPTS AND SKILLS	VISUAL ARTS CONCEPTS AND SKILLS
Duck for President	combinations, chance, majority, percentages, problem solving, real-life applications of mathematics	voting, history of voting, voting as a right and responsibility of citizens, electoral college	environmental issues on current election ballots	Mount Rushmore
If the World Were a Village: A Book about the World's People	prediction, estimation, data interpretation, graphing, pie charts	geography, world population distributions, literacy and hunger rates, religions and languages in the world, distribution of money and access to global resources	importance of nutrition, impact of malnutrition and famine; history of electricity	Richard Diebenkorn's aerial view artwork, artists' renditions of maps
The Train of States	histogram, stem-and-leaf plots, data interpretation	tourism and industry in states, state facts (capitals, dates of statehood, landmarks, historical significance, etc.)	history of trains as a source of transportation	collage of state facts, creation of state flags
"Invention" (a poem in *Where the Sidewalk Ends*); *Perfect Inventions = Perfect World*	real-life applications of mathematics, careers in mathematics	identification of scientific and technological advances, promoting the common good through civic action	exploration of a biographical piece	inventions and sketches of Leonardo da Vinci, collage of inventors, collage of careers

Sam and the Lucky Money (1995)

by Karen Chinn

Scholastic, ISBN #0439698898

Overview of Book:
Readers are reminded that giving is more important than receiving in this tale of a young boy who looks for ways to spend his $4 while walking through an American urban Chinatown during the Chinese New Year. Readers will enjoy the colorful illustrations that bring to life the sights and sounds of celebration of the Chinese New Year in a city.

Mathematical Concepts and Skills:
money, computation with money, ratio, multiplication

Social Studies Concepts and Skills:
individuals' wants and needs, role of money in everyday life, currencies of different countries, aspects of the Chinese New Year

Overview of Activities:
Students discuss the role of money and an individual's needs and wants. Students also explore and present various aspects of the Chinese New Year including its history, the artistry in its celebration, its celebratory foods, and the Chinese calendar. Students then create a budget for a one-week trip to China, determining the cost of various travel-related items in U.S. dollars and in Chinese yuans.

National Mathematics Standards (2000):

π

Students in grades 3 through 5 should "develop fluency in adding, subtracting, multiplying, and dividing whole numbers" and they should "develop and use strategies to estimate computations involving fractions and decimals in situations relevant to students' experiences" (Number and Operations Standard) (p. 392).

National Social Studies Standards (1994):

Social studies programs for early grades should include experiences that provide for the study of *global connections and interdependence,* so that the learner can "examine the relationships and tensions between personal wants and needs" (p. 70). Social studies programs for early grades should include experiences that provide for the study of *how people organize for the production, distribution, and consumption of goods and services,* so that the learner can "explain and demonstrate the role of money in everyday life," "distinguish between needs and wants," and "describe the influences of incentives, values, traditions, and habits on economic decisions" (p. 65).

Materials: Internet (or other informational resources)

Description of Activities:

1. Begin a discussion about the Chinese New Year. Record on the board any facts students might know about the Chinese New Year.

2. Read *Sam and the Lucky Money*. At the end of the book, ask students what is the author's message. How would they have responded in Sam's situation?

3. Ask students to each write a paragraph in which they explain the difference between one's needs and wants. Students give at least one example of something they want but may or may not need. Discuss the importance of society being more aware of one another's needs and how people can organize to help the needy. Discuss the role of money in everyday life. How does money help us to meet our needs and wants? Is it important or necessary to be wealthy?

4. Divide the class into four groups:

    • the historians (who research and present facts and statistics about the history and customs of the Chinese New Year);

    • the event planners (who research the various colors, decorations [e.g., paper lanterns, cloth dragon, etc.], and "music" [e.g., fire-crackers] used during the celebration of the Chinese New Year);

    • the chefs (who research the foods [e.g., Trays of Togetherness, etc.] eaten during the Chinese New Year);

    • the timekeepers (who research the Chinese calendar and how animals are associated with each year, the characteristics of each of the animals, etc.).

    Using the websites listed below or other informational resources, each group should develop some type of artifact (whether a PowerPoint presentation, posterboard presentation, diorama, collage, etc.), displaying their findings. All students in each group take part in presenting these findings.

5. Students record in their journals the five most interesting facts they learned about the Chinese New Year.

6. Remind students that, at the beginning of the story, *Sam and the Lucky Money*, Sam receives $4. Using the Currency Converter websites listed below, find out the exchange rate between the U.S. dollar and the Chinese yuan (pronounced "you an"). (For example, as of July 2007, one U.S. dollar was worth 7.56 Chinese yuan.) How much is $4 in Chinese yuans?

7. Students work in small groups and plan a one-week trip to China and create an accompanying budget of expenses. Students research the cost for an airline ticket, hotel accommodations, food, transportation, entertainment (museums, sight-seeing venues, etc.), passport fees, and other travel-related expenses. Students develop a two-column spreadsheet showing the cost of each item in U.S. dollars in the first column. Using the current exchange rate (between the U.S. dollar and the Chinese yuan), students compute the cost of each item in Chinese yuans, recording this figure in the second column of the spreadsheet. Students may use calculators to assist in their computations. Can students travel to China if they have a budget of 25,000 yuans?

Assessment:

- Did students actively participate in classroom discussions about wants vs. needs, the role of money, and the message set forth in *Sam and the Lucky Money*?

- Did students actively participate in the creation and the presentation of their findings on the Chinese New Year?

- Did students record in their journals five facts they learned about the Chinese New Year?

- Did students create an accurate budget and correctly convert between U.S. dollars and Chinese yuans?

Activity Extensions:

- Using the Chinese Calendar website listed below, students discover what animals correspond to their birth years. Students then create and interpret a class bar graph (or pictograph or pie chart) showing the frequency of each animal.

- Students explore the celebration of other holidays by various cultures.

- Using the Currency Converter websites listed below, students research and explore the names of other countries' currencies (e.g., Japanese yen, British pound, Mexican peso, etc.) as well as their value relative to the U.S. dollar. Students solve problems involving ratios and convert between and among the different currencies.

- Explore money in poetry by Shel Silverstein (e.g., "Smart" [2004], "The Googies Are Coming" [2004], and "Big Eating Contest" [1996]) and Jack Prelutsky (e.g., "Baloney Belly Billy" [1984]).

Cross-Curricular Connections:

Visual Arts

- Create a traditional Chinese New Year lantern.

- Work in groups to create a large paper dragon.

- Explore the design and artistry of various countries' paper currencies.

Science

- Explore the history and development of the Chinese calendar and compare it to other calendars, such as the Julian calendar, Gregorian calendar, etc. How did the Chinese and other civilizations record the passage of time?

Related Children's Literature

Adil, J. (2006). *Supply and demand*. Mankato, MN: Capstone Press.

Axelrod, A. (1997). *Pigs will be pigs: Fun with math and money*. New York: Aladdin Paperbacks.

Bouchard, D. (1999). *The dragon new year: A Chinese legend*. Atlanta: Peachtree.

Chinn, K. (1995). *Sam and the lucky money*. New York: Scholastic.

Crane, C. (2006). *D is for dragon: A China alphabet*. Chelsea, MI: Sleeping Bear Press.

Demi. (2003). *Happy, happy Chinese New Year!* New York: Crown Books for Young Readers.

Franco, B. (2003). *Super garage sale*. Vernon Hills, IL: ETA Cuisenaire.

Liatsos, S. (1999). *Poems to count on*. New York: Scholastic.

Mackey, L. (2004). *Money mama and the three little pigs*. Angoura Hills, CA: P4K.

Morrissey, T. (2005). *My mom is a dragon*. San Francisco: ThingsAsian Press.

Murphy, S. (1998). *The penny pot*. New York: Scholastic.

Prelutsky, J. (1984). *The new kid on the block*. New York: Scholastic.

Schwartz, D. (1989). *If you made a million*. New York: Lothrop, Lee & Shepard.

Scieszka, J., & Smith, L. (1995). *Math curse*. New York: Penguin Books.

Silverstein, S. (1996). *Falling up*. New York: HarperCollins.

Silverstein, S. (2004). *Where the sidewalk ends*. New York: HarperCollins.

Vaughan, M. (1996). *The dancing dragon*. New York: Mondo.

Viorst, J. (1988). *Alexander, who used to be rich last Sunday*. New York: Aladdin Paperbacks.

Williams, R. (2001). *The coin counting book*. Watertown, MA: Charlesbridge.

Related Instructional Resources

Brown, T. (1987). *Chinese new year*. New York: Holt.

Chan, H (2004). *Celebrating Chinese New Year: An activity book*. Cincinnati, OH: Asia for Kids.

Cribb, J. (2005). *Money* (Eyewitness books series). New York: Dorling Kindersley.

Dillon, S. (2003). *The Scholastic big book of holidays around the year*. New York: Scholastic.

Jones, L. (2003). *Kids around the world celebrate! The best feasts and festivals from many lands* (Kids around the world series). New York: Jossey-Bass.

Kindersley, A., & Kindersley, B. (1997). *Children just like me! Celebrations*. New York: DK Children.

Morrissey, T. (2006). *Hiss! Pop! Boom! Celebrating Chinese New Year*. San Francisco: ThingsAsian Press.

Press, J. (2001). *Around the world art & activities: Visiting the 7 continents through craft fun*. Charlotte, VT: Williamson.

Simmonds, N., Swartz, L., & Children's Museum, Boston. (2002). *Moonbeams, dumplings and dragon boats: A treasury of Chinese holiday tales, activities & recipes*. Fairbanks, AK: Gulliver Books.

Related Websites

Chinese Calendar

http://www.fi.edu/fellows/fellow1/apr99/calendar/index.html

Chinese New Year Facts and Statistics

http://www.educ.uvic.ca/faculty/mroth/438/CHINA/chinese_new_year.html
http://news.nationalgeographic.com/news/2001/01/0123-newyear.html
http://edsitement.neh.gov/view_lesson_plan.asp?id=381

Chinese New Year Lantern

http://www.newton.mec.edu/Angier/DimSum/china__dim_sum__spring_fes.html

Create a Graph Online

http://nces.ed.gov/nceskids/createagraph/

Currency Converter

http://www.gocurrency.com/currency-conversion.htm
http://finance.yahoo.com/currency?u

Exploring Coin Values with Shel Silverstein Poems

http://www.usmint.gov/kids/index.cfm?FileContents=/kids/teachers/LessonView.cfm&LessonPlanId=115
http://www.glc.k12.ga.us/BuilderV03/LPTools/LPShared/lpdisplay.asp?LPID=17755

Making Money and Minds

http://www.pbs.org/wgbh/nova/moolah/hotsciencemoolah/
http://www.usmint.gov/kids/coinnews/index.cfm

Math Poems—*Money*

http://www.tooter4kids.com/classroom/math_poems.htm

Virtual Manipulatives Library—Count the Money

http://nlvm.usu.edu/en/nav/frames_asid_325_g_2_t_1.html

The Great Divide (1999)

by Dayle Ann Dodds

Candlewick Press, ISBN #0763615927

Overview of Book:	Readers embark on a rhyming cross-country race and see the field of eighty contestants narrow page after page in a halving pattern in *The Great Divide*.
Mathematical Concepts and Skills:	division, writing number sentences, patterns, problem solving
Social Studies Concepts and Skills:	history of transportation, modes of transportation, creation of timelines
Overview of Activities:	Students gain practice with division and express the division equations articulated in *The Great Divide* as the story unfolds. Then, students explore, compare, contrast, discuss, and present various modes of transportation.
National Mathematics Standards (2000):	Students in grades 3 through 5 should "understand the various meanings of multiplication and division" and "the effects of multiplying and dividing whole numbers" (Number and Operations Standard) (p. 392). Students should also "express mathematical relationships using equations" (Algebra Standard) (p. 394).
National Social Studies Standards (1994):	Social studies programs for early grades should include experiences that provide for the study of *relationships among science, technology and society,* so that the learner can "identify and describe examples in which science and technology have changed the lives of people, such as in homemaking, childcare, work, transportation, and communication" (p. 67).
Materials:	paper, Internet (or other resources)
Description of Activities:	1. Begin reading *The Great Divide*. As the story unfolds, challenge students to record in their journals the equation (e.g., $80 \div 2 = 40$) that represents the current number of bikers and bikers remaining after each twist and turn.

2. At the end of the story, place students into four groups and play "Half Steps to One." Give each group a piece of paper. Announce the starting number and have one student in each group record this number on the paper. Students pass the paper clockwise to the next person, who will take that number, cut it in half, and record it on the paper. If students encounter a fractional result, ignore the fractional part, and round the number down (e.g., 25 cut in half is 12.5, so round down to 12.). Students continue passing the paper clockwise in their small groups until a student reaches 1. This student should raise his or her hand immediately and read aloud the computational results to check for accuracy (e.g., if the starting number is 60, students ought to record the following series of numbers on their paper: 60, 30, 15, 7, 3, 1.). If the halving steps are correct, this group wins.

3. Students might play "Quarter Steps to One" and change the divisor to 4, thus taking one quarter of the number each time. Students continually divide the resulting number by 4 until they reach 1.

4. Revisit the various modes of transportation that appear in *The Great Divide*, namely, bikes, boats, horses, hot air balloons, airplanes, and foot travel. Challenge students to think of other modes of transportation (e.g., automobile, truck, motorcycle, train, helicopter, monorail, submarine, steamboat, covered wagon, subway, rocket, etc.).

5. Students form small groups and research the history of a particular type of transportation. Students identify the evolution, benefits, and disadvantages of the mode of transportation. Students might create a PowerPoint presentation or develop large posters or a collage to share the findings with the class. Students should develop a timeline, complete with graphic images or illustrations, showing the evolution of their choice of transportation.

6. Allow students to enjoy poetry about transportation by reading such poems as "The Little Road," "The Bridge," "Bus Stop," "The Subway Train," and "My Legs and I" in Jacobs's (1993) book.

Assessment:
- Did students correctly record each division equation and divide accurately?

- Did students present an articulate, accurate, and complete history of their choice of transportation?

Activity Extensions:

- Explore the numeric pattern that results by tearing a piece of paper in half, in half again, and then in half again, etc. Students might develop a two-column table in which they keep track of the number of tears and the resulting number of pieces of paper. Can students articulate what the pattern is? (Answer: It is a doubling pattern.) Can students continue the pattern and guess how many pieces of paper would result after 10 tears? (Answer: $2^{10} = 1024$). After 20 tears? (Answer: $2^{20} = 1,048,576$). Can students express the equation that models the pattern? (Answer: The pattern is an exponential function; namely, $P = 2^T$ where P is the number of pieces of paper and T is the number of the tear.) Explain how exponential functions grow slowly in the beginning but then quickly increase.

- Explore the Women's History in Transportation website and see females' contribution to the advancement of transportation.

- Read a biography of Amelia Earhart (first woman to fly solo across the Atlantic Ocean), Harriet Quimby (first woman to fly solo across the English Channel), Bessie Coleman (first female African American pilot), or Sally Ride (first American woman in space).

- Enjoy poetry about transportation authored by Shel Silverstein (e.g., "Homemade Boat" [2004], "The Little Blue Engine" [2004], and "The Acrobats" [2004]) and Jack Prelutsky (e.g., "Nine Mice" [1984]).

Cross-Curricular Connections:

Visual Arts

- Explore pages 48–51 in *A Child's Book of Art* (Micklethwait, 1993) in which the author shows a variety of artistic masterpieces depicting means of travel. Challenge students to locate other pieces of artwork that depict modes of transportation.

Science

- Research which modes of transportation do and do not contribute to air pollution and noise pollution.

Related Children's Literature

Aird, H. (1986). *Henry Ford: Young man with ideas* (Childhood of famous Americans series). New York: Aladdin.

Borden, L., & Kroeger, M. (2004). *Fly high! The story of Bessie Coleman*. New York: Aladdin.

Bunting, E. (1990). *How many days to America: A Thanksgiving story*. Boston: Houghton Mifflin.

Dodds, D. (1999). *The great divide*. Cambridge, MA: Candlewick Press.

Erickson, P. (1997). *Daily life in a covered wagon*. New York: Penguin Young Readers.

Fraser, M. (1996). *Ten mile day: And the building of the Transcontinental Railroad*. New York: Holt.

Hirschmann, K. (2001). *Necco Sweethearts series: Math magic*. New York: Scholastic.

Hutchins, P. (1986). *The doorbell rang*. New York: Greenwillow Books.

Jacobs, L. (1993). *Is somewhere always far away? Poems about places*. New York: Holt.

Kupchella, R. (2004). *Girls Can! Make it happen*. Golden Valley, MN: Tristan.

McGovern, A. (1991). *If you sailed on the Mayflower in 1620*. New York: Scholastic.

Moss, M. (2001). *Brave Harriett*. San Diego: Harcourt.

Murphy, S. (1996). *Give me half!* New York: HarperCollins.

Murphy, S. (1997). *Divide and ride*. New York: HarperCollins.

Pallotta, J. (2003). *Hershey's kisses multiplication and division*. New York: Scholastic

Pinczes, E. (1993). *One hundred hungry ants*. Boston: Houghton Mifflin.

Pinczes, E. (1995). *A remainder of one*. Boston: Houghton Mifflin.

Prelutsky, J. (1984). *The new kid on the block*. New York: Scholastic.

Ryan, P. (1999). *Amelia and Eleanor go for a ride*. New York: Scholastic.

Scieszka, J., & Smith, L. (1995). *Math curse*. New York: Penguin Books.

Silverstein, S. (2004). *Where the sidewalk ends*. New York: HarperCollins.

Sutton, R. (2005). *Car* (Eyewitness books series). New York: Dorling Kindersley.

Related Instructional Resources

Bingham, C. (2006). *DK big book of transportation*. New York: Dorling Kindersley.

Conley, R. (2005). *The automobile* (Inventions that shaped the world series). New York: Scholastic.

Halpern, M. (2004). *Railroad fever: Building the Transcontinental Railroad 1830–1870*. Washington, DC: National Geographic Society.

Heap, C. (1996). *DK big book of trains*. New York: Dorling Kindersley.

Micklethwait, L. (1993). *A child's book of art: Great pictures: First words*. New York: Dorling Kindersley.

Oxlade, C. (1999). *Ships: A fascinating fact file and learn-it-yourself book* (Investigations series). London: Anness Publishing.

Wilkinson, P. (1995). *Transportation* (Ideas that changed the world series). New York: Chelsea House.

Related Websites

History of Automobiles
> http://inventors.about.com/library/inventors/blcar.htm
> http://www.ausbcomp.com/~bbott/cars/carhist.htm

History of Boats and Ships
> http://www.historyworld.net/wrldhis/PlainTextHistories.asp?groupid=104&HistoryID=aa14
> http://www.boatsafe.com/kids/navigation.htm

History of Trains
> http://www.csrmf.org/doc.asp?id=345
> http://www.pbs.org/wgbh/amex/tcrr/

History of Transportation
> http://www.si.edu/resource/faq/nmah/transportation.htm
> http://inventors.about.com/library/inventors/bl_history_of_transportation.htm
> http://americanhistory.si.edu/ONTHEMOVE/themes/story_48_1.html

Women's History in Transportation
> http://www.si.edu/resource/faq/nmah/transportation.htm

Activities Featuring Algebra

One Grain of Rice (1997)

by Demi

Scholastic, ISBN #059093998X

Overview of Book:
Learn the tale of Rani, a wise and resourceful village girl who outsmarts a greedy raja by requesting for her reward one grain of rice for thirty days.

Mathematical Concepts and Skills:
patterns, functions, estimation

Social Studies Concepts and Skills:
purpose of government, how government provides or does not provide for peoples' needs, characteristics of governments

Overview of Activities:
Students explore, estimate, and predict the results of a doubling pattern and express the pattern algebraically. Students then explore, discuss, compare, and contrast various forms of governance and how these entities meet (or do not meet) peoples' needs.

National Mathematics Standards (2000):
Students in grades 3 through 5 should "describe, extend, and make generalizations about geometric and numeric patterns." They should "represent and analyze patterns and functions using words, tables, and graphs" (Algebra Standard) (p. 394).

National Social Studies Standards (1994):
Social studies programs for early grades should include experiences that provide for the study of *how people create and change structures of power, authority, and governance*, so that the learner can "explain the purpose of government" and "give examples of how government does or does not provide for needs and wants of people, establish order and security, and manage conflict" (p. 63). Social studies programs for early grades should include experiences that provide for the study of *how people organize for the production, distribution, and consumption of goods and services*, so that the learner can "give examples that show how scarcity and choice govern our economic decisions" (p. 65).

Materials:
looseleaf (or ruled paper), calculators, world map

Description of Activities:

1. Students fold a piece of looseleaf (or ruled paper) in half vertically. Students label the column on the left "Number of the day" and label the column on the right "Grains of rice received." Begin reading *One Grain of Rice*. Pause after reading that Rani asks for "two grains of rice, the next day four grains of rice, and so on for thirty days."

2. Students complete the table they have created by recording the number of grains of rice Rani receives each day up until day five. Ask students if they notice a pattern in the number of grains of rice received. If this pattern were to continue, ask students to estimate how many grains of rice Rani would receive on day thirty. Let some students share their estimations and their thinking.

3. Challenge students to work collaboratively to express the (doubling) pattern by writing its corresponding number sentence or equation. (The pattern can be expressed as $N = 2^{(d-1)}$, where N = number of grains of rice received and d = the number of the day.)

4. Using this equation, students use calculators to compute the number of grains of rice Rani will receive on day thirty (536,870,912 grains). Students compare this number to their original estimations. How accurate were their estimations? Were students surprised at the enormity of this number and at how fast the doubling pattern grew? Explain that the equation that models the grains of rice Rani receives is an exponential function. Exponential functions begin by growing slowly, but then increase very quickly.

5. Finish reading *One Grain of Rice* so that students can compare their calculations (i.e., data entries in their tables of values) with the numbers in the story.

6. Ask students to describe the ruler in *One Grain of Rice*. The raja in the story considers himself to be fair, yet the story paints him as a selfish dictator.

7. Using the Outline Maps website or the Printable Maps website, give students a blank map and have them mark where India is located. Discuss India's form of government, which is a federal republic. Students research and discuss the characteristics of the Indian government.

8. Label the forms of governance of other countries on a map. Students should also compare and contrast aspects of a democratic society to one that is run by a different form of government, namely a tyrannical government. (Consider viewing the World Factbook—Guide to Country Profiles website for supplemental information.) What are the advantages and disadvantages to both? Students write a brief piece describing a day in the life of someone living under tyrannical governance.

Assessment:

- Did students make accurate estimations regarding the number of grains of rice Rani would receive and clearly explain their reasoning?

- Did students correctly compute the number of grains of rice received each day?

- Did students compose a number sentence or equation that modeled the doubling pattern?

- Did students articulate the forms of government in place in various parts of the world?

- Did students correctly articulate the characteristics of various governments?

- Did students clearly articulate the advantages and disadvantages of various forms of governance?

Activity Extensions:

- At the end of Demi's book, the author tells us that Rani received over one billion grains of rice. Challenge students to view their data, sum all of the grains of rice received cumulatively, and verify this. Refer to the final page in the book to see the author's calculations.

- Explore biographies of leaders (U.S. presidents, Adolf Hitler, Benito Mussolini, Queen Elizabeth, Mohandas Gandhi, etc.).

- Compare aspects of Indian culture to U.S. culture.

- Identify those countries that regularly face famine and discuss the implications. How can organizations and governments respond to address this situation?

- Students write their own folktales.

Cross-Curricular Connections:

Visual Arts

- Explore geometric patterns in Indian artwork.

Science

- Design a health unit focusing on the importance of nutrition and the impact of malnutrition and famine.

- Explore what rice is, its nutritional value, how it grows, and where.

- Design a unit focusing on the Indian animals featured in the story.

Related Children's Literature

Anno, M. (1999). *Anno's mysterious multiplying jar.* New York: Putnam Books.

Birch, D. (1988). *The king's chessboard.* New York: Puffin Books.

Demi. (1997). *One grain of rice.* New York: Scholastic.

Gelman, R. (2000). *Rice is life.* New York: Holt.

Losi, C. (1997). *The 512 ants on Sullivan Street.* New York: Scholastic.

Roca, N. (2002). *Boys and girls of the world: From one end to the other.* Hauppauge, NY: Barron's Educational Series.

Scillian, D. (2003). *P is for passport.* Chelsea, MI: Sleeping Bear Press.

Smith, D. (2002). *If the world were a village: A book about the world's people.* Tonawanda, NY: Kids Can Press.

Spier, P. (2002). *People.* New York: Doubleday.

Related Instructional Resources

D'Alusio, F. (1998). *Women in the material world.* San Francisco: Sierra Club Books.

Menzel, P. (1995). *Material world: A global family portrait.* San Francisco: Sierra Club Books.

Press, J. (2001). *Around the world art & activities: Visiting the 7 continents through craft fun.* Charlotte, VT: Williamson.

Related Websites

Outline Maps
http://www.eduplace.com/ss/maps/

Place Value using *One Grain of Rice* (Demi, 1997)
http://www.eduref.org/cgi-bin/printlessons.cgi/Virtual/Lessons/Mathematics/Arithmetic/ATH0033.html
http://www-history.mcs.st-and.ac.uk/history/BiogIndex.html

Printable Maps
http://www.nationalgeographic.com/xpeditions/atlas/

USA Rice Federation—International Site Links
http://www.usarice.com/international.html

The World Factbook—Guide to Country Profiles
https://www.cia.gov/cia/publications/factbook/docs/profileguide.html

"Safe?" (a poem in Falling Up) (1996)

by Shel Silverstein

HarperCollins, ISBN #0060248025

Maps & Globes (1985)

by Jack Knowlton

HarperCollins, ISBN #0064460495

Overview of Poem and Book:	Learn how to properly cross a street, with a focus on direction, in Silverstein's "Safe?" Then, in *Maps & Globes,* learn a brief history of the evolution of maps, the various types of maps, and features of maps and globes, such as the equator, lines of latitude and longitude, altitude, depth, and sea level.
Mathematical Concepts and Skills:	coordinate graphing, ordered pairs, plotting points, moving directionally
Social Studies Concepts and Skills:	map features (equator, lines of latitude and longitude, hemispheres), determining latitude and longitude, determining location and direction
Overview of Activities:	Students learn coordinate graphing by viewing a map (or globe) and using the lines of latitude and longitude to locate and travel between locations. Students then use a Cartesian coordinate system to record and reproduce the location of colors on state or international flags.
National Mathematics Standards (2000):	Students in grades 3 through 5 should "describe location and movement using common language and geometric vocabulary" and "make and use coordinate systems to specify locations and to describe paths." Students should also "find the distance between points along horizontal and vertical lines of a coordinate system" (Geometry Standard) (p. 396).
National Social Studies Standards (1994):	Social studies programs for early grades should include experiences that provide for the study of *people, places, and environments,* so that the learner can "interpret, use, and distinguish various representations of the earth, such as maps, globes, and photographs," "construct and use mental maps of locales, regions, and the world that demonstrate understanding of relative location, direction, size, and shape," and "estimate distance and calculate scale" (p. 54).

Materials: world map that shows the lines of latitude and longitude, globe, rulers, black markers, one-inch graph paper, colored pencils or crayons

Description of Activities:

1. Begin reading all or select pages (in particular, pages 12–27) of *Maps & Globes*, in which the author explains how a globe is a tiny map or model of our earth. Provide students with a world map that shows the lines of latitude and longitude (see World Maps websites below). Explain how the lines of latitude and longitude form an intersecting, imaginary network that is used to identify the exact location of any place on Earth.

2. Using a globe as a guide, show and describe how the lines of latitude (or parallels) indicate how far north or south something is relative to the equator (which is zero degrees latitude). The lines of longitude (or Meridians) indicate how far east or west something is relative to the Greenwich (or Prime) Meridian (which is zero degrees longitude). Using rulers, students locate and trace over in black marker the Prime Meridian and the equator on their maps. Describe how the equator divides the earth into the Northern and Southern hemispheres while the Prime Meridian divides the earth into the Eastern and Western hemispheres.

3. Using their maps, students locate and record the locations (in degrees latitude and degrees longitude) of various cities (e.g., Chicago, IL is located approximately at 41 degrees north latitude and 87 degrees west longitude; Sydney, Australia is located approximately at 34 degrees south latitude and 151 degrees east longitude). Encourage students to begin at the intersection of the equator and the Prime Meridian and then move up or down (to determine the city's north or south latitude) and then east or west (to determine the city's east or west longitude). Refer to the Lat and Lon Coordinates websites listed below to verify students' approximations.

4. Place students in pairs. One student selects two cities and then challenges his or her partner to explain how to move directionally from one location to the other on the map by following the lines of latitude and longitude. For example, if a student selects New York City (located approximately at 41 degrees north latitude and 73 degrees east longitude) and London (located approximately at 51 degrees north latitude and 5 degrees west longitude), his or her partner might say, "If I start at New York City, I could move approximately 10 degrees north latitude and then move approximately 70 degrees west longitude to arrive in London." Stduents take turns, giving each other practice with using a coordinate system, by moving along lines of latitude and longitude and identifying specific locations.

5. Introduce the Cartesian coordinate system, named after the French mathematician, Rene Descartes. Relate how the Cartesian coordinate system is similar to the network of lines of latitude and longitude on a globe or map since both allow for the identification of specific locations. Using graph paper and rulers, assist students in drawing and labeling an *x*-axis and *y*-axis and creating a scale on each axis. Explain how, when using a map or globe, one must know both the latitude and longitude to locate a point of interest. Similarly, with the Cartesian coordinate system, one must know the ordered pair, (*x*, *y*), to determine the location of a specific point. Provide students practice with plotting and locating coordinate pairs on their Cartesian grid.

6. Challenge students to create a list of coordinate pairs by sketching and coloring an international or state flag. Working in pairs, students visit one of the Flags websites listed below and choose a flag. (Flags that work well are two- or three-colored striped flags or those without emblems; e.g., Monaco or France.) Using one-inch graph paper, students create a Cartesian coordinate system (by drawing a scaled *x*- and *y*-axis), sketch a flag of their choice, and color it in accordingly. Students place the name of the flag at the top of the graph paper.

7. Students label the corners of the various colored areas with their corresponding coordinate pairs. Students record all of the coordinate pairs on a sheet of paper (that match each colored region) and give this information to another pair of students, who are challenged to recreate the map, using this list of coordinate pairs.

8. Students share their flag recreations with the class and discuss their accuracy.

Assessment:
- Did students locate the equator and Prime Meridian on their maps?
- Did students locate and correctly record the latitude and longitude of various cities?
- Did students accurately use directional words (north, south, east, west) when describing movement on a map?
- Did students accurately draw and scale a Cartesian coordinate system?
- Did students accurately record the coordinate pairs of the colors on their selected flag?
- Did students accurately recreate the colors in a flag by plotting the coordinate pairs on their graph paper?

Activity Extensions:

- As suggested on page 24 of *Maps & Globes*, students measure and compute the circumference of the earth (approximately 24,900 miles) by wrapping a piece a string end-to-end around the earth. Measure the length of the string and then multiply it by the scale factor printed on the globe in its legend.

- Read pages 15–17 in *Maps & Globes* and discuss the difficulty in creating a map (two-dimensional) of the world (three-dimensional). Explore various map projections using the websites listed below.

- Read a biography on Rene Descartes, inventor of the Cartesian coordinate system.

- Read a biography on famous cartographers and geographers including Gerardus Mercator, Arthur Robinson, Arno Peters, etc.

- Research careers that require knowledge of geography and cartography.

- Read various poems about maps, explorers, and map terminology in *A World of Wonders: Geographic Travels in Verse and Rhyme* (Lewis, 2002).

Cross-Curricular Connections:

Visual Arts

- Discuss the significance and meaning of color in the creation of flags. Use watercolors or another medium to create renditions of state or international flags.

- Visit the Six Contemporary Artists Who Use Maps in Their Work website and see several artists' (Alighiero Boetti, Kathy Prendergast, etc.) renditions of maps.

Science

- Explore the characteristics and habitats of organisms that live in the oceans, deserts, tropics, jungles, arctic, grasslands, etc.

- Discover and share facts regarding the deepest and oldest lake; the longest river; the highest mountain; the wettest, driest, coldest, and snowiest places; etc., in Jenkins's (1998) book.

Related Children's Literature

Adler, D. (1991). *A picture book of Christopher Columbus.* New York: Scholastic.

Asch, F. (1994). *The earth and I.* New York: Scholastic.

Bell, N. (1982). *The book of where: Or how to be naturally geographic* (A brown paper schoolbook series). Boston: Little, Brown.

Brocklehurst, R. (2004). *Usborne children's picture atlas.* New York: Scholastic.

Chesanow, N. (1995). *Where do I live?* Hauppauge, NY: Barron's Educational Series.

Gibbons, G. (1995). *Planet Earth/Inside out.* New York: Morrow.

Jenkins, S. (1998). *Hottest coldest highest deepest.* Boston: Houghton Mifflin.

Knowlton, J. (1985). *Maps & globes.* New York: HarperCollins.

Knowlton, J. (1988). *Geography from A to Z: A picture glossary.* New York: HarperCollins.

Kramer, S. (2004). *Who was Ferdinand Magellan?* (Who was . . . ? series). New York: Penguin Young Readers.

Lasky, K. (1994). *The librarian who measured the earth.* Boston: Little, Brown.

Leedy, L. (2003). *Mapping Penny's world.* New York: Holt.

Lewis, J. (2002). *A world of wonders: Geographic travels in verse and rhyme.* New York: Dial Books for Young Readers.

Rockwell, A. (1998). *Our earth.* New York: Scholastic.

Silverstein, S. (1996). *Falling up.* New York: HarperCollins.

Singer, M. (1991). *Nine o'clock lullaby.* New York: Scholastic.

St. George, J. (2005). *So you want to be an explorer?* New York: Penguin Young Readers Group.

Related Instructional Resources

Matthews, R. (2005). *Explorers* (Eyewitness books series). New York: Dorling Kindersley.

Press, J. (2001). *Around the world art & activities: Visiting the 7 continents through craft fun.* Charlotte, VT: Williamson.

Ryan, P. (1989). *Explorers and mapmakers.* New York: Lodestar Books.

Sipiera, P. (1991). *Globes* (A new true book series). Chicago: Children's Press.

Sobel, D. (1995). *Longitude: The true story of a lone genius who solved the greatest scientific problem of his time.* New York: Walker.

Taylor, B. (1993). *Maps and mapping* (Young discoveries series). New York: Kingfisher.

Related Websites

Cartesian Coordinate System

http://mathsfirst.massey.ac.nz/Algebra/CoordSystems/images/quadgrid2.png

http://www.easywms.com/easywms/files/Image/blog/programming/php/03fig02.jpg

Flags

http://www.50states.com/flag/

http://www.flags.net/

http://www.anbg.gov.au/flags/flags.html

Free Online Graph Paper

http://incompetech.com/beta/linedGraphPaper/easy.html

Lat and Lon Coordinates

http://www.infoplease.com/atlas/latitude-longitude.html

http://www.infoplease.com/ipa/A0001769.html

http://www.infoplease.com/ipa/A0001796.html

http://www.mapsofworld.com/utilities/world-latitude-longitude.htm

http://geocoder.us/

Maps and Map Projections

http://www.btinternet.com/~se16/js/mapproj.htm

http://www.nationalgeographic.com/features/2000/exploration/projections/index.html

http://geography.about.com/library/weekly/aa031599.htm

http://www.flourish.org/upsidedownmap/

http://www.nationalgeographic.com/xpeditions/atlas/

http://rockyweb.cr.usgs.gov/outreach/mapcatalog/

http://www.kidsdomain.com/kids/links/Maps.html

http://encyclopedia.kids.net.au/page/ma/Map_projection

Mercator Projections

http://science.nasa.gov/Realtime/rocket_sci/orbmech/mercator.html

http://worldatlas.com/aatlas/worldout.htm

http://www.warnercnr.colostate.edu/class_info/nr502/lg2/projection_descriptions/mercator.html

Outline Maps

http://www.eduplace.com/ss/maps/

Peters Projection

http://geography.about.com/library/weekly/aa030201a.htm

http://en.wikipedia.org/wiki/Gall-Peters_projection

http://encyclopedia.kids.net.au/page/ga/Gall-Peters_projection

Prime Meridian

http://worldatlas.com/aatlas/imagee.htm

http://wwp.greenwichmeridian.com/

Printable Maps

http://www.nationalgeographic.com/xpeditions/atlas/

Rene Descartes

http://www-history.mcs.st-andrews.ac.uk/Mathematicians/Descartes.html

Robinson Projection

http://www.manifold.net/doc/7x/robinson.htm

Six Contemporary Artists Who Use Maps in Their Work

http://www.artjunction.org/articles/mapartists.html

World Maps

http://worldatlas.com/aatlas/world.htm

http://www.mapquest.com/atlas/?region=index

More Activities Featuring Geometry

http://www.infoplease.com/atlas/mapindex.html

Mummy Math: An Adventure in Geometry (2005)

by Cindy Neuschwander

Holt, ISBN #0805075054

Mummies, Pyramids, and Pharaohs: A Book about Ancient Egypt (2004)

by Gail Gibbons

Little, Brown, ISBN #0316309281

Overview of Books:	In *Mummy Math*, follow two boys' journey through an Egyptian pyramid as they use their problem-solving skills and mathematical knowledge of two- and three-dimensional shapes to find the ancient pharaoh's burial chamber and a way out. Then, in *Mummies, Pyramids, and Pharaohs: A Book about Ancient Egypt*, discover various facts about Egyptian society and culture, including the construction of Egyptian homes and pyramids, clothing, farming methods, craftsmanship, hieroglyphics, religious practices, celebrations, and mummification.
Mathematical Concepts and Skills:	two- and three-dimensional shapes, polyhedra, prisms, pyramids, cones, cylinders, spheres, sorting, classification
Social Studies Concepts and Skills:	Egyptian culture, architecture, and geography, pyramids, maps
Overview of Activities:	Students explore various three-dimensional shapes and discern and distinguish attributes of pyramids, prisms, cones, cylinders, and spheres. Students also define and look for relationships between and among vertices, faces, and edges. Then, students divide into groups of architects, astronomers, cartographers, and art collectors and explore and present findings on the Great Pyramid at Giza.
National Mathematics Standards (2000):	Students in grades 3 through 5 should "identify, compare, and analyze attributes of two- and three-dimensional shapes and develop vocabulary to describe the attributes." They should also "classify two- and three-dimensional shapes according to their properties and develop definitions of classes of shapes such as triangles and pyramids" (Geometry Standard) (p. 396).

National Social Studies Standards (1994):

Social studies programs for early grades should include experiences that provide for the study of *the ways human beings view themselves in and over time,* so that the learner can "identify and use various sources for reconstructing the past, such as documents, letters, diaries, maps, textbooks, photos, and others." Learners should also "demonstrate an understanding that people in different times and places view the world differently" (p. 51).

Materials: real-life examples (or paper models) of cylinders (can), spheres (ball), cones (ice cream cone), prisms (shoe box, dice), and pyramids; blank map of Egypt; map of Egypt showing major cities, landmarks, etc.; Internet or other informational resources

Description of Activities:

1. Place several examples (real-life objects or paper models) of pyramids and prisms on a table, but do not identify them by name. Introduce these three-dimensional solids as polyhedra. In a separate pile on the table, place a cone, cylinder, and sphere and introduce these solids as *not* polyhedra. Ask students to observe the three-dimensional solids and record in their journals each solid's name (if they know it) and a description of each shapes' attributes. Challenge them to compose a definition of a polyhedron. (A polyhedron is a three-dimensional solid with plane [flat] faces; that is, it contains no curved surfaces or edges.) Explain that cones, spheres, and cylinders are not polyhedra because they have curved surfaces.

2. Remove the cones, cylinders, and spheres from the table. Challenge students to categorize the polyhedra into two subsets (one called "prisms" and the other called "pyramids"). Students work collaboratively to develop a definition of a prism and a pyramid, noting both their similarities and differences. (A prism is comprised of two parallel, congruent polygonal bases with parallelograms for faces. A pyramid has a polygonal base and its faces are triangles.)

3. After learning the mathematical definition of a prism and pyramid, ask students to record in their journals their definition of a face, vertex, and edge, as you point to each using one of the polyhedra. (A *face* of a three-dimensional solid is the two-dimensional shape serving as one of its sides. An *edge* is one of the line segments that make up a three-dimensional solid and occurs where two faces meet. A *vertex* is a point where faces meet.) Students share their definitions and work to develop a refined class definition of each term.

4. Read *Mummy Math*. Students identify the names of the solids as they appear in the book's illustrations.

5. At the end of the book, students create a "net" of the three-dimensional solids appearing in *Mummy Math* (e.g., cube, square pyramid, tetrahedron, etc.). A net is a sketch of what each shape might look like if flattened or unfolded. (Creating nets helps students see that a three-dimensional shape is made up two-dimensional shapes, where the two-dimensional shapes serve as faces of the three-dimensional shape.)

6. In their journals, students create a three-column table and count and record the number of faces, edges, and vertices for each of the three-dimensional solids for which they created a net. (The sketches students made in the prior step will help them complete the table of values.) Students work in small groups to determine the algebraic relationship among faces, vertices, and edges (faces + vertices = edges + 2).

7. Read *Mummies, Pyramids, and Pharaohs* allowing students to discover more about Egypt, Egyptian life and culture, and the pyramids.

8. Provide students with a blank map of Egypt (see Printable Blank Map of Egypt website below). Students mark on their maps the Nile, surrounding countries and bodies of water, major cities, location of the Great Pyramid, the "red land," and other important landmarks.

9. Embark on a classroom fact-finding mission, using the closing pages in *Mummies, Pyramids, and Pharaohs* (or using the Internet and other resources), regarding the Great Pyramid at Giza in Egypt, one of the Seven Wonders of the World. Until the early twentieth century, this was the tallest structure in the world. Divide the class into four groups:

    a. the architects, who research and present the mathematics of the pyramids, in particular, the immense dimensions of the pyramids and the Sphinx, number of stones used, materials used in creating the stones, etc. These students should relate the size of the pyramid to other more familiar structures as a means to demonstrate its enormity.

    b. the astronomers, who research and present findings on how the Great Pyramid at Giza was used as a sundial and to indicate solstices and equinoxes, its link to the constellation Orion, etc.

    c. the cartographers, who research and present maps of the location of the various pyramids, maps of the interiors of pyramids, secret rooms, burial chamber, etc.

d. the art collectors, who research and present findings on artifacts and treasures uncovered in sealed tombs of pyramids.

Each group should develop some type of artifact (whether a PowerPoint presentation, posterboard presentation, diorama, etc.), displaying their findings. All students in each group take part in presenting their findings.

10. Students record in their journals the five most interesting facts they learned about the Great Pyramid at Giza.

Assessment:
- Did students accurately name and describe the attributes of various three-dimensional solids?

- Did students provide an accurate definition of a polyhedron?

- Did students sort the polyhedra into two subsets, namely, prisms and pyramids?

- Did students accurately sketch the nets of the three-dimensional solids?

- Did students notice how two-dimensional shapes serve as the faces for three-dimensional solids?

- Did students accurately count the number of faces, vertices, and edges on solids?

- Did students discover the algebraic relationship among faces, vertices, and edges?

- Did students correctly locate on their maps of Egypt various landmarks, etc.?

- Did students actively participate and present accurate findings on Egyptian pyramids?

- Did students record in their journals at least five facts they know about Egypt?

Activity Extensions:
- Explore other classes of solids such as the Platonic Solids, Archimedean Solids, and the Kepler-Poinsot Solids by visiting the Platonic Solids website and the Paper Models of Polyhedra website.

- Students research Plato's reasoning for his naming of each of the Platonic Solids.

- Visit the Virtual Manipulatives Library—The Platonic Solids website where students can grab-and-drag a three-dimensional shape on the screen and observe and count the faces, edges, and vertices.

- Visit the Hieroglyphs Translator website and print your name or a secret message out in hieroglyphics. Students might code and then have a classmate decode a fact about Egypt written in your own hieroglyphic language.

- Explore and create a timeline of past Egyptian pharaohs and their accomplishments.

- Enjoy poetry about a mummy authored by Shel Silverstein (e.g., "The Mummy" [1996]).

Cross-Curricular Connections:

Visual Arts

- Visit the Create Art—Making 3D Shapes website and learn how to draw three-dimensional shapes.

- Look for three-dimensional shapes in various works of arts (e.g., Jacopo de Barberi's *Luca Pacioli*, Andy Warhol's *Big Torn Campbell's Soup Can*, Rene Magritte's *The Promenades of Euclid*, M.C. Escher's *Hand with Reflecting Sphere*, Albrecht Durer's *Melancolia I*, etc.).

- Explore how Mayan and Aztec civilizations decorated their pyramids and compare/contrast them to the Egyptian pyramids.

Science

- Research the process of mummification.

Related Children's Literature

Aliki. (1995). *Mummies made in Egypt*. New York: HarperTrophy.

Fisher, L. (1997). *The gods and goddesses of ancient Egypt*. New York: Holiday House.

Gibbons, G. (2004). *Mummies, pyramids, and pharaohs: A book about ancient Egypt*. New York: Little, Brown.

Hoban, T. (1986). *Shapes, shapes, shapes*. New York: Greenwillow Books.

Hoban, T. (2000). *Cubes, cones, cylinders, & spheres*. New York: Greenwillow Books.

Macaulay, D. (1982). *Pyramids*. Boston: Houghton-Mifflin.

Micklethwait, L. (2004). *I spy shapes in art*. New York: Greenwillow Books.

Milton, J. (1996). *Mummies* (All aboard reading series). New York: Grosset & Dunlap.

Murphy, S. (2001). *Captain invincible and the space shapes*. New York: HarperCollins.

Neuschwander, C. (2003). *Sir cumference and the sword in the cone: A math adventure*. Watertown, MA: Charlesbridge.

Neuschwander, C. (2005). *Mummy math: An adventure in geometry*. New York: Holt.

Silverstein, S. (1996). *Falling up*. New York: HarperCollins.

Related Instructional Resources

Biesty, S. (2005). *Egypt in spectacular cross-section*. New York: Scholastic.

Dineen, J. (1998). *Lift the lid on mummies: Unravel the mysteries of Egyptian tombs and make your own mummy!* (Lift the lid on series). Philadelphia: Running Press.

Hart, A., & Mantell, P. (1997). *Pyramids: 50 Hands-on activities to experience ancient Egypt*. Charlotte, VT: Williamson.

Honan, L. (1999). *Spend the day in ancient Egypt: Projects and activities that bring the past to life* (Spend the day in series). New York: Jossey-Bass.

Platt, R. (2003). *Hieroglyphics: The secrets of ancient Egyptian writing to unlock and discover* (Treasure chests series). Philadelphia: Running Press Kids.

Press, J. (2001). *Around the world art & activities: Visiting the 7 continents through craft fun*. Charlotte, VT: Williamson.

Related Websites

Art and the Platonic Solids

http://www.dartmouth.edu/~matc/math5.geometry/unit6/unit6.html

Create Art—Making 3D Shapes

http://www.sanford-artedventures.com/create/try_this_3d.html#

http://www.sanford-artedventures.com/create/tech_forms.html

Great Pyramid Statistics

http://www.crystalinks.com/gpstats.html

http://hypertextbook.com/facts/2003/PerkhaAhmed.shtml

http://www.plim.org/greatpyramid.html

Hieroglyphs Translator

http://magma.nationalgeographic.com/ngm/egypt/translator.html

Map of Egypt

http://worldatlas.com/webimage/countrys/africa/eg.htm

http://www.infoplease.com/atlas/country/egypt.html

Paper Models of Polyhedra

http://www.korthalsaltes.com/

Platonic Solids

http://www-groups.dcs.st-and.ac.uk/~history/Diagrams/PlatonicSolids.gif

http://www.mathsisfun.com/platonic_solids.html

http://www.georgehart.com/virtual-polyhedra/platonic_relationships.html

Platonic Solids and Art

http://www.dartmouth.edu/~matc/math5.geometry/unit6/unit6.
html#Polyhedra%20in%20Art%20&%20Architecture

Polyhedra Nets

http://www.mathsnet.net/geometry/solid/nets.html

http://www.korthalsaltes.com/

http://mathforum.org/alejandre/workshops/net.html

Printable Blank Map of Egypt

http://www.nationalgeographic.com/xpeditions/atlas/index.
html?Parent=africa&Rootmap=egypt&Mode=d

Virtual Manipulatives Library—The Platonic Solids

http://nlvm.usu.edu/en/nav/frames_asid_128_g_2_t_3.html?open=instructions

How Do You Know What Time It Is? (2003)

by Robert E. Wells

Whitman, ISBN #0807579408

Alice Yazzie's Year (2003)

by Ramona Maher

Tricycle Press, ISBN #1582460809

Overview of Books:	*Alice Yazzie's Year* details the eleventh year of a young Navajo girl's life, month by month, through poetic verse and richly southwestern illustrations. Then, in *How Do You Know What Time It Is?*, explore a concise history of time, clocks, and calendars and learn how time was measured and recorded by early civilizations, when clocks were first invented, and how time is measured in present day.
Mathematical Concepts and Skills:	measurement of time, estimation, prediction
Social Studies Concepts and Skills:	comparing and contrasting different stories or accounts about events, Navajo people and culture
Overview of Activities:	Students gain practice with predicting and estimating how many times they can complete a task in the span of one minute. Students then learn about the various ways to measure time, both past and present. Students explore facts about and report on the Navajo people and culture.
National Mathematics Standards (2000):	Students in grades 3 through 5 should "select and apply appropriate standard units and tools to measure length, area, volume, weight, time, temperature, and the size of angles." Students should "understand that measurements are approximations and understand how differences in units affect precision" (Measurement Standard) (p. 400).

National Social Studies Standards (1994):

Social studies programs for early grades should include experiences that provide for the study of *culture and cultural diversity,* so that the learner can "describe ways in which language, stories, folktales, music, and artistic creations serve as expressions of culture and influence behavior of people living in a particular culture" (p. 49). Social studies programs for early grades should also include experiences that provide for the study of *the ways human beings view themselves in and over time,* so that the learner can "demonstrate an understanding that different people may describe the same event or situation in diverse ways," "read and construct simple time-lines," and "compare and contrast different stories or accounts about past events, people, places, or situations" (p. 51).

Materials:

stopwatches (or watches with a second hand), Internet (or other resources)

Description of Activities:

1. Challenge students to predict the length of one minute. Students close their eyes so they cannot see a clock or watch and are not swayed by their classmates' responses. Announce "Start!" Students raise their hand when they think one minute has elapsed. How accurate were their predictions of the length of one minute?

2. Students work in pairs and record how many times they estimate they can write their name, tie their shoe, and count to 99 by nines in one minute. Both students time each other and record their data. How accurate were their predictions?

3. Besides using a stopwatch, challenge students to list in their journals other ways people can keep track of time (observing the moon phases, observing the movement of stars, sundials, hourglass, pendulum clock, atomic clock, calendars, etc.). Read *How Do You Know What Time It Is?* and allow students to learn a brief history of how people from centuries ago kept track of the passage of time.

4. Students now focus on the passage of time in terms of calendar months, while exploring facts about the Navajo people. Record on the board the English and corresponding Navajo name for each of the months (as done in *Alice Yazzie's Year*). Assist students in pronouncing the Navajo months' names.

5. Begin a discussion by asking students what they know about the Navajo Nation, which currently is the largest tribe in North America (e.g., Where is the Navajo Nation located? What is another name for the Navajo? Who is the current (or past) leader of the Navajo Nation?, etc.). Refer to the Navajo Nation websites listed below for information about the Navajo Nation regarding its history, government, economy, geography, culture, etc. Also, reference the closing pages of *Alice Yazzie's Year* for facts about the Navajo people.

6. Read all or select passages from *Alice Yazzie's Year*. Perhaps select the current month, or fall months, for example. Share with students the corresponding illustration for each month, allowing them to visually experience the southwestern influence evident in the illustrations.

7. After reading specific passages detailing various months in Alice's life, students write a short verse or paragraph describing what might occur in their lives during the same months. Students share their creative writing samples with the class and make comparisons between their lives and that of Alice. How is life on a Navajo reservation different from students' life? The same?

8. Students work in small groups and research an aspect of the Navajo Nation, such as its history, government and leadership, economy, music, art, folktales and legends, etc. Students locate at least five facts about their topic. Students create a PowerPoint presentation or develop large posters or a collage, in the spirit of southwestern colors and style, and share their findings with the class.

Assessment:
- Did students make reasonable estimations for what can be done in the span of one minute?
- Did students compose a short verse or paragraph detailing occurrences in their lives?
- Did students participate in discussions about the similarities and differences between their lives and that of Alice's?
- Did students gather at least five pertinent pieces of information about their topic and articulately present their topic to the class?

Activity Extensions:
- Students work in small pairs and are assigned a means of measuring time (e.g., shadow stick, water clocks, sundial, hourglass, pendulum clock, watch, atomic clock, quartz crystals, calendars, etc.). Students research their topic and present their findings to the class (including the inventors of the device, how the device works, etc.).

- Research various types of calendars (Gregorian, Julian, Solar, Chinese, Hebrew, etc.).

- Research the Y2K problem that faced the world's computers in the late 1990s.

- Bring a world map to class. Point out the various time zones and demonstrate how to read time as you cross time zones.

- Read *The Navajo Year, Walk through Many Seasons* (Flood, 2006) and learn about the events, sights, and sounds that occur throughout the year on the Navajo Reservation.

- Read *How the Stars Fell into the Sky* (Oughton, 1992), a Navajo tale explaining why the night sky appears as it does.

- Report on current events in the Navajo Nation by selecting and reading a headline from the Navajo Nation newspaper, *Navajo Times*.

- Research and present facts about other Native American tribes.

Cross-Curricular Connections:

Visual Arts

- Students create a southwestern illustration to accompany their creative writing samples.

- Explore the work of Navajo artists using the Navajo Artists websites listed below.

- Explore the artwork and crafts of Native Americans such as kachina dolls, turquoise jewelry, pottery, quilts, etc.

- Explore the geometry in Navajo and Native American quilts.

- Explore the "melting clocks" appearing in many of Salvador Dali's works.

Science

- Read *Arctic Lights, Arctic Nights* (Miller, 2003) and enjoy a month-by-month description of Fairbanks, Alaska, which experiences some of the world's most extreme temperatures and light variations.

- Make a sundial or place a sundial (or shadow stick) outside. Teach students how to read time using a sundial. Over the course of a few hours, allow students to make readings using the sundial to test its accuracy.

- Explore how early civilizations observed moon phases to keep track of time.

Related Children's Literature

Anno, M. (1987). *Anno's sundial*. New York: Philomel Books.

Anno, M. (1999). *All in a day*. New York: Putnam.

Blood, C., & Link, M. (1990). *The goat in the rug*. New York: Aladdin.

Bruchac, H. (2001). *Heart of a chief*. New York: Puffin Books.

Bruchac, H. (2002). *Navajo long walk: Tragic story of proud people's forced march from homeland*. Washington, DC: National Geographic Books.

Chainan, M. (1998). *The chief's blanket*. Tiburon, CA: Kramer.

Edmonds, W. (1994). *Big book of time*. New York: Readers Digest Kids.

Flood, N. (2006). *The Navajo year, walk through many seasons*. Flagstaff, AZ: Salina Bookshelf.

Maestro, B. (1999). *The story of clocks and calendars*. New York: HarperCollins.

Maher, R. (2003). *Alice Yazzie's year*. Berkeley, CA: Tricycle Press.

Miles, M. (1985). *Annie and the old one*. Boston: Little, Brown.

Miller, D. (2003). *Arctic nights, arctic lights*. New York: Walker.

Morgan, R. (1999). *In the next three seconds*. New York: Puffin Books.

Oughton, J. (1992). *How the stars fell into the sky: A Navajo legend*. Boston: Houghton Mifflin.

Pluckrose, H. (1995). *Time*. New York: Scholastic.

Roessel, M. (1993). *Kinaalda: A Navajo girl grows up*. Minneapolis: Lerner.

Roessel, M. (1995). *Songs from the loom: A Navajo girl learns to weave*. Minneapolis: Lerner.

Santella, A. (2003). *The Navajo* (True books: American Indian series). Chicago: Children's Press.

Schoberle, C. (1994). *Day lights, night lights*. New York: Simon & Schuster.

Scieszka, J., & Smith, L. (1995). *Math curse*. New York: Penguin Books.

Wells, R. (2003). *How do you know what time it is?* Morton Grove, IL: Whitman.

Related Instructional Resources

Harris, V. (1997). *Using multiethnic literature in the K–8 classroom*. Norwood, MA: Christopher-Gordon.

Mobley, C. (1994). *Navajo rugs and blankets: A coloring book*. Tucson, AZ: Rio Nuevo.

Slapin, B., & Seale, D. (1992). *Through Indian eyes: The native experience in books for children*. Philadelphia: New Society.

Related Websites

Calendar Facts
> http://webexhibits.org/calendars/timeline.html

Franklin Institute—TimeKeepers
> http://sln.fi.edu/time/keepers/index.html

History of Time and Clocks
> http://home.rochester.rr.com/kjmpage/clocktimeline.html
> http://www.clockinc.com/History_of_clock_time.asp
> http://inventors.about.com/od/cstartinventions/a/clock.htm
> http://www.which-clocks.com/history.html

NASA Kids—Sundials
> http://kids.msfc.nasa.gov/earth/sundials/sundials.asp

Native American Tribes
> http://www.nativeculturelinks.com/indians.html
> http://www.nativeamericainc.com/

Navajo Artists
> http://www.nativeartistsunited.org/artists.html

Navajo Nation
> http://www.navajo.org/
> http://www.lapahie.com/Navajo_Map_Lg.cfm

***Navajo Times* Newspaper**
> http://www.navajotimes.com/

Salvador Dali
> http://www.salvadordalimuseum.org/home.html
> http://www.artcyclopedia.com/artists/dali_salvador.html

Stopwatch
> http://www.shodor.org/interactivate/activities/stopwatch/

Tell Time Anywhere in the World
> http://www.worldtimeserver.com/current_time_in_AR-SJ.aspx

Tell Time with Your Feet
> http://www.math.csusb.edu/faculty/susan/timefeet.html

Virtual Manipulatives Library—Analog and Digital Clocks
> http://nlvm.usu.edu/en/nav/frames_asid_316_g_2_t_4.html

Virtual Manipulatives Library—What Time Will It Be?
> http://nlvm.usu.edu/en/nav/frames_asid_318_g_2_t_4.html

Duck for President (2004)

by Doreen Cronin

Simon & Schuster Books for Young Readers, ISBN #0439671442

Overview of Book:	After becoming tired of working for Farmer Brown, Duck pursues a political career and discovers the hardships of running for various offices.
Mathematical Concepts and Skills:	combinations, chance, majority, percentages, problem solving, real-life applications of mathematics
Social Studies Concepts and Skills:	voting, history of voting, voting as a right and responsibility of citizens, electoral college
Overview of Activities:	Students discuss various aspects of voting with a focus on our rights and responsibilities as members of a democratic society to vote. They also discuss the role and duties of the president and learn how the electoral college works. Students experience the mathematics involved in voting by engaging in a problem-solving activity in which they determine different combinations of electoral votes that sum to 270. Students also solve voting scenarios to enhance their understanding of percentages.
National Mathematics Standards (2000):	Students in grades 3 through 5 should "develop fluency in adding, subtracting, multiplying, and dividing whole numbers" (Number and Operations Standard) (p. 392). They should "recognize and apply mathematics in contexts outside of mathematics" (Connections Standard) (p. 402). They should "apply and adapt a variety of appropriate strategies to solve problems" (Problem Solving Standard) (p. 402).
National Social Studies Standards (1994):	Social studies programs for early grades should also include experiences that provide for the study of *the ideals, principles, and practices of citizenship in a democratic republic,* so that the learner can "identify examples of the rights and responsibilities of citizens," "explain actions citizens can take to influence public policy decisions," and "explain how public policies and citizen behaviors may or may not reflect the stated ideals of a democratic republican form of government" (p. 73). Social studies programs for early grades should also include experiences that provide for the study of *how people create and change structures of power, authority, and governance,* so that the learner can "explain the purpose of government," and "distinguish among local, state, and national government and identify representative leaders at these levels such as mayor, governor, and president" (p. 63).

Materials: map (or list) indicating the number of electoral votes per state (see websites listed below), red and blue crayons

Description of Activities:

1. Facilitate a discussion regarding voting by asking such questions as: What is the legal voting age in the United States? When were women granted the right to vote? What amendment granted women the right to vote? Why do people vote? Why don't people vote? What percentage of people typically votes in presidential elections? What types of elections are there? Have you ever voted for something? If applicable, discuss any recent election results relative to their city, state, or school.

2. Discuss why voting is important, emphasizing that voting is a right and responsibility of U.S. citizens (see PBS Kids—Why Vote? website for discussion ideas). Refer to the What a Difference One Vote Makes website and explore elections in which candidates have won by the margin of one vote.

3. Read *Duck for President*.

4. At the end of the book, after learning of Duck's political hardships, begin a discussion about whether students would want to serve as president and why. Ask students to articulate what the president's responsibilities are, what the job entails, what knowledge and traits make a successful president, etc.

5. Discuss how in a presidential election, the electoral college, which is comprised of 538 members, elects the president as opposed to the popular vote. In a two-person presidential election, if a candidate wins at least 270 electoral votes (over one-half of the total vote), that individual becomes president. If three or more candidates are running for the presidency, and no one wins the absolute majority (over one-half of the total vote), the president is chosen by the House of Representatives. If this is the case, each state gets one vote, and the candidate who wins a majority of votes (i.e., twenty-six states) is named president.

6. Visit one of the U.S. Electoral Votes websites listed below and provide students with a map (or list) indicating the number of electoral votes per state. Challenge students to work in small groups to determine and record in their journals different combinations of state electoral votes that sum to the majority of 270. Students share their solutions and strategies for summing to 270 with their classmates.

7. Discuss how Congress (which is comprised of senators and the members of the House of Representatives) is expected to vote the way the people vote, but this does not always happen. Discuss the historic elections (in 1824, 1876, 1888, and 2000) in which a candidate won the majority of the popular vote, but lost the presidency, since he did not have the majority of electoral votes.

8. Challenge students to solve more problems involving the mathematics of voting by visiting the Figure This!—What Percentage Does It Take to Win a Vote? website, where students' understanding of percentages is challenged as they determine whether a majority rules.

Assessment:
- Did students participate in the discussion about voting and the roles and duties of the president?

- Did students determine and explain at least one way to sum the electoral votes to 270?

- Did students accurately solve additional problems dealing with percentages encountered in the voting process?

Activity Extensions:
- Hold a mock election in class.

- Visit the History of Voting website and research and present the findings on the history of voting, the individuals (in particular, females) who played important roles in terms of voting rights, etc. Or visit the Voting Rights Timeline website and research and present findings of important documented events.

- Research and present the findings of a biography on a women's voting rights activist (e.g., Susan B. Anthony, Julia Ward Howe, Lucretia Mott, Alice Paul, Elizabeth Cadt Stanton, Lucy Stone, etc.).

- Create a book, complete with illustrations, that features on each page each student's response to the prompt, "If I were president of the United States, I would . . ."

- Visit the PBS Kids—Cast Your Vote website, which allows students to select and vote on important issues, after which they receive a Future Voter's Card.

Cross-Curricular Connections:

Visual Arts

- Visit images of and locate facts about Mount Rushmore, located in South Dakota and created by the sculptor Gutzon Borglum, which features the heads of former presidents Washington, Jefferson, Theodore Roosevelt, and Lincoln.

Science

- Research and discuss which environmental issues are on current (or recently passed) election ballots. Students discuss the implications of both sides of the issue and then take a class vote.

Related Children's Literature

Christelow, E. (2004). *Vote!* New York: Clarion Books.

Cronin, D. (2004). *Duck for president.* New York: Simon & Schuster Books for Young Readers.

Davis, G. (2004). *Wackiest White House pets.* New York: Scholastic.

Davis, K. (2002). *Don't know much about the presidents.* New York: HarperCollins.

Donovan, S. (2003). *Running for office: A look at political campaigns* (How government works series). Minneapolis: Lerner.

Fritz, J. (1999). *You want women to vote, Lizzie Stanton?* New York: Putnam Juvenile.

Fuqua, N. (2004). *First pets: Presidential best friends.* New York: Scholastic.

Goldman, D. (2004). *Presidential losers.* Minneapolis: Lerner.

Gordon, P., & Snow, R. (2004). *Kids learn America! Bringing geography to life with people, places & history.* Charlotte, VT: Williamson.

Grandfield, L. (2003). *America votes: How our president is elected.* Tonawanda, NY: Kids Can Press.

Grodin, E. (2004). *D is for democracy: A citizen's alphabet.* Chelsea, MI: Sleeping Bear Press.

Hoose, P. (2001). *We were there, too! Young people in U.S. history.* New York: Farrar Straus Giroux.

Krull, K. (2004). *A woman for president: The story of Victoria Woodhull.* New York: Walker Books for Young Readers.

Landau, E. (2003). *The president's work: A look at the executive branch* (How government works series). Minneapolis: Lerner.

Lay, K. (2004). *Crown me!* New York: Holiday House.

McCully, E. (1998). *The ballot box battle.* New York: Dragonfly Books.

O'Neal, Z. (2001). *A long way to go: A story of women's right to vote* (Once upon America series). New York: Puffin Books.

Provensen, A. (1997). *The buck stops here: The president of the United States of America.* New York: Browndeer Press Paperbacks.

Rubel, D. (1994). *Scholastic encyclopedia of the presidents and their times.* New York: Scholastic.

Scillian, D. (2001). *A is for America: An American alphabet.* Chelsea, MI: Sleeping Bear Press.

Smith, R., & Smith, M. (2005). *N is for our nation's capital: A Washington, DC, alphabet* (Discover America state by state alphabet series). Chelsea, MI: Sleeping Bear Press.

Sobel, S. (1999). *How elections works.* Hauppauge, NY: Barron's Educational Series.

Sobel, S. (1999). *How the U.S. government works.* Hauppauge, NY: Barron's Educational Series.

Sobel, S. (2001). *Presidential elections: And other cool facts.* Hauppauge, NY: Barron's Educational Series.

Sullivan, G. (1987). *Facts and fun about the presidents.* New York: Scholastic.

Thimmesh, C. (2004). *Madame President: The extraordinary, true, (and evolving) story of women in politics.* Boston: Houghton Mifflin.

Related Instructional Resources

Cheney, L. (2005). *A time for freedom: What happened when in America.* New York: Simon & Schuster.

Davis, K. (2004). *Don't know much about the 50 states* (Don't know much about series). New York: HarperTrophy.

Devrian Global Industries. (2006). *States activities book.* Union, NJ: Author.

Hauser, J. (2004). *Little hands celebrate America: Learning about the USA through crafts & activities.* Charlotte, VT: Williamson.

Murphy, F. (2002). *Our country.* New York: Scholastic Professional Books.

Related Websites

Children's Literature that Teaches about Elections
> http://www.education-world.com/a_curr/curr271.shtml

Electoral College
> http://www.votescount.com/books/elecoll.htm

Federal Election Commission
> http://www.fec.gov/
> http://www.fec.gov/pages/96to.htm
> http://www.eac.gov/election_resources/htmlto5.htm

Figure This!—What Percentage Does It Take to Win a Vote?
> http://www.figurethis.org/challenges/c36/challenge.htm

History of Voting
> http://www2.edgate.com/elections/inactive/history_of_the_vote/

Mount Rushmore
> http://www.mtrushmore.net/

PBS Kids—Cast Your Vote
> http://pbskids.org/democracy/vote/castvote.html

PBS Kids—The Democracy Project
> http://pbskids.org/democracy/

PBS Kids—Why Vote?
> http://pbskids.org/zoom/fromyou/elections/elections101.html

Presidents of the United States of America
> http://www.worldalmanacforkids.com/explore/presidents.html
> http://www.whitehouse.gov/history/presidents/

U.S. Electoral Votes
> http://www.worldatlas.com/webimage/countrys/namerica/usstates/electorl.htm
> http://www.vote-smart.org/election_president_electoral_college.php

Voting Rights Timeline
> http://www.lbjlib.utexas.edu/johnson/lbjforkids/civil_voting_timeline.shtm

What a Difference One Vote Makes
> http://pbskids.org/democracy/vote/index.html

Women's Suffrage
> http://womenshistory.about.com/od/suffrage/

If the World Were a Village:
A Book about the World's People (2002)

by David J. Smith

Kids Can Press, ISBN #1550747797

Overview of Book:

In Smith's book, the world is presented as if it were a village of one hundred people. Through the use of vividly colorful illustrations, Smith presents eye-opening statistics that dramatically portray the inequities in our world.

Mathematical Concepts and Skills:

prediction, estimation, data interpretation, graphing, pie charts

Social Studies Concepts and Skills:

geography, world population distributions, literacy and hunger rates, religions and languages in the world, distribution of money and access to global resources

Overview of Activities:

Students predict and explore world population distributions using maps and pie charts. Students also predict and graph various world data, such as literacy rates, access to resources, the distribution of wealth, types of food, different languages, and types of religions. Students discuss the implications of expanding populations and their impact on the environment and resources.

National Mathematics Standards (2000):

π

Students in grades 3 through 5 should "collect data using observations, surveys, and experiments." Students should "represent data using tables and graphs such as line plots, bar graphs, and line graphs." Students should also "propose and justify conclusions and predictions that are based on data" (Data Analysis and Probability Standard) (p. 400).

National Social Studies Standards (1994):

Social studies programs for early grades should include experiences that provide for the study of *people, places, and environments* so that the learner can "use appropriate resources, data sources, and geographical tools such as atlases, data bases, grid systems, charts, graphs, and maps to generate, manipulate, and interpret information" (p. 54). Social studies programs for early grades should also include experiences that provide for the study of *how people organize for the production, distribution, and consumption of goods and services,* so that the learner can "give examples that show how scarcity and choice govern our economic decisions" (p. 65). Social studies programs for early grades should include experiences that provide for the study of *relationships among science, technology, and society,* so that the learner can "identify and describe examples in which science and technology have changed the lives of people," and can "suggest ways to monitor science and technology in order to protect the physical environment, individual rights, and the common good" (p. 67). Social studies programs for early grades should include experiences that provide for the study of *global connections and interdependence,* so that the learner can "explore causes, consequences, and possible solutions to persistent, contemporary, and emerging global issues, such as pollution and endangered species" (p. 70).

Materials: map of the world, bags of one hundred beans for each group of four, blank paper, rulers, protractors, markers, sticky notes, copied pages from *If the World Were a Village*

Description of Activities:

1. Give each group of four students a map of the world and a bag of one hundred precounted beans (see the Outline Maps website or Printable Maps website listed below). Read the first two sentences of *If the World Were a Village* in which the reader learns that the world's population is 6 billion, 200 million. Explain that the one hundred beans in students' bags represent the one hundred people in the author's global village. Assist students in understanding that one bean represents 62 million people. Thus, the entire bag of one hundred beans represents 6.2 billion, the world's population. Students place the one hundred beans on various countries and continents as a means to represent the world's population.

2. Students share their predictions for their global population distributions. Ask such questions as: Where on your map are most of the beans located? The fewest? Are there continents or countries on which no beans are placed? How many people do you estimate live in certain countries or on particular continents?, etc.

3. Share the population data in Smith's book appearing on page 8. Using spreadsheet software (or by visiting the Create a Graph Online website), consider preparing in advance a pie chart to provide students with a visual representation of the data (as this is a more powerful way to view all of the statistics in Smith's book). Discuss the accuracy of students' population predictions. Discuss the implications of population densities (especially in such places as India, China, etc.) and the impact on resources, the environment, pollution, etc.

4. Copy select "theme" pages from Smith's book in which a different topic is presented (food; languages; wealth; access to electricity, clean air, and water; etc.). Using a sticky note, cover the numerical data, but leave the text introducing and describing the topic uncovered. Distribute one "theme" page to each group of students. Students discuss the topic and, using the Create a Graph Online website, generate a pie chart representing their prediction of what the data will look like. (Older students should create a pie chart by hand.)

5. Each group presents its pie chart to the class, after which the teacher reveals the actual data from Smith's book. Discuss the implications of each group's topic. (The teacher might want to create a pie chart in advance for each theme page as a means to assist students in comparing their graphs to a graph of the actual data.)

6. Students predict what the global village will be like in the future by exploring the statistics found on page 29 in Smith's book. Students discuss the data, notice the doubling pattern, and then make predictions about the population of the global village in the next one hundred years. Students create a line graph showing the population (y-axis) over time (x-axis). What are the implications if the population of the world continues to increase at this rate? Facilitate a discussion.

Assessment:

- Did students make reasonable predictions when representing world population distributions?

- Did students notice the unequal distribution of populations worldwide and articulate the implications of this?

- Did students make reasonable predictions about their topic?

- Did students make accurate pie charts and line graphs and interpret them accurately?

- Did students articulate the implications of the inequities and disparities in our world?

Activity Extensions:

- Students work in pairs and, using the Internet or a world almanac, locate an interesting world statistic, not discussed in *If the World Were a Village*. Students create a pie chart and then share the statistic with the class. For example, students might research and graph blood types, forms of world governance, number of cell phone subscribers worldwide, etc.

- Students explore maps, the history of maps, and mapmaking.

Cross-Curricular Connections:

Visual Arts

- Explore the artwork of the twentieth-century American painter and abstract expressionist Richard Diebenkorn, many of whose paintings are aerial landscape views (e.g., *Cityscape I*, Berkeley series, etc.).

- Visit the Six Contemporary Artists Who Use Maps in Their Work website and view several artists' (Alighiero Boetti, Kathy Prendergast, etc.) renditions of maps.

Science

- Design a health unit focusing on the importance of good nutrition and the impact of malnutrition and famine.

- Explore the history of electricity and its role in advancing society.

Related Children's Literature

Garrison, J., & Tubesing, A. (1996). *A million visions of peace: Wisdom from the Friends of Old Turtle*. New York: Scholastic.

Hoose, P. (2002). *It's our world, too!* New York: Farrar Straus Giroux.

Kincade, S. (1992). *Our time is now* (Young people changing the world). Upper Saddle River, NJ: Pearson Foundation.

Lewis, B. (1992). *Kids with courage: True stories about young people making a difference*. Minneapolis: Free Spirit.

Pershing Accelerated School Students. (2002). *We dream of a world*. New York: Scholastic.

Roca, N. (2002). *Boys and girls of the world: From one end to the other*. Hauppauge, NY: Barron's Educational Series.

Scillian, D. (2003). *P is for passport*. Chelsea, MI: Sleeping Bear Press.

Smith, D. (2002). *If the world were a village: A book about the world's people*. Tonawanda, NY: Kids Can Press.

Smith, D. (2003). *Mapping the world by heart*. Watertown, MA: Snyder.

Spier, P. (1980). *People*. New York: Doubleday.

Related Instructional Resources

D'Alusio, F. (1998). *Women in the material world*. San Francisco: Sierra Club Books.

Lewis, B. (1995). *The kid's guide to service projects: Over 500 service ideas for young people who want to make a difference*. Minneapolis: Free Spirit.

Lewis, B. (1998). *The kid's guide to social action: How to solve social problems you choose—and turn creative thinking into positive action*. Minneapolis: Free Spirit.

Menzel, P. (1995). *Material world: A global family portrait*. San Francisco: Sierra Club Books.

Press, J. (2001). *Around the world art & activities: Visiting the 7 continents through craft fun*. Charlotte, VT: Williamson.

Ward, R. (2004). K–8 preservice teachers' journey into the global village: Exploring real-world data using children's literature and technology. *Arizona Reading Journal, 31*(1), 43–47.

Related Websites

Create a Graph Online
> http://nces.ed.gov/nceskids/createagraph/

Maps and Map Projections
> http://www.btinternet.com/~se16/js/mapproj.htm
> http://www.nationalgeographic.com/features/2000/exploration/projections/index.html
> http://www.flourish.org/upsidedownmap/

Outline Maps
> http://www.eduplace.com/ss/maps/

Printable Maps
> http://www.nationalgeographic.com/xpeditions/atlas/

Richard Diebenkorn
> http://www.artchive.com/artchive/ftptoc/diebenkorn_ext.html

Six Contemporary Artists Who Use Maps in Their Work
> http://www.artjunction.org/articles/mapartists.html

U.S. Census Data and Statistics
> http://www.census.gov/
> http://www.census.gov/compendia/statab/

Virtual Manipulatives Library—Pie Chart
> http://nlvm.usu.edu/en/nav/frames_asid_183_g_2_t_5.html?open=activities

World Data and Statistics
> http://www.infoplease.com/
> http://www.worldbank.org/data/
> http://www.cia.gov/cia/publications/factbook/
> http://www.wri.org/
> http://www.unicef.org/
> http://www.un.org/
> http://plasma.nationalgeographic.com/places/index.html
> http://www.pbs.org/wgbh/nova/worldbalance/eart-nf.html
> http://mapping.com/gv/
> http://www.prb.org/
> http://www.readtofeed.org/

The Train of States (2004)

by Peter Sis

Greenwillow Books, ISBN #0060578386

Overview of Poem and Book:

Hop from car to car on this train of states and learn each state's bird, flower, tree, capital, and date of statehood, along with a multitude of interesting state facts and figures.

Mathematical Concepts and Skills:

histogram, stem-and-leaf plots, data interpretation

Social Studies Concepts and Skills:

tourism and industry in states, state facts (capitals, dates of statehood, landmarks, historical significance, industry, tourism, etc.)

Overview of Activities:

Students create and then compare and contrast a histogram with a stem and leaf plot. Students then create a classroom state train, labeled with facts about the states (e.g., capital, tourism, industry, major landmarks, etc.).

National Mathematics Standards (2000):

Students in grades 3 through 5 should "collect data using observations, surveys, and experiments." Students should "represent data using tables and graphs such as line plots, bar graphs, and line graphs." Students should "compare different representations of the same data and evaluate how well each representation shows important aspects of the data." Students should also "propose and justify conclusions and predictions that are based on data" (Data Analysis and Probability Standard) (p. 400).

National Social Studies Standards (1994):

Social studies programs for early grades should include experiences that provide for the *study of people, places, and environments* so that the learner can "use appropriate resources, data sources, and geographical tools such as atlases, data bases, grid systems, charts graphs, and maps to generate, manipulate, and interpret information" and "locate and distinguish among varying landforms and geographic features, such as mountains, plateaus, islands, and oceans" (p. 54).

Materials:

map of the United States, listing of the dates of statehood (see websites listed below), graph paper, rulers, 9" × 12" white paper, 11" × 14" red and blue paper, markers

Description of Activities:

1. Prior to class, examine all or select pages from *The Train of States*. Announce particular states' names appearing on each page and challenge students to name the state capital before sharing it with the class. Challenge students to locate that state on a map of the United States and to also name other facts they know about that state (e.g., landmarks, historical significance, climate, etc.). Consider sharing with students some of the interesting facts appearing on pages in the book either in text or via illustrations (e.g., appearing on the page featuring New York are illustrations of the four presidents born in that state, namely Franklin D. Roosevelt, Theodore Roosevelt, Martin van Buren, and Millard Fillmore; a sketch of the Statue of Liberty and Manhattan, etc.).

2. Ask students to predict during which century (1700s, 1800s, or 1900s) the largest number of states became states and to explain their reasoning.

3. Distribute to students a list of the dates of statehood using one of the Dates of Statehood websites listed below. Students use this data to create and label a histogram showing the frequencies of dates of statehood by century (1700s, 1800s, and 1900s). (Consider using graph paper to help students create their histograms.)

4. After creating their histograms, students interpret their graph by answering questions such as: What century saw the most states join the United States? The least? Did their predictions match the data? How many times more states became states in the 1700s as compared to the 1800s? To the 1900s?, etc. Students should explain their reasoning when responding to each question.

5. Using *The Train of States* Fact Sheet, students create three stem-and-leaf plots, one for each century (1700s, 1800s, and 1900s). Students interpret their graphs by answering questions such as: During what century and decade did the largest number of states become states? The fewest? Were there years during which no territories became states? If so, when? During what year did most territories become states? How many times more states became states in 1860 than in 1820?, etc. Students should explain their reasoning when responding to each question.

6. Ask students to compare their stem-and-leaf plots to their histograms. Which graph do they think better represents the data? Why? What information can you glean from a histogram that you cannot from a stem-and-leaf plot? What information can you glean from a stem-and-leaf plot that you cannot from a histogram?

7. Place students in pairs and assign each pair a state. Each pair draws its state on a piece of white 9" × 12" paper, labels it, labels its capital, and lists its date of statehood. Students also include pertinent information about that state (e.g., landmarks, geographic features, climate, major industry, etc.) using an almanac, the Internet, or some other resource. Glue the individual pieces of 9" × 12" white paper onto larger (11" × 14") red or blue paper, creating a "patriotic" border. Students share their work with their classmates in small groups or with the whole class.

8. Create a train of states (alternating between red and blue) by hanging each piece of artwork around the perimeter of the classroom.

Assessment:

- Did students recall state capitals and locate states on a map?

- Did students know other facts about the states (e.g., landmarks, historical significance, etc.)?

- Did students accurately create and interpret their histograms and stem-and-leaf plots?

- Did students create a state train with accurate facts?

Activity Extensions:

- Using the Create a Graph Online website, students create a pie chart showing the dates of statehood by decade. Students compare and contrast this graphical representation of the data to their histogram and stem-and-leaf plots and discuss which graph best displays the data.

- Enjoy poetry about transportation authored by Shel Silverstein (e.g., "Homemade Boat" [2004], "The Little Blue Engine" [2004], and "The Acrobats" [2004]) and Jack Prelutsky (e.g., "Nine Mice" [1984]).

Cross-Curricular Connections:

Visual Arts

- Make a collage of a state capturing facts and figures about the state.

- Make state flags using watercolors or construction paper.

Science

- Explore the history of trains as a source of transportation.

Related Children's Literature

Aliki. (1963). *The story of Johnny Appleseed*. New York: Aladdin Paperbacks.

Bateman, T. (1989). *Red, white, blue, and Uncle Who? The stories behind some of America's patriotic symbols*. New York: Holiday House.

Buller, J., & Schade, S. (2005). *The first ladies* (Smart about series). New York: Grosset & Dunlap.

Buller, J., Schade, S., Cocca-Leffler, M., Holub, J., Kelley, T., & Regan, D. (2003). *Smart about the fifty states: A class report*. New York: Grosset & Dunlap.

Cheney, L. (2002). *America: A patriotic primer*. New York: Simon & Schuster Books for Young Readers.

Cheney, L. (2003). *A is for Abigail: An almanac of amazing American women*. New York: Simon & Schuster Books for Young Readers.

Cheney, L. (2006). *Our fifty states: A family adventure across America*. New York: Simon & Schuster Books for Young Readers.

Davis, G. (2004). *Wackiest White House pets*. New York: Scholastic.

Fuqua, N. (2004). *First pets: Presidential best friends*. New York: Scholastic.

Keenan, S. (2004). *O, say can you see? America's symbols, landmarks, and important words*. New York: Scholastic.

Keller, L. (2002). *Scrambled states of America*. New York: Holt.

Scieszka, J., & Smith, L. (1995). *Math curse*. New York: Penguin Books.

Scillian, D. (2002). *One nation: America by the numbers*. Chelsea, MI: Sleeping Bear Press.

Scillian, D. (2003). *P is for passport*. Chelsea, MI: Sleeping Bear Press.

Silverstein, S. (2004). *Where the sidewalk ends*. New York: HarperCollins.

Sis, P. (2004). *The train of states*. New York: Greenwillow Books.

Waller, A. (1994). *Betsy Ross*. New York: Scholastic.

Related Instructional Resources

Cheney, L. (2005). *A time for freedom: What happened when in America*. New York: Simon & Schuster.

Davis, K. (2004). *Don't know much about the 50 states* (Don't know much about series). New York: HarperTrophy.

Devrian Global Industries. (2006). *States activities book*. Union, NJ: Devrian Global Industries.

Gordon, P., & Snow, R. (2004). *Kids learn America! Bringing geography to life with people, places & history*. Charlotte, VT: Williamson.

Hauser, J. (2004). *Celebrate America: Learning about the USA through crafts & activities*. Charlotte, VT: Williamson.

Murphy, F. (2002). *Our country*. New York: Scholastic Professional Books.

Press, J. (2001). *Around the world art & activities: Visiting the 7 continents through craft fun*. Charlotte, VT: Williamson.

Related Websites

Create a Graph Online
> http://nces.ed.gov/nceskids/createagraph/

Dates of Statehood
> http://www.50states.com/statehood.htm
> http://www.enchantedlearning.com/usa/states/statehood.shtml
> http://www.1930census.com/united_states_50_states_by_statehood.php

Stem and Leaf Plots
> http://math.about.com/library/weekly/aa051002a.htm

U.S. Data and Statistics
> http://www.globalcomputing.com/StatesContent.htm
> http://www.50states.com/
> http://www.whitehousehistory.org/
> http://www.census.gov/
> http://www.census.gov/compendia/statab/
> http://plasma.nationalgeographic.com/places/index.html
> http://www.infoplease.com/

Virtual Manipulatives Library—Histogram
> http://nlvm.usu.edu/en/nav/frames_asid_183_g_2_t_5.html?open=activities

Activities Featuring Connections

"Invention" (a poem in Where the Sidewalk Ends) (2004)

by Shel Silverstein

HarperCollins, ISBN #0060572345

Perfect Inventions = Perfect World (2000)

by Fifth-Grade Students of Holly Springs Elementary School, Pickins, S.C.

Scholastic, ISBN #0439260663

Overview of Poem and Book: Learn about the obstacles one can encounter during the process of invention in Silverstein's "Invention." Then in *Perfect Inventions = Perfect World*, the authors, elementary school students who view themselves as future leaders, scientists, and inventors, propose various inventions, machines, and technology that will protect and advance the planet while filling it with peace and happiness.

Mathematical Concepts and Skills: real-life applications of mathematics, careers in mathematics

Social Studies Concepts and Skills: identification of scientific and technological advances, promoting the common good through civic action

Overview of Activities: Students learn of the potential inventions of young students wanting to make the earth a better place. Students then brainstorm and work collaboratively to design and illustrate a potential invention, with a focus on improving the quality of life and protecting the environment.

National Mathematics Standards (2000): Students in grades 3 through 5 should "recognize and apply mathematics in contexts outside of mathematics" (Connections Standard) (p. 402). Students should also "communicate their mathematical thinking coherently and clearly to peers, teachers, and others" and "use the language of mathematics to express mathematical ideas precisely" (Communication Standard) (p. 402).

National Social Studies Standards (1994):

Social studies programs for early grades should include experiences that provide for the study of *interactions among individuals, groups, and institutions,* so that the learner can "show how groups and institutions work to meet individual needs and promote the common good (p. 60)." Social studies programs for early grades should also include experiences that provide for the study of *relationships among science, technology, and society,* so that the learner can "identify and describe examples in which science and technology have changed the lives of people, such as homemaking, childcare, work, transportation, and communication" (p. 67). Finally, social studies programs for early grades should include experiences that provide for the study of *the ideals, principles, and practices of citizenship in a democratic republic,* so that the learner can "recognize and interpret how the 'common good' can be strengthened through various forms of citizen action" (p. 73).

Materials: Internet (or library resources), posterboard, crayons or markers

Description of Activities:

1. Read the short poem "Invention" by Shel Silverstein to set the stage for the upcoming activity on developing a potential invention. Briefly discuss obstacles inventors might encounter as they develop and put to the test new ideas and the importance of perseverance.

2. Introduce the book *Perfect Inventions = Perfect World* to students, describing how the book was written by fifth graders who describe themselves in the opening page as "the next generation of leaders, scientists, and inventors." Remind students that they, too, are our future and can thus impact our planet, its environment, and its people, in both positive and negative ways. Engage students in a discussion of how they impact our planet by asking such questions as: What are you doing now to protect the environment? Do you recycle? Do you conserve energy by not leaving on lights? Do you waste food? Water? Do you participate in volunteer organizations? Charitable organizations? After-school activities that foster good citizenship? Remind students that their actions today leave a lasting impact on others and the planet, and thus they are in charge of making decisions for the common good.

3. Share with the class several of the clever and original ideas of inventions described and illustrated in *Perfect Inventions = Perfect World.* Note how the names of the students' inventions are derived from the Greek and Latin roots (which is why the names of the inventions may seem unfamiliar or awkward to pronounce). As you share various inventions, allow students to judge whether they think the invention is possible, beneficial, practical, etc. Also, students should explain what content knowledge and skills they would need (e.g., in math, science, geography, medicine, botany, zoology, etc.) to make the invention a reality.

4. Students work in small groups and brainstorm ideas of potential inventions. Each group selects one invention and, in the spirit of *Perfect Inventions = Perfect World*, names the invention using Greek or Latin roots, describes it, and illustrates it using their posterboard and markers. Each group then presents its invention to the class and describes what math (or other content knowledge) students might need to know to make the invention a reality. To help direct students, consider narrowing the focus to an invention that would help their school, neighborhood, state, a certain country, etc.

Assessment:

*   Did students develop a potential original invention, complete with a name, description, and illustration, and which would benefit the common good?

*   Did students clearly articulate the mathematical and other content knowledge needed to create their potential original invention?

Activity Extensions:

*   Visit the U.S. Patent and Trademark Office website and research the patent process, how many patents are in existence, who has received the greatest number of patents, the first women to receive a patent, etc. Also, research the difference between a patent, trademark, and copyright.

*   Research and present the findings of a biography on an inventor (e.g., Archimedes, Johannes Gutenberg, Milton S. Hershey, Thomas L. Jennings, etc.).

*   Share with students some of the interesting inventions, and the stories behind inventions of girls and women in *Girls Think of Everything: Stories of Ingenious Inventions by Women* (e.g., windshield wipers, Kevlar, space bumper, etc.). (The introductory pages to the book provide an engaging look at the accomplishments of women and the evolution of inventions.) Discuss the mathematical knowledge, and other content knowledge, these female inventors possessed to create such inventions.

*   Discuss students' choices of future careers. Focus on the math they will need to know to perform well in these jobs. Also, discuss how these jobs contribute to society, to the environment, or to the common good.

Cross-Curricular Connections:

Visual Arts

- Research and present the inventions and sketches of the great artist, Leonardo da Vinci.

- Create a collage of individuals who have changed our world for the better through their inventions.

- Create a collage containing images of careers in which the goal is to protect or better our world and/or environment.

Science

- Explore a biography of a famous scientist or inventor (e.g., Madame Curie, Benjamin Franklin, Thomas Edison, Jonas Salk, etc.).

Related Children's Literature

Barretta, G. (2006). *Now and Ben: The modern inventions of Ben Franklin?* New York: Holt.

DeMauro, L. (2002). *Thomas Edison: A brilliant inventor* (Time for kids series). New York: HarperCollins.

Fifth-Grade Students of Holly Springs Elementary School, Pickens, S.C. (2000). *Perfect inventions = perfect world.* New York: Scholastic.

Garrison, J., & Tubesing, A. (1996). *A million visions of peace: Wisdom from the Friends of Old Turtle.* New York: Scholastic.

Harper, C. (2001). *Imaginative inventions: The who, what, when, where, and why of roller skates, potato chips, marbles and pie (and more!).* Boston: Little, Brown.

LaFontaine, B. (1998). *Great inventors and inventions* (100 things you should know about series). London: Dover.

Marzollo, J. (1994). *My first book of biographies: Great men and women every child should know.* New York: Scholastic.

Reimer, L., & Reimer, W. (1995). *Mathematicians are people, too.* Palo Alto, CA: Dale Seymour.

Satterfield, K. (2005). *Benjamin Franklin: A man of many talents* (Time for kids series). New York: HarperCollins.

Schonberg, M. (2005). *I is for idea: An inventions alphabet.* Chelsea, MI: Sleeping Bear Press.

Silverstein, S. (2004). *Where the sidewalk ends.* New York: HarperCollins.

St. George, J. (2002). *So you want to be an inventor?* New York: Penguin.

Thimmesh, C. (2000). *Girls think of everything: stories of ingenious inventions by women.* Boston: Houghton Mifflin.

Thimmesh, C. (2002). *The sky's the limit: Stories of discovery by women and girls.* Boston: Houghton Mifflin.

Turvey, P. (1994). *Inventions: Inventors and ingenious ideas* (Timelines series). London: Franklin Watts.

Wood, R. (2003). *Great inventions* (Discoveries series). New York: Barnes & Noble Books.

Wulffson, D. (2001). *Kid who invented the trampoline: More surprising stories about inventions.* New York: Penguin Young Readers Group.

Related Instructional Resources

Inventor and Inventions Series (Benchmark Books)

Brewer, D. (2004). *Inventions* (100 things you should know about series). New York: Barnes & Noble Books.

Casey, S. (2005). *Kids inventing! A handbook for young inventors.* San Francisco: Jossey-Bass.

Egan, L. (1999). *Inventors and inventions.* New York: Scholastic.

Flack, J. (1989). *Inventing, inventions, inventing.* Portsmouth, NH: Libraries Unlimited.

Kassinger, R. (2002). *Build a better mousetrap: Make classic inventions, discover your problem-solving genius, and take the inventor's challenge.* Hoboken, NJ: Wiley.

Lewis, B. (1995). *The kid's guide to service projects: Over 500 service ideas for young people who want to make a difference.* Minneapolis: Free Spirit.

Saunders, H. (1988). *When are we ever gonna have to use this?* Palo Alto, CA: Dale Seymour.

Related Websites

Birth Places of Famous Mathematicians

     http://www-groups.dcs.st-and.ac.uk/~history/BiogIndex.html

Biographies of Scientists

     http://www.blupete.com/Literature/Biographies/Science/Scients.htm

     http://www.infoplease.com/spot/scibio8.html

     http://www.maths.tcd.ie/pub/HistMath/Links/SciBiog.html

Biographies of Women in Science

     http://www.awm-math.org/biographies.html#sciencebios

Great Inventors

     http://library.thinkquest.org/5847/homepage.htm

     http://library.christchurch.org.nz/Kids/Inventions/WhoInvented/

     http://www.enchantedlearning.com/inventors/medicine.shtml

U.S. Patent and Trademark Office

     http://www.uspto.gov/

Women Inventors

     http://inventors.about.com/library/blwomeninventors.htm

     http://inventors.about.com/od/womeninventors/index_a.htm

     http://www.ideafinder.com/features/classact/women.htm

Literature-Based Mathematics and Visual Arts Activities

The Mathematics-Visual Arts Connection

The arts (visual art, music, movement, and drama) present an ideal and unique forum through which children and students can express their ideas, thoughts, and emotions. In particular, the visual arts, which range from "drawing, painting, sculpture, and design, to architecture, film, video, and folk arts" (MENC, 1994, p. 33), embody mathematics, as students can explore such interrelated concepts as patterns, line, shape, and form. A growing body of evidence documents that learning in the arts involves principles shared with other academic disciplines (Bransford et al., 2004; Deasy, 2002; Fiske, 1999; Scripp, 2002). Thus, integrating the arts with other content areas is mounting (Bickley-Green, 1995; Efland, 2002; McDonald & Fisher, 2006; Muller & Ward, 2007; Phillips

& Bickley-Green, 1998; Walling, 2005; Ward & Muller, 2006). Further, in learning the characteristics of and mathematics embedded in the visual arts, students can collaboratively engage in communicating, reasoning, and investigating, activities that both the NCTM (1989, 2000) and MENC (1994) strongly advocate. In his book *Arts with the Brain in Mind*, Jensen (2001) argues that the "visual arts seem to be strongest when used as a tool for academic learning" (p. 58). Further, Eisner (1998, 2004) cites many studies that report strong links between visual learning and improvement in reading and creativity.

> "The visual arts embody interrelated mathematics concepts such as patterns, line, shape, and form."

This chapter articulates a variety of literature-based activities that integrate concepts and skills used and learned in the study of mathematics with those in the visual arts. While engaged in these activities, students will discover and gain practice with such mathematics concepts and skills as counting, place value, fractions, adding fractions with like and unlike denominators, reducing fractions, mixed numbers, improper fractions (Number and Operations Standard); patterns, pattern recognition (Algebra Standard); two- and three-dimensional shapes, polygons, prisms, pyramids, points, lines, line segments, angles, perspective, transformations, tessellations, spatial reasoning, symmetry (Geometry Standard); area, perimeter, angle measurement, scale (Measurement Standard); and sorting, classification, combinations, chance, likelihood, probability, randomness, sampling with replacement, law of large numbers, data collection and interpretation, graphing (Data Analysis and Probability Standard).

Art concepts and skills featured in this chapter include line, shape, color, value, texture, form space, art history, and using various art mediums. While exploring mathematics, students will simultaneously learn about and mimic the work of such artists as M. C. Escher, Henri Matisse, Joan Miro, Piet Mondrian, Pablo Picasso, Georges Seurat, and others.

The integrated literature-based activities also provide students with many opportunities to predict, estimate, problem solve, and reason (Problem Solving and Reasoning and Proof Standards) as well as communicate and use various representations to organize, record, model, and interpret mathematical ideas

(Communication and Representation Standards). Further, students will also discover and explore real-life applications of mathematics and the visual arts and careers in mathematics and the visual arts (Connections Standard).

Remember to check the appendix for ideas and samples of assessment rubrics.

Matrix of Mathematics and Visual Arts Activities

BOOK TITLE	MATHEMATICAL CONCEPTS AND SKILLS	VISUAL ARTS CONCEPTS AND SKILLS	SCIENCE CONCEPTS AND SKILLS	SOCIAL STUDIES CONCEPTS AND SKILLS
The Dot; A Million Dots; Georges Seurat (Getting to Know the World's Greatest Artists Series)	counting, place value, magnitude of numbers, estimation	color, value, texture, form, creating art (Seurat-like artwork), art history (work of Georges Seurat and pointillism)	magnification	historical forms of counting and place value
Ed Emberley's Picture Pie: A Circle Drawing Book; Henri Matisse: Drawing with Scissors	fractions, adding fractions with like and unlike denominators, reducing fractions, mixed numbers, improper fractions, estimation	line, shape, color, texture, value, creating art (Matisse-like artwork), art history (work of Henri Matisse)	chromatics	paper-cutting traditions
Tessellations: The History and Making of Symmetrical Designs; A Cloak for the Dreamer	tessellations, patterns, transformations (translations, rotations, reflections, glide reflections)	line, shape, color, creating art (tessellations), art history (work of M. C. Escher)	tessellations in nature and architecture	tessellations in Native American rugs and blankets, North American quilts
Zoo in the Sky: A Book of Animal Constellations	shapes, polygons, angles, points, line segments	line, shape, form, creating art (chalk sketch)	astronomy, identification of animals, animal characteristics and habitats	geography, cartography, exploration of a biographical piece on an astronomer
I Spy Shapes in Art; Picasso (Getting to Know the World's Greatest Artists Series)	two- and three-dimensional shapes, attributes of polygons and solids	line, shape, color, texture, form, space, creating art (Picasso-like artwork), art history (work of Picasso and cubism)	two- and three-dimensional shapes in nature	two- and three-dimensional shapes in architecture
Grandfather Tang's Story: A Tale Told with Tangrams	shapes, transformations (slides, flips, and turns), spatial reasoning	line, shape, color, creating art (watercolor and ink painting), art history (Chinese tangram stories)	habitat and characteristics of animals in China	study of China, storytelling as a folk tradition

BOOK TITLE	MATHEMATICAL CONCEPTS AND SKILLS	VISUAL ARTS CONCEPTS AND SKILLS	SCIENCE CONCEPTS AND SKILLS	SOCIAL STUDIES CONCEPTS AND SKILLS
Snowflake Bentley	line symmetry, reflections, hobbies and careers that use math	line, shape, color, creating art (paper snowflakes), art history (*papel picado*, "perforated paper" from Mexico)	weather, seasons, snowflakes, microscopes	careers and hobbies that use mathematics and science, symmetry in flags, paper-cutting traditions
Follow the Line; Mondrian (Great Modern Masters Series)	shapes, angles, line segments, lines, perpendicular lines	line, shape, color, creating art (Mondrian-like artwork), art history (work of Mondrian and abstract period)	chromatics	lines of latitude and longitude
Madlenka; Zoom	perspective, area, perimeter, angle measure, scale	line, shape, form, space, creating art (drawing using perspective)	telescopes and microscopes	map projections
Probably Pistachio; Miro: Earth and Sky (Art for Children Series); *Joan Miro* (Famous Artists Series)	likelihood, probability, randomness, sampling with replacement, prediction, law of large numbers	line, shape, color, form, space, creating art (surrealist art), art history (work of Joan Miro)	stars and constellations	geography of the Catalonia region of Spain

The Dot (2003)

by Peter Reynolds

Candlewick Press, ISBN #0763619612

A Million Dots (2006)

by Andrew Clements

Simon & Schuster Books for Young Readers, ISBN #0689858248

Georges Seurat
(Getting to Know the World's Greatest Artists Series) (2002)

by Mike Venezia

Children's Press, ISBN #0516278134

Overview of Books:	Enjoy the heart-warming tale of a teacher's inspiration and her belief in a young budding artist's talents in *The Dot*. In *A Million Dots,* come see what a million dots actually looks like and explore the magnitude of numbers while learning a variety of interesting and astonishing number facts and trivia. Then, in *Georges Seurat,* explore Seurat's artwork, which features pointillism, a style of painting consisting of dots placed close to one another.
Mathematical Concepts and Skills:	counting, place value, magnitude of numbers, estimation
Visual Arts Concepts and Skills:	color, value, texture, form, creating art (Seurat-like artwork), art history (work of Georges Seurat and pointillism)
Overview of Activities:	Students visually and numerically explore place value and the magnitude of numbers through the use of pictures and number facts. Students then create their own artwork in the spirit of Seurat's pointillism.
National Mathematics Standards (2000):	Students in grades 3 through 5 should "understand the place-value structure of the base-ten number system and be able to represent and compare whole numbers and decimals." Students should also "develop and use strategies to estimate the results of whole-number computations and to judge the reasonableness of such results" (Number and Operations Standard) (p. 392).

National Visual Arts Standards (1994):

Students should understand and apply media, techniques, and processes (Content Standard 1) and "use different media, techniques, and processes to communicate ideas, experiences, and stories" (Achievement Standard c) (p. 34); choose and evaluate a range of subject matter, symbols, and ideas (Content Standard 3) and "select and use subject matter, symbols, and ideas to communicate meaning" (Achievement Standard b) (p. 34); make connections between visual arts and other disciplines (Content Standard 6) and "identify connections between the visual arts and other disciplines in the curriculum" (Achievement Standard b) (p. 35).

Materials: calculators, 9" × 12" paper, coloring medium (Do-a-Dot pens or tempera paint and Q-tips)

Description of Activities:

1. Read *The Dot* to set the stage for the upcoming activities.

2. Read the opening page of *A Million Dots* where the author shows an illustration of ten, one hundred, five hundred, and then one thousand dots. Ask students to estimate how more pages they think would be needed to display one million dots. How long do they think it would take to count one million dots? Students share their reasoning.

3. Continue reading *A Million Dots* and allow students to view select pages of the many, many dots, assisting them in visually understanding how many pages are needed to capture one million dots. Also, take time to visit and discuss some of the interesting statistics and number facts appearing on each page.

4. Introduce pointillism, a style of painting invented by Georges Seurat, in which he used tiny dots of pure, unmixed colors that, when seen from a distance merge, creating the effect of blended colors. Read all or select excerpts from the biography, *Georges Seurat*. Let students view some of Seurat's works featuring pointillism (e.g., *Sunday Afternoon on the Island of La Grande Jatte, Invitation to the Sideshow,* and *Young Woman Powdering Herself*).

5. Students work in pairs and estimate the number of dots of paints used in all (or a portion) of Seurat's *Sunday Afternoon on the Island of La Grande Jatte*. (The picture measures 81" × 120" and each dot is approximately 1/16 of an inch in size.) Do students think this painting contains a million dots? (There are approximately 2,488,320 dots!) Students share their estimation and measurement strategies with the class and defend their reasoning.

6. Discuss and show a picture of the color wheel, which is made up of the primary colors (red, yellow, and blue) and the colors one obtains by mixing these colors (orange, green, and purple). On the color wheel,

each color lies opposite its complementary color, resulting in the creation of three main pairs: red/green, blue/orange, and yellow/purple. Seurat purposefully used complementary colors in his artwork because, when seen side by side, the colors contrast strongly, resulting in a brighter appearance.

7. Using 9" × 12" white paper and a coloring medium (e.g., Do-a-Dot pens or tempera paint and Q-tips), students create their own artwork in the style of Seurat's pointillism. Ask students to find objects in the classroom to serve as their subject matter. Students share their work with the class and discuss their choice of subject matter and color. Students discuss whether the style of art known as pointillism captures their subject matter well.

8. Challenge students to estimate and then compute the number of dots used in their artwork.

Assessment:

- Did students gain a better visual perspective and understanding of the magnitude of large numbers?

- Did students closely approximate the number of dots in Seurat's artwork?

- Did students create a painting in the spirit of Seurat's pointillism?

- Did students closely approximate the number of dots in their artwork?

Activity Extensions:

- Students visually experience our base ten system by exploring the Powers of Ten website or the Science, Optics, and You website. Students travel the universe with the click of a button, making leaps in powers of ten.

- Students compare and contrast the style of painting known as pointillism (comprised of dots and contrasting colors) with impressionist painting (comprised of brush strokes and softer colors).

- Students explore the life and artwork of pop artist Roy Lichtenstein and how he used Benday dots in many of his works (e.g., *Reflections: Nurse, Mural with Blue Brushstroke, Explosion*). Students create their own artwork in the spirit of Lichtenstein.

Cross-Curricular Connections:

Science

- Research and report on how visual acuity changes using magnification with magnifying glasses, microscopes, binoculars, and telescopes.

Social Studies

- Compare and contrast historical forms of counting and place value.

Related Children's Literature

Clements, A. (2006). *A million dots*. New York: Simon & Schuster Books for Young Readers.

Gag, W. (1996). *Millions of cats*. New York: Penguin Putnam Books.

Harris, N. (2004). *How big?* Oxfordshire, UK: Orpheus Books.

Nolan, H. (1995) *How much, how many, how far, how heavy, how long, how tall is 1000?* Tonawanda, NY: Kids Can Press.

Packard, E. (2000). *Big numbers: And pictures that show just how big they are!* Brookefield, CT: Millbrook Press.

Reynolds, P. (2003). *The dot*. Cambridge, MA: Candlewick Press.

Reynolds, P. (2004). *Ish*. Cambridge, MA: Candlewick Press.

Rosen, S. (1992). *How far is a star?* Minneapolis: Carolrhoda Books.

Schwartz, D. (1985). *How much is a million?* New York: Lothrop, Lee & Shepard Books.

Schwartz, D. (1989). *If you made a million*. New York: Lothrop, Lee & Shepard Books

Schwartz, D. (1998). *G is for googol: A math alphabet book*. Berkeley, CA: Tricycle Press.

Schwartz, D. (1999). *On beyond a million*. New York: Random House.

Schwartz, D. (2003). *Millions to measure*. New York: HarperCollins.

Scieszka, J., & Smith, L. (1995). *Math curse*. New York: Penguin Books.

Tang, G. (2003). *Math-terpieces: The art of problem solving*. New York: Scholastic.

Venezia, M. (2001). *Roy Lichtenstein* (Getting to know the world's greatest artists series). New York: Scholastic.

Venezia, M. (2002). *Georges Seurat* (Getting to know the world's greatest artists series). New York: Children's Press.

Walker, L. (1994). *Roy Lichtenstein: The artist at work*. New York: Lodestar Books.

Wells, R. (1993). *Is a blue whale the biggest thing there is?* Morton Grove, IL: Whitman.

Wells, R. (1995). *What's smaller than a pygmy shrew?* Morton Grove, IL: Whitman.

Wells, R. (2000). *Can you count to a googol?* Morton Grove, IL: Whitman.

Related Instructional Resources

Aigner-Clark, J.. (2004). *Baby Einstein: The ABCs of art*. New York: Hyperion Books for Children.

Dickins, R. (2005). *The children's book of art: An introduction to famous paintings*. London: Usborne.

Evans, J., & Skelton, T. (2001). *How to teach art to children*. Monterey, CA: Evan-Moor.

Kohl, M., & Solga, K. (1996). *Discovering great artists: Hands-on art for children in the styles of the great masters*. Bellingham, WA: Bright Ring.

Krull, K. (1995). *Lives of the artists: Masterpieces, messes*. San Diego: Harcourt Brace.

Micklethwait, L. (1993). *A child's book of art: Great pictures: First words*. New York: Dorling Kindersley.

Renshaw, A., & Ruggi, G. (2005). *The art book for children*. New York: Phaidon Press.

Scieszka, J., & Smith, L. (2005). *Seen art?* New York: Viking Press.

Williams, D. (1995). *Teaching mathematics through children's art*. Portsmouth, NH: Heinemann.

Related Websites

Can You Say Really Big Numbers?
http://www.mathcats.com/explore/reallybignumbers.html

Create Art
http://www.sanford-artedventures.com/create/create.html

Georges-Pierre Seurat
http://www.ibiblio.org/wm/paint/auth/seurat/

Have Some Fun with Optical Mixing
http://www.telfairartyfacts.org/kids/impressionism/impress6.htm

How Much Is Million? Lesson
http://www.lessonplanspage.com/MathHowMuchMillion-HundredNumberSense2.htm

Major Modern and Contemporary Visual Artists
http://www.the-artists.org/index.cfm

Paint a Color Wheel
http://www.sanford-artedventures.com/create/tech_paint_wheel.html

Pointillism Practice Page
http://www.epcomm.com/center/point/point.htm

Powers of Ten
http://microcosm.web.cern.ch/microcosm/P10/english/welcome.html

Roy Lichtenstein
http://www.artcyclopedia.com/artists/lichtenstein_roy.html
http://www.lichtensteinfoundation.org/

Science, Optics, and You
http://micro.magnet.fsu.edu/primer/java/scienceopticsu/powersof10/index.html

Study Art
http://www.sanford-artedventures.com/study/study.html

Teach Art
http://www.sanford-artedventures.com/teach/teach.html

Ed Emberley's Picture Pie: A Circle Drawing Book (1984)

by Edward Emberley

Little, Brown, ISBN #0316234265

Henri Matisse: Drawing with Scissors (2002)

by Keesia Johnson and Jane O'Connor

Grosset & Dunlap, ISBN #044842519X

Overview of Books: As the opening pages describe, *Ed Emberley's Picture Pie* book colorfully illustrates how a circle, divided into many fractional sectors, can be used to make patterns and pictures of animals, trees, fish, etc. Then, in *Henri Matisse: Drawing with Scissors*, learn about the life and artwork of Henri Matisse, best known for his artwork exhibiting bold colors and shapes.

Mathematical Concepts and Skills: fractions, adding fractions with like and unlike denominators, reducing fractions, mixed numbers, improper fractions, estimation

Visual Arts Concepts and Skills: line, shape, color, texture, value, creating art (Matisse-like artwork), art history (work of Henri Matisse)

Overview of Activities: Students gain practice with identifying and estimating fractional parts as well as adding fractions with like and unlike denominators. Students then create a piece of artwork in the spirit of Henri Matisse.

National Mathematics Standards (2000):

Students in grades 3 through 5 should "develop understanding of fractions as parts of unit wholes" and "use visual models, benchmarks, and equivalent forms to add or subtract commonly used fractions and decimals" (Number and Operations Standard) (p. 392).

National Visual Arts Standards (1994):

Students should understand and apply media, techniques, and processes (Content Standard 1) and "use different media, techniques, and processes to communicate ideas, experiences, and stories" (Achievement Standard c) (p. 34); choose and evaluate a range of subject matter, symbols, and ideas (Content Standard 3) and "select and use subject matter, symbols, and ideas to communicate meaning" (Achievement Standard b) (p. 34); reflect upon and assess the characteristics and merits of their work and the work of others (Content Standard 5) and "understand there are different responses to specific artworks" (Achievement Standard c) (p. 34); make connections between visual arts and other disciplines (Content Standard 6) and "identify connections between the visual arts and other disciplines in the curriculum" (Achievement Standard b) (p. 35).

Materials: fraction circles, copied pages from *Picture Pie*, brightly colored construction paper, large pieces of butcher paper, scissors, glue sticks

Description of Activities:

1. Read the opening two pages of *Ed Emberley's Picture Pie* in which the author shows how a circle can be divided into pie sectors and used to make various pictures.

2. Distribute a set of fraction circles to each student. Place students in groups of three or four and distribute to each group a page copied out of *Ed Emberley's Picture Pie*. Challenge students to make two or more shapes on the page by collaboratively using their fraction circles.

3. After constructing their shapes, ask students to first estimate the sum of all of the fraction pieces and then compute the sum of all the pieces. This will require students to add fractions with like and unlike denominators as well as work with mixed numbers and improper fractions. Students should reduce their fractional solution to lowest terms. Students compare their visual estimation of the sum of all of the fraction pieces to the sum they computed. How accurate were their estimations?

4. Share the life and artwork of Henri Matisse by reading *Henri Matisse: Drawing with Scissors* to the class. Take time to allow students to view and discuss the artwork of Matisse and how his artwork changed over the course of his lifetime. Consider projecting some of his artwork for students to view by accessing the Henri Matisse websites listed below. Compare the bold colors and shapes used in Matisse's artwork to the colorful art in Emberley's *Picture Pie* book.

5. Focus on the latter part of Matisse's life during which, because of his failing health, he could not stand for long periods of time in front of an easel. Confined to a wheelchair, he continued to work, energetically "drawing with scissors" as he referred to it, creating some of his most famous masterpieces: large-scale paper cutouts (e.g., *The Snail, The Sheaf,* and *Blue Nude III*). Matisse would cut shapes out of boldly colored paper and then have his assistant place and then glue them.

6. Place students in groups of four and give each group several pieces of brightly colored construction paper, scissors, gluesticks, and one large piece of butcher paper. Students collaboratively think of a subject matter to "paint" and then cut large shapes out of the construction paper to capture their subject matter, Then, one at a time, each student in the group takes a shape, obtains advice from the other group members as to where to place that shape, and then glues the shape into place on their large piece of butcher paper. Students take turns playing Matisse and then his assistant until all the pieces are pasted on the butcher paper and the work of art is completed. Groups then share and describe their Matisse-like masterpieces with the class.

7. Challenge students to view their Matisse masterpieces and to estimate what fractional amount of each color was used.

Assessment:

- Did students reasonably estimate and then sum all of their fraction pieces?

- Were students' strategies for adding the fraction pieces logical and efficient?

- Did students accurately add fractions with like and unlike denominators?

- Did students properly compute using mixed numbers and improper fractions?

- Did students reduce their fraction to its lowest terms?

- Did students notice the similarities between Emberley's illustrations and the artwork of Matisse?

- Did students create Matisse-like artwork?

- Did students reasonably estimate the amount of each color used in their Matisse-like work?

Activity Extensions:

- Students explore *The Hershey's Milk Chocolate Fractions Book* (Pallotta, 1999) and gain experience working with a rectangular unit as a whole, and then cutting it into fractional rectangular sectors, as opposed to fractional pie sectors.

- Print off a color copy of artwork by Roy Lichtenstein (e.g., *Red Barn*) or Paul Klee (e.g., *Zitronin*). Students first estimate what fractional amount of each color appears in the work of art. Copy grid or graph paper onto a clear transparency and ask students to place the transparency over the color print. Students count each of the colored squares to determine what fractional amount of each color appears. Students compare their results to their initial estimations.

- Enjoy poetry about color authored by Shel Silverstein (e.g., "Colors" [2004], and "The Painter" [1981]).

Cross-Curricular Connections:

Science

- Investigate chromatics, the science of color through paint mixing, prisms, and rainbows.

Social Studies

- Investigate other paper-cutting traditions, such as *jianzhi* (China), *kirigami* or *monkiri* (Japan), *scherenschnitte* (Germany and Switzerland), *silhouette* (France), and *wycinanki* (Poland).

Related Children's Literature

Appel, J., & Guglielmo, A. (2006). *Feed Matisse's fish.* New York: Sterling.

Emberley, E. (1984). *Ed Emberley's picture pie: A circle drawing book.* Boston: Little, Brown.

Emberley, E. (2006). *Ed Emberley's picture pie 2: A drawing book and stencil.* Boston: Little, Brown.

Gifford, S. (2003). *Piece = part = portion.* Berkeley, CA: Tricycle Press.

Johnson, K., & O'Connor, J. (2002). *Henri Matisse: Drawing with scissors.* New York: Grosset & Dunlap.

Matthews, L. (1979). *Gator pie.* New York: Dodd, Mead.

The Metropolitan Museum of Art. (2004). *Museum 1 2 3.* New York: Little, Brown.

The Metropolitan Museum of Art. (2005). *Museum shapes.* New York: Little, Brown.

Micklethwait, L. (1993). *I spy two eyes: Numbers in art.* New York: Greenwillow Books.

Micklethwait, L. (2004). *I spy shapes in art.* New York: Greenwillow Books.

Murphy, S. (1996). *Give me half!* New York: HarperCollins.

Pallotta, J. (1999). *The Hershey's milk chocolate fractions book.* New York: Scholastic.

Pallotta, J. (2002). *Apple fractions.* New York: Scholastic.

Pinczes, E. (2001). *Inch worm and a half.* Boston: Houghton Mifflin.

Pomerantz, C. (1984). *The half birthday party.* New York: Clarion.

Scieszka, J., & Smith, L. (1995). *Math curse.* New York: Penguin Books.

Scieszka, J., & Smith, L. (2005). *Seen art?* New York: Viking Press.

Silverstein, S. (1981). *A light in the attic.* New York: HarperCollins.

Silverstein, S. (2004). *Where the sidewalk ends.* New York: HarperCollins.

Tang, G. (2003). *Math-terpieces: The art of problem solving.* New York: Scholastic.

Venezia, M. (1997). *Henri Matisse* (Getting to know the world's greatest artists series). New York: Children's Press.

Venezia, M. (2001). *Roy Lichtenstein* (Getting to know the world's greatest artists series). New York: Children's Press.

Walker, L. (1994). *Roy Lichtenstein: The artist at work.* New York: Lodestar Books.

Winter, J. (1998). *My name is Georgia.* Orlando, FL: Silver Whistle.

Related Instructional Resources

Aigner-Clark, J. (2004). *Baby Einstein: The ABCs of art.* New York: Hyperion Books for Children.

Dickins, R. (2005). *The children's book of art: An introduction to famous paintings.* London: Usborne.

Evans, J., & Skelton, T. (2001). *How to teach art to children.* Monterey, CA: Evan-Moor.

Greenberg, D. (1999). *Funny & fabulous fraction stories.* New York: Scholastic.

Kohl, M., & Solga, K. (1996). *Discovering great artists: Hands-on art for children in the styles of the great masters.* Bellingham, WA: Bright Ring.

Krull, K. (1995). *Lives of the artists: Masterpieces, messes.* San Diego: Harcourt Brace.

Long, L. (2001). *Fabulous fractions: Games and activities that make math easy and fun.* Hoboken, NJ: Wiley.

Micklethwait, L. (1993). *A child's book of art: Great pictures: First words.* New York: Dorling Kindersley.

Renshaw, A., & Ruggi, G. (2005). *The art book for children.* New York: Phaidon Press.

Williams, D. (1995). *Teaching mathematics through children's art.* Portsmouth, NH: Heinemann.

Related Websites

Famous Artists
http://library.thinkquest.org/J001159/famart.htm

Fraction Circles
http://www.eduplace.com/state/pdf/hmm/trb/3/3_40.pdf

Henri Matisse
http://www.artcyclopedia.com/artists/matisse_henri.html
http://www.geocities.com/Paris/LeftBank/4208/
http://www.artchive.com/artchive/m/matisse/snail.jpg
http://www.ibiblio.org/wm/paint/auth/matisse/

Major Modern and Contemporary Visual Artists
http://www.the-artists.org/index.cfm

Paul Klee—*Zitronin*
http://www.fantasyarts.net/Paul_Klee_Paintings.htm

Roy Lichtenstein
http://www.artcyclopedia.com/artists/lichtenstein_roy.html
http://www.lichtensteinfoundation.org/

Virtual Manipulatives Library—Adding Fractions
http://nlvm.usu.edu/en/nav/frames_asid_106_g_3_t_1.html

Virtual Manipulatives Library—Comparing Fractions
http://nlvm.usu.edu/en/nav/category_g_3_t_1.html

Virtual Manipulatives Library—Equivalent Fractions
http://nlvm.usu.edu/en/nav/frames_asid_105_g_3_t_1.html

Virtual Manipulatives Library—Fractions Pieces
http://nlvm.usu.edu/en/nav/frames_asid_274_g_3_t_1.html?open=activities

Tessellations: The History and Making of Symmetrical Designs (2001)

by Pam Stephens

Crystal, ISBN #1562902431

A Cloak for the Dreamer (1994)

by Aileen Friedman

Scholastic, ISBN #0590489879

Overview of Books:	In *Tessellations: The History and Making of Symmetrical Designs,* follow your tour guide, Paul E. Gon, through a history of tessellations and the tessellated artwork of M. C. Escher while learning the math and art used when creating tessellations. In *A Cloak for the Dreamer*, enjoy a tale (with a message) about three sons of a tailor commissioned to design a cloak for the archduke. The creation of the cloaks demonstrates the meaning of what a tessellation is and is not.
Mathematical Concepts and Skills:	tessellations, patterns, transformations (translations, rotations, reflections, glide reflections)
Visual Arts Concepts and Skills:	line, shape, color, creating art (tessellations), art history (work of M. C. Escher)
Overview of Activities:	Students explore the mathematical concept of transformations and how performing one or more transformations results in the creation of a tessellation. Students also view and explore some of the tessellated artwork of the Dutch artist M. C. Escher.
National Mathematics Standards (2000): π	Students in grades 3 through 5 should "describe, extend, and make generalizations about geometric and numeric patterns" (Algebra Standard) (p. 394). They should also "predict and describe the results of sliding, flipping, and turning two-dimensional shapes" (Geometry Standard) (p. 396).

National Visual Arts Standards (1994): Students should understand and apply media, techniques, and processes (Content Standard 1) and "use different media, techniques, and processes to communicate ideas, experiences, and stories" (Achievement Standard c) (p. 34); use knowledge of structures and functions (Content Standard 2) and "know the differences among visual characteristics and purposes of art in order to convey ideas" (Achievement Standard a) (p. 34); choose and evaluate a range of subject matter, symbols, and ideas (Content Standard 3) and "select and use subject matter, symbols, and ideas to communicate meaning" (Achievement Standard b) (p. 34); make connections between visual arts and other disciplines (Content Standard 6) and "identify connections between the visual arts and other disciplines in the curriculum" (Achievement Standard b) (p. 35).

Materials: index cards precut into 2" × 2" squares (approximately four for each student), paper, scissors, tape, glue sticks, construction paper

Description of Activities:

1. Share with students some examples of M. C. Escher's tessellated artwork using the websites or other resources listed below. Ask students what features they notice in Escher's work (e.g., repeating patterns of the same shape). Introduce the concept of a tessellation, which is a repeating pattern with no gaps and no overlaps created by performing one or more transformations. Share more examples of tessellations using the websites or other resources listed below (in particular, see examples of student-made tessellations in *Tessellation Winners: Escher-Like Original Student Art, the First Contest* [Dale Seymour Publications, 1991].

2. Follow the instructions appearing on pages 18–37 in *Tessellations: The History and Making of Symmetrical Designs* and, using index cards precut into 2" × 2" squares, guide students in the creation of a tessellation by performing such transformations as a translation (slide), reflection (flip), rotation (turn), and glide reflection.

3. Using construction paper, students work independently and create tessellations by performing one or more transformations on a 2" × 2" square. Students should share their artwork with the class, challenging them to determine what transformation was used to create the tessellated pattern.

4. Read *A Cloak for the Dreamer* as a means to reinforce how some shapes tessellate (e.g., rectangles, hexagons) while others do not (e.g., circles). Students should articulate why shapes do or do not tessellate.

Assessment:

- Did students correctly perform the various transformations (translations, reflections, rotations, and glide rotations)?

- Did students accurately create their own tessellations?

- Did students correctly identify what transformation(s) was used to create other students' tessellated patterns?

- Can students articulate what a tessellation is and distinguish a pattern that is a tessellation from one that is not?

- Can students articulate the connection between math and art in the creation of tessellations?

Activity Extensions:

- Explore various Escher works and challenge students to determine what transformation or combination of transformations were used to create the tessellations in his artwork.

- Challenge students to find real-life examples of tessellations (floor tile, brick wall, honeycomb, etc.).

- Enjoy poetry about reflections authored by Shel Silverstein (e.g., "Reflection" [1981]).

Cross-Curricular Connections:

Science

- Find examples of tessellations that occur in nature (e.g., honeycombs, snake skin, armadillo shell, etc).

- Investigate how tessellations are used in architecture to improve strength in design (e.g., locking bricks in ancient pyramids).

Social Studies

- Look for tessellations in the weaving patterns of Native American rugs and blankets and North American quilts.

Related Children's Literature

Brumbeau, J. (2001). *The quiltmaker's gift*. New York: Scholastic.

Brumbeau, J. (2004). *The quiltmaker's journey*. New York: Orchard Books.

Friedman, A. (1994). *A cloak for the dreamer*. New York: Scholastic.

Micklethwait, L. (2004). *I spy shapes in art*. New York: Greenwillow Books.

Roza, G. (2005). *An optical artist: Exploring patterns and symmetry*. New York: PowerKids Press.

Silverstein, S. (1981). *A light in the attic*. New York: HarperCollins.

Stephens, P. (2001). *Tessellations: The history and making of symmetrical design*. Aspen, CO: Crystal.

Related Instructional Resources

Dale Seymour Publications. (1991). *Tessellation winners: Escher-like original student art, the first contest*. Palo Alto, CA: Author.

Dale Seymour Publications. (1997). *Tessellation teaching masters*. Palo Alto, CA: Author.

Dickins, R. (2005). *The children's book of art: An introduction to famous paintings*. London: Usborne.

Escher, M. (2004). *M. C. Escher: The graphic work*. Hohenzollernring, Germany: Taschen.

Evans, J., & Skelton, T. (2001). *How to teach art to children*. Monterey, CA: Evan-Moor.

Kohl, M., & Solga, K. (1996). *Discovering great artists: Hands-on art for children in the styles of the great masters*. Bellingham, WA: Bright Ring.

Krull, K. (1995). *Lives of the artists: Masterpieces, messes*. San Diego: Harcourt Brace.

Micklethwait, L. (1993). *A child's book of art: Great pictures: First words*. New York: Dorling Kindersley.

Press, J. (2001). *Around the world art & activities: Visiting the 7 continents through craft fun*. Charlotte, VT: Williamson.

Renshaw, A., & Ruggi, G. (2005). *The art book for children*. New York: Phaidon Press.

Scieszka, J., & Smith, L. (2005). *Seen art?* New York: Viking Press.

Shattschneider, D. (2005). *M. C. Escher: Visions of symmetry*. Petaluma, CA: Pomegranate.

Shattschneider, D., & Walker, W. (2005). *M. C. Escher kaleidocycles*. New York: Abrams.

Williams, D. (1995). *Teaching mathematics through children's art*. Portsmouth, NH: Heinemann.

Related Websites

Iproject—Make Your Own Tessellation
>http://www.iproject.com/escher/teaching/maketessel.html

Major Modern and Contemporary Visual Artists
>http://www.the-artists.org/index.cfm

M. C. Escher
>http://www.mcescher.com/
>http://www.artcyclopedia.com/artists/escher_mc.html

Tessellations
>http://britton.disted.camosun.bc.ca/jbsymteslk.htm
>http://mathforum.org/sum95/suzanne/tess.intro.html
>http://www.tessellations.org/
>http://mathforum.org/sum95/suzanne/tess.intro.html
>http://library.thinkquest.org/16661/escher/tessellations.1.html

Virtual Manipulatives Library—Reflections
>http://nlvm.usu.edu/en/nav/frames_asid_297_g_2_t_3.html?open=activities

Virtual Manipulatives Library—Rotations
>http://nlvm.usu.edu/en/nav/frames_asid_299_g_2_t_3.html?open=activities

Virtual Manipulatives Library—Tessellations
>http://nlvm.usu.edu/en/nav/frames_asid_163_g_2_t_3.html?open=activities

Virtual Manipulatives Library—Translations
>http://nlvm.usu.edu/en/nav/frames_asid_301_g_2_t_3.html?open=activities

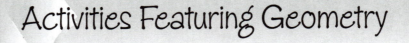

Activities Featuring Geometry

Zoo in the Sky: A Book of Animal Constellations (1998)

by Jacqueline Mitton

National Geographic Society, ISBN #079227069X

Overview of Book: Readers will be captivated by the vibrant and shimmering illustrations of ten familiar animal constellations, each accompanied by poetic text detailing the legend of the constellation. Mitton's book concludes with a brief description of stars and constellations, and its front and back covers are illustrated with a map of the northern and southern skies.

Mathematical Concepts and Skills: shapes, polygons, angles, points, line segments

Visual Arts Concepts and Skills: line, shape, form, creating art (chalk sketch)

Overview of Activities: Students explore maps of the nighttime sky in search of shapes and polygons within the constellations. Students also gain practice with locating and identifying acute, right, and obtuse angles. Students then gain practice with drawing lines, line segments, and angles by creating their own constellation. A classroom nighttime sky is created by adjoining all the individual constellations and hanging them on a wall.

National Mathematics Standards (2000): Students in grades 3 through 5 should "identify, compare, and analyze attributes of two-dimensional shapes and develop vocabulary to describe the attributes" (Geometry Standard) (p. 396). Students should also "understand such attributes as length, area, weight, volume, and size of an angle" and "select and apply appropriate standard units and tools to measure length, area, volume, weight, time, temperature, and the size of angles" (Measurement Standard) (p. 398).

National Visual Arts Standards (1994): Students should understand and apply media, techniques, and processes (Content Standard 1) and "use different media, techniques, and processes to communicate ideas, experiences, and stories" (Achievement Standard c) (p. 34); choose and evaluate a range of subject matter, symbols, and ideas (Content Standard 3) and "select and use subject matter, symbols, and ideas to communicate meaning" (Achievement Standard b) (p. 34); and make connections between visual arts and other disciplines

(Content Standard 6) and "identify connections between the visual arts and other disciplines in the curriculum" (Achievement Standard b) (p. 35).

Materials: map of the night sky (inside front and back cover of *Zoo in the Sky*), highlighters, small star stickers (ten per student), rulers, pencils, white and yellow chalk, black construction paper

Description of Activities:

1. Prior to reading *Zoo in the Sky*, begin a discussion by asking students if they have ever gazed at clouds during the day or the stars at night and have seen patterns, objects, or shapes in the skies.

2. Read *Zoo in the Sky* to students and allow them to learn the names of various constellations and to also observe the patterns and shapes people of centuries ago saw in the stars.

3. Provide students with a map of the night sky and ask them to find constellations containing shapes and polygons. For example, a trapezoid can be seen in the constellation, Sagittarius, while a pentagon is apparent in Cygnus. Younger students might be encouraged to look for simple shapes, such as triangles, squares, and rectangles, while older students can be challenged to find quadrilaterals, pentagons, and hexagons as well as various types of angles (acute, right, and obtuse).

4. Using a highlighter, students trace the outline of any shape (or angle) they spot within the constellations. Students record their findings in their journals, listing the name of the constellation, the shape seen in the constellation, and a description of the shape in terms of its attributes.

5. In small groups or as a whole class, students share their findings. By exploring the constellations in this fashion, students not only will learn the names of various polygons (and angles), but the teacher can introduce to older learners other terminology related to polygons, including points, line segments, convex, concave, regular, nonregular, and congruent.

6. Create and hang a night sky in your own classroom. Students think of an animal or mythical creature to serve as their constellation. Their constellation should be an original idea and not an animal seen in *Zoo in the Sky*.

7. Revisit a few pages in *Zoo in the Sky* and explain to students that the stars form a very basic foundation for the actual picture. For example, students locate Ursa Major (the Great Bear) on their map of the night sky and compare this to the illustration of the Great Bear on page 4. Encourage students to notice how shapes, lines, and points (stars) make up this constellation as well as others.

8. Students use their pencils and rulers to draw an outline of an animal constellation on a piece of black construction paper. Students place star stickers on main points along the lines and angles of their animal form. Students trace over the lead pencil sketch with white chalk.

9. Students use pieces of yellow chalk to draw more complex figures of animals or mythical creatures around the constellations. Students name and label their constellations in English and, if a Latin dictionary is available, with the corresponding Latin name underneath.

10. Students share their pieces of artwork in small groups or as a whole class, describing their component shapes and sharing their names.

11. Hang the students' constellations on a large wall side by side in a rectangular fashion, creating a night sky of the students' artwork.

Assessment:
- Did students notice patterns and shapes in the constellations?
- Did students correctly identify polygons (or angles) by name?
- Did students correctly describe the attributes of various shapes and polygons?
- Did students create original constellations using straight lines, angles, shapes, and points?
- Did students provide appropriate labels/names for their constellations?

Activity Extensions:
- Tap into students' creative writing skills by asking them to write descriptive stories to accompany their constellation artwork that describe the figures. Staple or tape these descriptions onto the backs of the black construction paper. Allow each student to present his or her story to the class, challenging the listeners to add a twist to the origin plot, perhaps connecting it to other original stories presented by students.

- Ask students to describe what they think a star is and record their responses on the chalkboard. Prompt them by asking: What do stars look like? Why do they twinkle? How big is a star? The sun is a star, but the earth is a planet. How is a star different from a planet? After several responses are recorded on the chalkboard, encourage students to develop a group consensus on what they think a star is. Then, read Mitton's description of a star to the students (located at the end of *Zoo in the Sky*). Also, visit some of the websites or books listed below for more age-appropriate information about stars. Ask students to record their definitions of a star in their journals based on the discussion and information shared.

- Enjoy poetry about stars authored by Shel Silverstein (e.g., "Somebody Has To" [1981]).

Cross-Curricular Connections:

Science

- Begin a unit on astronomy (e.g., stars and constellations, distance, location, rotation of planets, solar system, Milky Way galaxy, universe, history of astronomy).

- Identify animals and their characteristics, as well as their habitats, especially those included in the book.

Social Studies

- Study geography as it relates to astronomy (e.g., hemispheres, equator, poles, distance, location, etc.).

- Investigate ancient cartography.

- Explore a biography of an important astronomer (e.g., Galileo, Johannes Kepler, Copernicus, Tycho Brahe, etc.).

Related Children's Literature

Barner, B. (2002). *Stars! Stars! Stars!* San Francisco: Chronicle Books.

Berger, M., & Berger, G. (1999). *Do stars have points? Questions and answers about stars and planets.* New York: Scholastic.

Branley, F. (1981). *The sky is full of stars.* New York: HarperCollins.

Branley, F. (2002). *The sun: Our nearest star.* New York: HarperCollins.

Brown, M. (1998). *I like stars.* New York: Golden Books.

Driscoll, M. (2004). *A child's introduction to the night sky.* New York: Black Dog & Leventhal.

Gallant, R. (1991). *The constellations: How they came to be.* New York: Four Winds Press.

Gibbons, G. (1999). *Stargazers.* New York: Holiday House.

Kerrod, R. (2002). *The book of constellations: Discover the secrets in the stars.* Hauppauge, NY: Barron's Educational Series.

Krupp, E. (1991). *Beyond the blue horizon: Myths and legends of the sun, moon, stars, and planets.* New York: HarperCollins.

Krupp, E., & Krupp, R. (1989). *The Big Dipper and you.* New York: Morrow.

Love, A., & Drake, J. (2004). *The kids' book of the night sky.* Tonawanda, NY: Kids Can Press.

Mitton, J. (1998). *Zoo in the sky: A book of animal constellations.* Washington, DC: National Geographic Society.

Mitton, J. (2004). *Once upon a starry night: A book of constellations.* Washington, DC: National Geographic Society.

Pearce, Q., & Fraser, M. (1991). *The stargazer's guide to the galaxy.* New York: RGA.

Rey, H. (1980). *The stars: A new way to see them.* Boston: Houghton Mifflin.

Rey, H. (1982). *Find the constellations.* Boston: Houghton Mifflin.

Ridpath, I. (1988). *Star tales.* New York: Universe Books.

Sasaki, C. (2003). *The constellations: Stars and stories.* New York: Sterling.

Silverstein, S. (1981). *A light in the attic.* New York: HarperCollins.

Sipiera, P., & Sipiera, D. (1997). *Constellations.* Danbury, CT: Scholastic.

Stott, C. (2003). *I wonder why stars twinkle (and other questions about space).* New York: Kingfisher.

Taylor, H. (1997). *Coyote places the stars.* New York: Aladdin.

Thompson, C. (1989). *Glow in the dark constellations: A field guide for young stargazers.* New York: Grosset & Dunlap.

Turnbull, S. (2003). *Usborne beginners: Sun, moon, and stars.* New York: Scholastic.

Related Instructional Resources

Chartrand, M., Tirion, W., & Mechler, G. (1995). *National Audubon Society pocket guide to constellations of the northern skies.* New York: Knopf.

Driscoll, M. (2004). *A child's introduction to the night sky: The story of the stars, planets, and constellations—and how you can find them in the sky.* New York: Black Dog & Leventhal.

Heifetz, M., & Tirion, W. (2004). *A walk through the heavens: A guide to stars and constellations and their legends.* New York: Cambridge University Press.

Kohl, M., & Solga, K. (1996). *Discovering great artists: Hands-on art for children in the styles of the great masters.* Bellingham, WA: Bright Ring.

Levitt, I., & Marshall, R. (1992). *Star maps for beginners: 50th anniversary edition.* New York: Fireside.

Pasachoff, J., & Percy, J. (Eds.). (2005). *Teaching and learning astronomy: Effective strategies for educators worldwide.* New York: Cambridge University Press.

Renshaw, A., & Ruggi, G. (2005). *The art book for children.* New York: Phaidon Press.

Williams, D. (1995). *Teaching mathematics through children's art.* Portsmouth, NH: Heinemann.

Related Websites

Astronomy for Kids
> http://www.kidsastronomy.com/

Build the Big Dipper
> http://ology.amnh.org/astronomy/stufftodo/dipper.html?src=schol_space

The Constellations and Their Stars
> http://www.astro.wisc.edu/~dolan/constellations/constellations.html
> http://www.dustbunny.com/afk/index.html
> http://nasaexplores.nasa.gov/extras/constellations/constellation.html

Make a Star Finder
> http://spaceplace.nasa.gov/en/kids/st6starfinder/st6starfinder.shtml

Stargazing
> http://ology.amnh.org/astronomy/stufftodo/stargazing.html?src=schol_space

I Spy Shapes in Art (2004)

by Lucy Micklethwait

Greenwillow Books, ISBN #0060731931

Picasso (Getting to Know the World's Greatest Artists Series) (1988)

by Mike Venezia

Children's Press, ISBN #0516422715

Overview of Books: *I Spy Shapes in Art*, which contains fourteen masterpieces from such artists including O'Keeffe, Matisse, and Escher, entices readers in a game of seek-and-find for two- and three-dimensional shapes. In *Picasso*, readers enjoy a brief biography of the twentieth-century Spanish cubist painter and sculptor, Pablo Picasso, while exploring his many masterpieces and changing styles of painting.

Mathematical Concepts and Skills: two- and three-dimensional shapes, attributes of polygons and solids

Visual Arts Concepts and Skills: line, shape, color, texture, form, space, creating art (Picasso-like artwork), art history (work of Picasso and cubism)

Overview of Activities: Students gain practice with identifying and describing the similarities and differences between two- and three-dimensional shapes and explore how three-dimensional shapes are created from two-dimensional shapes. After discussing a style of artwork developed by Pablo Picasso called cubism, students create two pieces of artwork, one that exemplifies analytical cubism, the other synthetic cubism.

National Mathematics Standards (2000):

Students in grades 3 through 5 should "identify, compare, and analyze attributes of two- and three-dimensional shapes and develop vocabulary to describe the attributes." They should also "classify two- and three-dimensional shapes according to their properties and develop definitions of classes of shapes such as triangles and pyramids" (Geometry Standard) (p. 396).

National Visual Arts Standards (1994):

Students should understand and apply media, techniques, and processes (Content Standard 1) and "use different media, techniques, and processes to communicate ideas, experiences, and stories" (Achievement Standard c) (p. 34); use knowledge of structures and functions (Content Standard 2)

and "know the differences among visual characteristics and purposes of art in order to convey ideas" (Achievement Standard a) (p. 34); choose and evaluate a range of subject matter, symbols, and ideas (Content Standard 3) and "select and use subject matter, symbols, and ideas to communicate meaning" (Achievement Standard b) (p. 34); make connections between visual arts and other disciplines (Content Standard 6) and "identify connections between the visual arts and other disciplines in the curriculum" (Achievement Standard b) (p. 35).

Materials: examples of two- and three-dimensional shapes, pencils, crayons or colored pencils, lined posterboard, unruled posterboard, rulers, newspapers, magazines, wallpaper and fabric scraps, scissors, glue

Description of Activities:

1. Begin reading *I Spy Shapes in Art*. For each shape that appears on each page, students record in their journals the name of the shape, a description of the shape's attributes, and a real-life example of the shape.

2. At the end of the book, revisit each page and ask students to describe and discuss the attributes they recorded for each shape and the real-life example they identified for each shape.

3. Place several examples of two- and three-dimensional shapes on a table (e.g., a lid for a circle, a ball for a sphere, a die for a cube, a picture of a yield sign for a triangle, a picture of a pyramid for a square pyramid, etc.). Challenge students to divide the collection of shapes into two separate and distinct groups (or subsets). Ask students to describe and discuss the similarities and differences between the shapes to assist them in the sorting process. Ask questions such as: How is a circle different from a sphere? A square different from a cube?, etc.

4. Once the set of shapes has been sorted into two smaller subsets, encourage students to see how two-dimensional shapes form the faces of the three-dimensional solids (e.g., six square faces make a cube).

5. Introduce the style of painting known as cubism developed by Pablo Picasso. Show several images of Picasso's cubist works (e.g., *Three Musicians, Portrait of D. H. Kahnweiler, Girl with a Mandolin*), and let students guess why his style of artwork is named cubism. The first

period of cubism (1909–1912) was referred to as analytical cubism. Following this, Picasso and another artist named Georges Braque developed a period of artwork known as synthetic cubism in which they adhered objects and materials (such as sandpaper, newspaper, and wallpaper) on their paintings. Thus, the technique of collage was born.

6. Share the life and artwork of Pablo Picasso by reading *Picasso* to the class. Take time to allow students to view more of and discuss Picasso's artwork and the many phases of his artwork using the Picasso websites below.

7. Students create a piece of artwork in the spirit of Picasso's analytical cubism by lightly tracing a pencil sketch on lined posterboard. Students then use crayons or colored pencils to color in the individual squares on the grid. Students must use only one color per square, which will result in an angular, "cube-like" appearance. Students share their work and discuss what they like and dislike about the form of art known as analytical cubism.

8. Provide students with a piece of unruled posterboard, scissors, glue, newspapers, magazines, and fabric and wallpaper scraps. Students gain practice working in the spirit of Picasso's synthetic cubism style by creating a collage of some subject matter, or even a self-portrait. Once completed, students share and discuss their artwork with the class and how this style of cubism captures their subject matter.

9. Students compare and contrast the two forms of cubism. Which do they find more aesthetically pleasing? Which captures one's subject better? Facilitate a discussion.

Assessment:
- Did students correctly identify attributes of and sort two- and three-dimensional shapes?
- Did students identify real-life examples of each shape?
- Did students see how three-dimensional shapes are constructed from two-dimensional shapes?
- Did students create Picasso-like works in the spirit of analytic cubism and synthetic cubism?
- Did students describe, compare, and contrast Picasso's two styles of cubism?

Activity Extensions:

- Using nets, create a mobile of the five Platonic Solids (tetrahedron, cube, octahedron, dodecahedron, and icosahedron), which are a special family of three-dimensional shapes. Discuss what the Platonic Solids are, their history, and what characteristics make them such a special class of shapes.

- Using the resources and websites listed below, explore how the artists Henri Matisse, Wassily Kandinsky, and Joan Miro used shapes in their artwork.

- Enjoy poetry about shapes authored by Shel Silverstein (e.g., "Shapes" [1981]).

Cross-Curricular Connections:

Science

- Locate and identify two- and three-dimensional shapes that occur in nature.

Social Studies

- Investigate the use of two- and three-dimensional shapes in architecture.

Related Children's Literature

Appel, J., & Guglielmo, A. (2006). *Feed Matisse's fish.* New York: Sterling.

Bargallo, E. (2006). *My name is Picasso.* Hauppauge, NY: Barron's Educational Series.

Burns, M. (1994). *The greedy triangle.* New York: Scholastic.

Dodds, D. (1994). *The shape of things.* Cambridge, MA: Candlewick Press.

Froman, R. (1975). *Angles are as easy as pie.* New York: Crowell.

Greene, R. (1997). *When a line bends . . . A shape begins.* New York: Scholastic.

Hoban, T. (1986). *Shapes, shapes, shapes.* New York: Greenwillow Books.

Hoban, T. (2000). *Cubes, cones, cylinders, & spheres.* New York: Greenwillow Books.

Johnson, K., & O'Connor, J. (2002). *Henri Matisse: Drawing with scissors.* New York: Grosset & Dunlap.

Kelley, T. (2002). *Pablo Picasso: Breaking all the rules* (Smart about art series). New York: Grosset & Dunlap.

Ljungkvist, L. (2006). *Follow the line.* New York: Penguin.

Maltbie, P. (2005). *Picasso and Minou.* Watertown, MA: Charlesbridge.

Mason, A. (1994). *Picasso: An introduction to the artist's life and work* (Barron's famous artist series). London: Aladdin Books.

The Metropolitan Museum of Art. (2005). *Museum shapes.* New York: Little, Brown.

Micklethwait, L. (1993). *I spy two eyes: Numbers in art.* New York: Greenwillow Books.

Micklethwait, L. (2004). *I spy shapes in art.* New York: Greenwillow Books.

Neuschwander, C. (2005). *Mummy math: An adventure in geometry.* New York: Holt.

Ross, N. (1995). *Miro* (Famous artists series). Hauppauge, NY: Barron's Educational Series.

Scarborough, K. (2001). *Pablo Picasso* (Artists in their times series). New York: Scholastic.

Scieszka, J., & Smith, L. (2005). *Seen art?* New York: Viking Press.

Silverstein, S. (1981). *A light in the attic.* New York: HarperCollins.

Tang, G. (2003). *Math-terpieces: The art of problem solving.* New York: Scholastic.

Venezia, M. (1988). *Picasso* (Getting to know the world's greatest artists series). Chicago: Children's Press.

Venezia, M. (1997). *Henri Matisse* (Getting to know the world's greatest artists series). New York: Children's Press.

Related Instructional Resources

Aigner-Clark, J. (2004). *Baby Einstein: The ABCs of art.* New York: Hyperion Books for Children.

Aston, P. (2006). *Coloring book Kandinsky.* New York: Prestel.

Dickins, R. (2005). *The children's book of art: An introduction to famous paintings.* London: Usborne.

Evans, J., & Skelton, T. (2001). *How to teach art to children.* Monterey, CA: Evan-Moor.

Jeffett, W., Miro, J., & Coyle, L. (2002). *The shape of color: Joan Miro's painted sculptures.* London: Scala.

Kohl, M., & Solga, K. (1996). *Discovering great artists: Hands-on art for children in the styles of the great masters.* Bellingham, WA: Bright Ring.

Krull, K. (1995). *Lives of the artists: Masterpieces, messes.* San Diego: Harcourt Brace.

Micklethwait, L. (1993). *A child's book of art: Great pictures: First words.* New York: Dorling Kindersley.

Renshaw, A., & Ruggi, G. (2005). *The art book for children.* New York: Phaidon Press.

Williams, D. (1995). *Teaching mathematics through children's art.* Portsmouth, NH: Heinemann.

Related Websites

Eye on Art—Cubism
http://www.eyeconart.net/history/cubism.htm

Famous Artists
http://library.thinkquest.org/J001159/famart.htm

Henri Matisse
http://www.artcyclopedia.com/artists/matisse_henri.html
http://www.ibiblio.org/wm/paint/auth/matisse/

Interactive Cubism
http://www.mrpicassohead.com/create.html

Joan Miro
http://www.artcyclopedia.com/artists/miro_joan.html

Major Modern and Contemporary Visual Artists
http://www.the-artists.org/index.cfm

Pablo Picasso
http://www.artchive.com/artchive/P/picasso.html
http://picasso.csdl.tamu.edu/picasso/
http://www.picasso.fr/anglais/

Platonic Solids
http://www-groups.dcs.st-and.ac.uk/~history/Diagrams/PlatonicSolids.gif
http://www.mathsisfun.com/platonic_solids.html

Polyhedra Nets
http://mathforum.org/alejandre/workshops/net.html
http://www.korthalsaltes.com/

Virtual Manipulatives Library—The Platonic Solids
http://nlvm.usu.edu/en/nav/frames_asid_128_g_2_t_3.html?open=instructions

Wassily Kandinsky
http://www.artcyclopedia.com/artists/kandinsky_wassily.html
http://www.glyphs.com/art/kandinsky/comp8640.jpg
http://www.ibiblio.org/wm/paint/auth/kandinsky/

Grandfather Tang's Story: A Tale Told with Tangrams (1990)

by Ann Tompert

Dragonfly Books, ISBN #0517885581

Overview of Book: Under the shade of an old tree, a grandfather shares a tale with his granddaughter about two foxes that continually transform into different animals. Throughout the story, tangrams are arranged in various orientations to illustrate the characters in the story. The moral of the story focuses on rivalry and friendship.

Mathematical Concepts and Skills: shapes, transformations (slides, flips, and turns), spatial reasoning

Visual Arts Concepts and Skills: line, shape, color, creating art (watercolor and ink painting), art history (Chinese tangram stories)

Overview of Activities: Students work with tangrams and identify relationships between and among the various tangram shapes as well as create animal shapes illustrated in Tompert's book. Students then create a watercolor and ink picture and story in the tradition of Chinese tangram storytelling.

National Mathematics Standards (2000): Students in grades 3 through 5 should "investigate, describe, and reason about the results of subdividing, combining, and transforming shapes" and "predict and describe the results of sliding, flipping, and turning two-dimensional shapes" (Geometry Standard) (p. 396).

National Visual Arts Standards (1994): Students should understand and apply media, techniques, and processes (Content Standard 1) and "use different media, techniques, and processes to communicate ideas, experiences, and stories" (Achievement Standard c) (p. 34); use knowledge of structures and functions (Content Standard 2) and "use visual structures and functions of art to communicate ideas" (Achievement Standard c) (p. 34); understand the visual arts in relation to history and cultures (Content Standard 4) and "identify specific works of art as belonging to particular cultures, times, and places" (Achievement Standard b) (p. 34); make connections between the visual arts and other disciplines (Content Standard 6) and "identify connections between the visual arts and other disciplines in the curriculum" (Achievement Standard b) (p. 35).

Materials: tangrams, outlines of animal shapes from *Grandfather Tang's Story* (on overhead transparencies or on paper), watercolor paints and paintbrushes, large construction or watercolor paper, black pens or fine-line markers, pencils, scissors

Description of Activities:

1. Give each student a set of tangrams. Students count and name each of the seven tangram pieces and name attributes of each shape. Define and explore the relationships between and among the seven pieces; for example, students might notice that the two small (or large) triangles, when placed adjacent to one another, can form a triangle, square, or parallelogram. Thus, a triangle is one-half the area of a square (or parallelogram).

2. Challenge students to see if it is possible to create a square by using exactly two tangram pieces, and then three pieces, and then four pieces, etc., and then all seven pieces. This will give students practice with transformations by performing slides, flips, and turns as they orient the individual pieces to form a square.

3. Begin reading *Grandfather Tang's Story*. Allow students to create some or all of the animals as the story unfolds, by placing an outline of each animal on the overhead. Or, after the story ends, distribute paper copies of the outlines of some of the animals to students and let them create the animal shapes. Students share the strategies they used in solving each tangram puzzle (e.g., Which piece did they use first? Next? Did they see a pattern or clue in the outline of the animal shape that helped them place the tangram pieces?).

4. At the end of the book, revisit select illustrations with students, encouraging them to notice the illustrator's use of watercolor and ink. Students work in groups of five or six and develop a story they could tell using the tangram pieces, watercolors, and ink. Each student is responsible for one page (text and illustration) in the story.

5. Before making their watercolor and ink illustrations, students should first experiment with the tangram pieces to create new forms. The forms can be animals (not ones featured in the book), human or mythical figures, plants or trees, or other objects (e.g., automobiles, buildings, etc.). The only limitation is that all of the tangrams are used once to create a form. As the students are working with the tangram pieces, students should be thinking of stories that they could tell with the tangrams they are creating. Students record their stories on paper and create an accompanying watercolor and ink illustration.

6. When the paintings are dry, students attach their written stories to the bottoms of their watercolor pictures. Students share their stories in either small groups or as a whole class.

Assessment:

- Did students correctly name and identify the attributes of each tangram piece?

- Did students notice the relationships between and among the various tangram pieces?

- Did students create shapes and animals using tangrams?

- Did students explain the strategies they used in creating their shape or animal tangrams?

- Did students work collaboratively to develop and tell a story that supported their watercolor and ink illustration?

Activity Extensions:

- Bind each story into a class book entitled *Tangram Tales*, and maintain it in the classroom library.

- Give students more practice with performing transformations (slides, flips, and turns) by taking various tangram shapes, tracing them, and then performing each transformation several times and noticing the results.

- Enjoy poetry about reflections including "Reflection" (Silverstein, 1981), "Mirror" (Lewis, 1998), or "egamI rorriM ruoY mA I" (Prelutsky, 1996).

Cross-Curricular Connections:

Science
- Investigate the habitat and characteristics of animals in China.

Social Studies
- Begin a unit of study on China (e.g., geography, history, culture, etc.).

- Discuss the use of storytelling as a folk tradition.

Related Children's Literature

Campbell E. (2005). *Tangram magician*. Melbourne, FL: Blue Apple.

Flournoy, V. (1985). *The patchwork quilt*. New York: Dial Books for Young Readers.

Lewis, J. (1998). *Doodle dandies: Poems that take shape*. New York: Aladdin.

Maccarone, G. (1997). *Three pigs, one wolf, and seven magic shapes*. New York: Scholastic.

Marsh, V. (1996). *Story puzzles: Tales in the tangram tradition*. Fort Atkinson, WI: Highsmith Press.

Prelutsky, J. (1996). *A pizza the size of the sun*. New York: Scholastic.

Ringgold, F. (1996). *Tar beach*. New York: Dragonfly Books.

Silverstein, S. (1981). *A light in the attic*. New York: HarperCollins.

Tompert, A. (1990). *Grandfather Tang's story: A tale told with tangrams*. New York: Dragonfly Books.

Walton, P. (2000). *The warlord's puzzle*. Gretna, LA: Pelican.

Related Instructional Resources

Bando, I. (1995). *Geometry and fractions with tangrams*. Vernon Hills, IL: Learning Resources.

Elfers, J., & Schuyt, M. (2000). *Tangrams: 1600 ancient Chinese puzzles*. New York: Barnes & Noble.

Ford, B. E. (1990). *Tangrams: The magnificent seven piece puzzle*. Vallejo, CA: Tandora's Box Press.

Ford, B. E. (1990). *The master revealed: A journey with tangrams*. Vallejo, CA: Tandora's Box Press.

Goodnow, J. (1994). *Math discoveries with tangrams*. Grand Rapids, MI: Ideal School Supply Company.

Kohl, M., & Solga, K. (1996). *Discovering great artists: Hands-on art for children in the styles of the great masters*. Bellingham, WA: Bright Ring.

Martschinke, J. (1997). *Tangrammables: A tangram activity book*. Vernon Hills, IL: Learning Resources.

Mogard, S. (1992). *Windows to tangrams: Reproducible activities*. Covina, CA: American Teaching Aids.

Press, J. (2001). *Around the world art & activities: Visiting the 7 continents through craft fun*. Charlotte, VT: Williamson.

Read, R. (1965). *Tangrams: 330 puzzles*. Mineola, NY: Dover.

Renshaw, A., & Ruggi, G. (2005). *The art book for children*. New York: Phaidon Press.

Slocum, J., Botermans, J., Gebhardt, D., Ma, M., Ma, X., Raizer, H., Sonnevald, D., van Splunteren, C. (2003). *The tangram book*. New York: Sterling.

Related Websites

Interactive Tangrams

    http://enchantedmind.com/puzzles/tangram/tangram.html

    http://www.kidscom.com/games/tangram/tangram.html

    http://illuminations.nctm.org/LessonDetail.aspx?ID=L152

    http://www.channel4.com/learning/microsites/P/puzzlemaths/tangrams.shtml

    http://www.tygh.co.uk/tan/tan.htm

    http://teams.lacoe.edu/documentation/classrooms/amy/geometry/5-6/activities/tangrams/tangrams.html

Smart Books: *Grandfather Tang's Story*

    http://www.k-state.edu/smartbooks/Lesson019.html

Snowflake Bentley (1998)

by Jacqueline Briggs Martin

Houghton Mifflin, ISBN #0395861624

Overview of Book:	Readers will enjoy the biography of Wilson Bentley, also nicknamed "Snowflake Bentley," who, as a young boy, was fascinated with ice crystals and recorded their unique characteristics through micro-photography over the course of his lifetime.
Mathematical Concepts and Skills:	line symmetry, reflections, hobbies and careers that use math
Visual Arts Concepts and Skills:	line, shape, color, creating art (paper snowflakes), art history (*papel picado*, "perforated paper" from Mexico)
Overview of Activities:	Students discuss and explore line symmetry in snowflakes and in other objects. Students create snowflakes out of coffee filters, mark the lines of symmetry, and then make a mobile. Students continue experimenting with symmetry by creating a *papel picado*.
National Mathematics Standards (2000):	Students in grades 3 through 5 should "identify and describe line and rotational symmetry in two- and three-dimensional shapes" (Geometry Standard) (p. 396).
National Visual Arts Standards (1994):	Students should understand and apply media, techniques, and processes (Content Standard 1) and "use different media, techniques, and processes to communicate ideas, experiences, and stories" (Achievement Standard c) (p. 34); use knowledge of structures and functions (Content Standard 2) and "know the differences among visual characteristics and purposes of art in order to convey ideas" (Achievement Standard a) (p. 34); understand the visual arts in relation to history and cultures (Content Standard 4) and "identify specific works of art as belonging to particular cultures, times, and places" (Achievement Standard b); make connections between visual arts and other disciplines (Content Standard 6) and "identify connections between the visual arts and other disciplines in the curriculum" (Achievement Standard b) (p. 35).
Materials:	hand mirrors or miras, blank Venn diagram for each student, white coffee filters, construction paper, 8.5" × 11" scrap paper, scissors, tape, gluesticks, string or yarn, hangers, teacher-made examples of *papel picado* created prior to class, multicolored tissue paper

Description of Activities:

1. Visit the Original Wilson Bentley Images of Snowflakes website listed below and ask students to describe characteristics of snowflakes. Students should notice how snowflakes are symmetric, as well as six-sided and unique. Encourage students to define what symmetry means and give examples of real-life objects that are symmetric.

2. Using a small hand mirror or a mira, describe and demonstrate how, like snowflakes, certain letters of the alphabet have line symmetry. A letter (or object) has line symmetry if it can be cut in half by a line (called a line of reflection or a line of symmetry) such that there is a mirror image of the letter on both sides of the line. Lines of reflections might by horizontal (e.g., in the letters B and D), vertical (e.g., in the letters A and W), or diagonal (e.g., in the letter O). The letters M and B each have one line of reflection. Other letters, like H and O, have more than one line of symmetry. Some letters have no symmetry and are called asymmetric or nonsymmetric (e.g., the letters G, L).

3. Give each student a Venn diagram printed from the Blank Venn Diagram website listed below. Students label the circle on the left as "Letters with vertical line symmetry" and the circle on the right as "Letters with horizontal line symmetry." Students determine in which portion of the Venn diagram the letters of the alphabet belong. Students should notice that some letters fall into the overlapping section of the Venn diagram, since they have both vertical and horizontal line symmetry. Letters with no vertical or horizontal symmetry belong outside of the two circles.

4. Read *Snowflake Bentley*. At the end of the story, encourage students to think of and discuss other hobbies and careers that involve mathematics and science.

5. Using white coffee filters, students create a snowflake by folding a coffee filter in half three times and then cutting it. Students should predict what they think their snowflake will look like after cutting it but prior to opening it up. After cutting and unfolding the filter, students should carefully glue the filter onto a piece of blue construction paper. Students can remove the excess construction paper surrounding the snowflake by cutting around the filter, but leaving a thin border. Using a ruler and marker, students mark the lines of symmetry. Students compare and contrast their snowflakes and discuss similarities and differences in their shape and appearance.

6. Using string, tape, and hangers (or dowel rods), students collaborate to create a snowflake mobile using the snowflakes they just created.

7. Students engage in another paper cutting that allows them to further explore symmetry by creating a *papel picado* (Spanish for "perforated paper"), which is a Mexican form of paper cutting. Traditionally, many layers of tissue paper are stacked on top of one another, and a hammer and small chisels, *fierritos*, are used to cut designs into the paper. The individual pieces of paper are then separated and hung as banners or flags to celebrate important Mexican festivals and holidays. Typical holidays that incorporate *papel picado* are Easter, Christmas, *Día de los Muertos* ("Day of the Dead"), weddings, *quinceañeras* (fifteenth birthday of females), and christenings. Common symbols cut into *papel picado* banners are human and animal figures, flowers, foliage, skeletons, angels, crosses, and words or phrases associated with the event. The borders for the banners are often ornate, with scalloped edging or zigzag fringe.

8. Before creating their *papel picado* banners, students fold a piece of 8.5" × 11" scrap paper accordion style and experiment making cuts and designs in the paper. Encourage students to notice and articulate the symmetry (or nonsymmetry) in their resulting cuts after they unfold the paper (e.g., a triangle cut when unfolded appears as a diamond shape, semicircle cuts appear as circles, etc.).

9. Students think of a Mexican holiday or festival for which they would like to create a *papel picado* banner. Students select two colored pieces of tissue paper and place one on top of the other. Fold the stacked tissue paper accordion style and cut a design into the tissue paper, using symbols representative of that holiday.

10. Students decorate their classroom with their *papel picado* banners by folding and securing (using tape) the top one inch of their *papel picado* banners over a piece of yarn or string. (Or, students can make a single hole punch in the top corners of their banner and thread yarn through the holes.)

11. In small groups or as a whole class, students explain the holiday or event they chose to represent, the colors they chose to represent the holiday, the symbols they used to signify the event, and the symmetrical and nonsymmetrical designs and shapes in their banners.

Assessment:
- Did students provide a working definition of symmetry?
- Did students identify symmetric objects in real life or nature?
- Did students correctly locate lines of symmetry in letters and correctly place letters in the Venn diagram?

- Did students notice and mark the lines of symmetry in their snowflakes?

- Did the students choose appropriate colors and symbols for their papel picado banners representative of their chosen holiday or festival?

- Did students distinguish between symmetrical and nonsymmetrical figures, both in discussion and in the creation of their banners?

Activity Extensions:

- Students locate pictures of objects with reflective symmetry (facial photo, butterfly, corporate logo, etc.) and create a collage. Students draw the line of reflection(s) on each photo.

- Enjoy poetry about snow (e.g., "Snowman" [Silverstein, 2004]).

- Enjoy poetry about reflections, including "Reflection" (Silverstein, 1981), "Mirror" (Lewis, 1998), or "egamI rorriM ruoY mA I" (Prelutsky, 1996).

Cross-Curricular Connections:

Science

- Begin a unit on weather and seasons, starting with snow and winter.

- Learn how to use microscopes and discuss the impact that microscopes have had on science.

Social Studies

- Explore careers and hobbies that use mathematics and science.

- Explore symmetry in flags and the meaning of colors and symbols in state, national, and international flags.

- Investigate other paper-cutting traditions, such as *jianzhi* (China), *kirigami* or *monkiri* (Japan), *scherenschnitte* (Germany and Switzerland), *silhouette* (France), and *wycinanki* (Poland).

Related Children's Literature

Birmingham, D. (1988). *M is for mirror*. Norfolk, UK: Tarquin.

Birmingham, D. (1991). *Look twice!* Norfolk, UK: Tarquin.

Chorao, K. (2001). *Shadow night*. New York: Dutton Children's Books.

Gibbons, G. (1989). *Monarch butterfly*. New York: Scholastic.

Jonas, A. (1987). *Reflections*. New York: Greenwillow Books.

Lewis, J. (1998). *Doodle dandies: Poems that take shape*. New York: Aladdin.

Lomas Garza, C., Rohmer, H., Schecter, D., & Alarcon, F. X. (1999). *Magic windows/Ventanas mágicas*. San Francisco: Children's Book Press.

Martin, J. (1998). *Snowflake Bentley*. Boston: Houghton Mifflin.

Murphy, J. (2000). *Blizzard! The storm that changed America*. New York: Scholastic.

Murphy, S. (2000). *Let's fly a kite*. New York: Scholastic.

Prelutsky, J. (1996). *A pizza the size of the sun*. New York: Scholastic.

Silverstein, S. (1981). *A light in the attic*. New York: HarperCollins.

Silverstein, S. (2004). *Where the sidewalk ends*. New York: HarperCollins.

Sitomer, M., & Sitomer, H. (1970). *What is symmetry?* New York: Crowell.

Related Instructional Resources

Bentley, W. (2000). *Snowflakes in photographs*. Mineola, NY: Dover.

Bentley, W., & Humphreys, W. (1962). *Snow crystals*. Mineola, NY: Dover.

Higham, C. (2004). *Snowflakes for all seasons*. Layto, UT: Gibbs Smith.

Keilstrup, M. (1997). *Elegant designs for paper cutting*. Mineola, NY: Dover.

Kohl, M., & Solga, K. (1996). *Discovering great artists: Hands-on art for children in the styles of the great masters*. Bellingham, WA: Bright Ring.

Lomas Garza, C. (1999). *Making magic windows: Creating papel picado/cut-paper art*. San Francisco: Children's Book Press.

Press, J. (2001). *Around the world art & activities: Visiting the 7 continents through craft fun*. Charlotte, VT: Williamson.

Reed, B. L. (1987). *Easy-to-make decorative paper snowflakes*. Mineola, NY: Dover.

Renshaw, A., & Ruggi, G. (2005). *The art book for children*. New York: Phaidon Press.

Williams, D. (1995). *Teaching mathematics through children's art*. Portsmouth, NH: Heinemann.

Related Websites

Blank Venn Diagram
> http://home.att.net/%7Eteaching/graphorg/venn.pdf

Flags
> http://www.usflags.com/browsestore.asp?CategoryID=6
> http://www.flags.net/indexa.htm

Kaleidoscope
> http://www.pbs.org/parents/creativity/sensory/kaleidoscope.html

Original Wilson Bentley Images of Snowflakes
> http://www.snowflakebentley.com/snowflakes.htm

Papel Picado
> http://www.crizmac.com/free_resources/papelpicado.cfm
> http://www.dltk-kids.com/world/mexico/mpapel_picado.htm
> http://www.nps.gov/tuma/PapelPicado.html
> http://www.mexconnect.com/mex_/travel/dpalfrey/dppapelpicado.html
> http://www.art.unt.edu/ntieva/news/vol_7/issue3/96falp11.htm
> http://pbskids.org/zoom/activities/do/papelpicado.html

Snowflake Bentley
> http://www.vickiblackwell.com/lit/bentley.html
> http://snowflakebentley.com/museum.htm
> http://www.snowflakebentley.com/

Snowflakes and How to Make a Snowflake
> http://www.kinderart.com/seasons/dec7.shtml
> http://snowflakes.lookandfeel.com/
> http://www.papersnowflakes.com/
> http://pbskids.org/zoom/activities/sci/snowflake.html
> http://ms-t-inc.com/pdf-file/snowflak.pdf
> http://www.protozone.net/ASHOCK/AJSNOW.html

Symmetry
> http://www.emints.org/ethemes/resources/S00000202.shtml
> http://www.hbschool.com/activity/show_me/e673.htm
> http://www.pbs.org/teachersource/mathline/concepts/designandmath/activity2.shtm
> http://regentsprep.org/Regents/math/symmetry/Photos.htm
> http://www.bbc.co.uk/schools/gcsebitesize/maths/shape/symmetryrev2.shtml

Virtual Manipulatives Library—Reflections
> http://nlvm.usu.edu/en/nav/frames_asid_206_g_1_t_3.html?open=activities

Follow the Line (2006)

by Laura Ljungkvist

Penguin, ISBN #0670060496

Mondrian (Great Modern Masters Series) (1997)

by Jose Maria Faerna

Abrams, ISBN #0810946874

Overview of Books: Readers can do as the title of Ljungkvist's book suggests and "follow the line" that continually stretches from the front cover, through each and every page, and onto the back cover. While following the line extending from page to page, students can count, identify shapes, and make observations, prompted by the questions printed on each page. In Faerna's *Mondrian,* readers learn about the life and artwork of the twentieth-century Dutch abstract painter, Piet Mondrian, whose work primarily consists of intersecting vertical and horizontal lines and rectangles painted in the primary colors as well as black, white, and gray.

Mathematical Concepts and Skills: shapes, angles, line segments, lines, perpendicular lines

Visual Arts Concepts and Skills: line, shape, color, creating art (Mondrian-like artwork), art history (work of Mondrian and the abstract period)

Overview of Activities: Students explore acute, obtuse, and right angles and how lines and line segments create shapes and angles. Students then explore how the Dutch artist, Piet Mondrian, used a series of perpendicular lines and primary colors to create his abstract work. Students create a Mondrian-style painting.

National Mathematics Standards (2000):

Students in grades 3 through 5 should "build and draw geometric objects" and "create and describe mental images of objects, patterns, and paths." They should "identify, compare, and analyze attributes of two- and three-dimensional shapes and develop vocabulary to describe the attributes." They should also "recognize geometric ideas and relationships and apply them to other disciplines" (Geometry Standard) (p. 396). Students in grades 3 through 5 should "understand such attributes as length, area, weight, volume, and size of angle and select and apply an appropriate type of unit for measuring each attribute" (Measurement Standard) (p. 398).

National Visual Arts Standards (1994): Students should understand and apply media, techniques, and processes (Content Standard 1) and "describe how different materials, techniques, and processes cause different responses" (Achievement Standard b) (p. 33); use knowledge of structures and functions (Content Standard 2) and "know the differences among visual characteristics and purposes of art in order to convey ideas" (Achievement Standard a) (p. 34); choose and evaluate a range of subject matter, symbols, and ideas (Content Standard 3) and "select and use subject matter, symbols, and ideas to communicate meaning" (Achievement Standard b) (p. 34); make connections between visual arts and other disciplines (Content Standard 6) and "identify connections between the visual arts and other disciplines in the curriculum" (Achievement Standard b) (p. 35).

Materials: copies of select page(s) out of *Follow the Line*, highlighters, protractors, graph paper, rulers, 9" × 12" white construction paper, thick black markers; red, yellow, and blue crayons or colored pencils

Description of Activities:

1. Begin by asking students to provide their own working definitions and illustrations of a line, line segment, shape, and angle. Record select responses and sketches on the board.

2. Show students the front cover of *Follow the Line*. Trace with your finger how the line begins with the letter *F* in *Follow* and continues through the rest of the title, then off of the cover, and onto the inside cover, and then onto the successive pages, creating shapes and angles as it continues. By doing this, students will witness examples of a line, line segments, angles, and shapes. Revisit the responses and drawings on the board. Students work collaboratively to achieve a consensus on a definition for each of the terms.

3. Provide students with a copy of select page(s) out of *Follow the Line*. With students, highlight particular examples of acute, right, and obtuse angles, without using the angle names. Students compare, contrast, and describe the appearance of these three types of angles. (Older students might even measure the size of each angle using a protractor.) Challenge students to classify the angles into categories based on their size (or measure). Introduce the terms *acute, right,* and *obtuse angle*. Challenge students to locate examples of all three angles in the classroom.

4. Using the book *Mondrian,* as well as the related websites, show samples of the artwork of the twentieth-century Dutch abstract artist, Piet Mondrian, in particular his *Composition* paintings (pp. 40–61). Mondrian used several intersecting horizontal and vertical lines in his works. Students should notice that the intersecting (or perpendicular) lines in Mondrian's *Composition* paintings form right angles.

5. Ask students why they think Mondrian is labeled an abstract painter as compared to an impressionist, surrealist, etc., and what meaning or message is depicted in his artwork. Share biographical informational about Mondrian by reading excerpts from *Mondrian.*

6. Students create a Mondrian-style painting. Using a thick black marker and ruler, students trace horizontal and vertical lines on a 9" × 12" sheet of white construction paper, creating different-sized square and rectangular regions. Using red, yellow, and blue crayons or colored pencils, students color in the regions (also leaving some regions white, as did Mondrian).

7. Hang the students' artwork and let students compare and contrast their work. Which Mondrian-like pieces are most visually appealing? Why?

Assessment:
- Did students provide a working definition and sketch of a line, line segment, angle, and shape?

- Did students correctly identify and measure acute, right, and obtuse angles?

- Did students' artwork closely mimic Mondrian's style?

Activity Extensions:
- Explore the concept of area by using graph paper to create Mondrian-style paintings and then computing the area of each individual rectangle. Students should find that the sum of the areas of all of the (nonoverlapping) rectangles equals the area of the entire piece of paper.

- Students estimate what fractional part of their Mondrian-like artwork is red, blue, etc.

- Visit the Mondrimat website and let students experiment with color and shape by creating their own online artwork in the spirit of Mondrian.

Cross-Curricular Connections:

Science

- Since primary colors are important in Mondrian's work, investigate chromatics, the science of color through paint-mixing, prisms, and rainbows.

Social Studies

- Explore lines of latitude and longitude on a globe.

Related Children's Literature

Burns, M. (1994). *The greedy triangle*. New York: Scholastic.

Dodds, D. (1994). *The shape of things*. Cambridge, MA: Candlewick Press.

Faerna, J. (1997). *Mondrian* (Great modern masters series). New York: Adams.

Froman, R. (1975). *Angles are as easy as pie*. New York: Crowell.

Greene, R. (1997). *When a line bends . . . A shape begins*. New York: Scholastic.

Ljungkvist, L. (2006). *Follow the line*. New York: Penguin.

Scieszka, J., & Smith, L. (2005). *Seen art?* New York: Viking Press.

Tang, G. (2003). *Math-terpieces*. New York: Scholastic.

Related Instructional Resources

Dickins, R. (2005). *The children's book of art: An introduction to famous paintings*. London: Usborne.

Evans, J., & Skelton, T. (2001). *How to teach art to children*. Monterey, CA: Evan-Moor.

Kohl, M., & Solga, K. (1996). *Discovering great artists: Hands-on art for children in the styles of the great masters*. Bellingham, WA: Bright Ring.

Krull, K. (1995). *Lives of the artists: Masterpieces, messes*. San Diego: Harcourt Brace.

Micklethwait, L. (1993). *A child's book of art: Great pictures: First words*. New York: Dorling Kindersley.

Renshaw, A., & Ruggi, G. (2005). *The art book for children*. New York: Phaidon Press.

Scieszka, J., & Smith, L. (2005). *Seen art?* New York: Viking Press.

Williams, D. (1995). *Teaching mathematics through children's art*. Portsmouth, NH: Heinemann.

Related Websites

KidPort—Measuring Angles

http://www.kidport.com/Grade5/Math/MeasureGeo/MeasuringAngles.htm

Laura Ljungkvist

http://www.followtheline.com/home

http://www.followtheline.com/fun-1.html

Major Modern and Contemporary Visual Artists

http://www.the-artists.org/index.cfm

Mondrimat

http://www.stephen.com/mondrimat/

Piet Mondrian

http://www.artcyclopedia.com/artists/mondrian_piet.html

http://www.storyboardtoys.com/gallery/Piet-Mondrian.htm

http://www.fiu.edu/~andiaa/cg2/chronos.html

http://www.mossfoundation.org/page.php?id=81

http://www.ibiblio.org/wm/paint/auth/mondrian/

Piet Mondrian Coloring Page

http://www.enchantedlearning.com/paint/artists/mondrian/coloring/matrix.shtml

http://www.enchantedlearning.com/artists/mondrian/coloring/matrix.shtml

Study Art

http://www.sanford-artedventures.com/study/study.html

Teach Art—Forms in Architecture Lesson Plan

http://www.sanford-artedventures.com/teach/lp_forms_in_arch_contents.html

http://www.sanford-artedventures.com/teach/lp_lots_of_lines.html

Madlenka (2000)

by Peter Sis

Scholastic, ISBN #0374399697

Zoom (1995)

by Istvan Banyai

Puffin Books, ISBN #0140557741

Overview of Books:	In *Madlenka,* celebrate the wonders of different people, places, and cultures while enjoying aerial views and perspectives of city skyscrapers seen through Madlenka's eyes, as she announces to her richly varied New York City neighborhood block that her tooth is loose. Then, in the wordless book *Zoom,* embark on an ever-surprising visual journey into perspective, beginning with a close-up view of a rooster's comb and ending up in outer space.
Mathematical Concepts and Skills:	perspective, area, perimeter, angle measure, scale
Visual Arts Concepts and Skills:	line, shape, form, space, creating art (drawing using perspective)
Overview of Activities:	Students gain practice with perspective by developing a blueprint of their ideal room. They also construct three-dimensional models using linking cubes and draw the structures from different perspectives. Students learn the art technique of one-point perspective and design a cityscape. Students then explore the work of famous artists known for their work with perspective.
National Mathematics Standards (2000):	Students in grades 3 through 5 should "understand such attributes as length, area, weight, volume, and size of angle and select and apply the appropriate type of unit for measuring each attribute." Students should also "develop strategies for estimating the perimeters, areas, and volumes of irregular shapes" (Measurement Standard) (p. 398). Also, students in grades 3 through 5 should "build and draw geometric objects" as well as "identify and build a two-dimensional representation of a three-dimensional object" (Geometry Standard) (p. 396).

National Visual Arts Standards (1994):

Students should understand and apply media, techniques, and processes (Content Standard 1) and "describe how different materials, techniques, and processes cause different responses" (Achievement Standard b) (p. 33); use knowledge of structures and functions (Content Standard 2) and "know the differences among visual characteristics and purposes of art in order to convey ideas" (Achievement Standard a) (p. 34); reflect upon and assess the characteristics and merits of their work and the work of others (Content Standard 5) and "describe how people's experiences influence the development of specific artworks" (Achievement Standard b) (p. 34); make connections between visual arts and other disciplines (Content Standard 6) and "identify connections between the visual arts and other disciplines in the curriculum" (Achievement Standard b) (p. 35).

Materials:

lined posterboard, 1" graph paper, rulers, linking cubes, paper, colored pencils (or crayons or oil paints)

Description of Activities:

1. Read *Madlenka*. Allow students to enjoy the illustrations that capture young Madlenka's perspective of her world. Discuss how many of the illustrations, in particular, the ones appearing early on in the book, are a bird's-eye view of Madlenka's world, and thus give the reader a perspective of her world as a child surrounded by formidable skyscrapers and tall city buildings.

2. Students develop a blueprint of their ideal room. Consider obtaining actual blueprints for students to view. Encourage students to think and work as architects to develop criteria for designing their rooms. Using lined posterboard to develop scaled drawings, students note where walls, windows, and doors are located, as well as their height and width. Students should also discuss placement of furniture, outlets, switches, etc., and how much paint and carpeting they might need. Let students determine the shape of their ideal room as well as the room's minimum or maximum square footage, which will require them to discuss, understand, and apply the concepts of area and perimeter.

3. Students share and discuss their blueprints with the class.

4. Introduce the term *perspective* as it is used in art. Perspective is a technique used by artists to create the illusion of depth by means of converging lines. That is, artists purposefully draw and arrange lines on a page (two-dimensions) to make an image appear three-dimensional. Revisit some of the illustrations in *Madlenka* (e.g., front cover, inside front cover, opening page of text, etc.), in which structures are viewed from different angles and vantage points.

5. Distribute rulers, pencils, and lined posterboard to students. Guide them step-by-step in learning the technique of one-point perspective by creating a cityscape:

   a. Hold the lined posterboard landscape style (lengthwise). Draw a horizontal line about 1″ up from the bottom of the posterboard.

   b. Draw four or five rectangles of different heights and widths whose bases are located along the horizontal line. The rectangles serve as the fronts or faces of the buildings.

   c. Place a point somewhere along the top of the posterboard. This point will be known as the vanishing point.

   d. Using their rulers, students draw lines from the top vertices (corners) of each of the rectangles (buildings) to the vanishing point. These lines are called convergence lines. If one of these lines passes through a building, do not draw that line.

   e. Create the side and back of the city buildings by drawing lines parallel to the front lines of the buildings.

   f. Erase the extra lines that connect to the vanishing point.

   g. Students use colored pencils (or crayons) to finish detailing their city buildings, creating windows, doors, etc.

   Once completed, students share their cityscapes with the class.

6. View the work of various artists who used the technique of perspective, such as Leonardo da Vinci (*Adoration of the Magi*), Masaccio (*The Holy Trinity*), Donatello (*Feast of Herod*), and Albrecht Durer (*St. Jerome dans sa Cellule*). Can students identify the horizon in the artwork? The location of the vanishing point? The lines of convergence?

Assessment:
- Did students create an appropriately scaled room?
- Did students correctly measure and compute area and perimeter?
- Did students create a cityscape using one-point perspective?
- Did students identify the horizon, the vanishing point, and lines of convergence in other artworks?

Activity Extensions:
- Explore perspective and the magnitude of numbers by visiting the Powers of Ten website, which allows users to visually experience changing perspectives and our base-ten system. The user begins in a garden and, using the on-screen ruler, leaps outwards by positive powers of ten and eventually travels to the universe and beyond with the click of the mouse.

- Explore the Science, Optics, and You website and travel through the universe toward Earth by leaping in powers of ten. Encourage students to watch the powers of ten decrease and the resulting perspectives.

- Read Banyai's *Re-Zoom* (1998) and enjoy more viewing perspectives.

- Enjoy poetry about perspective authored by Shel Silverstein (e.g., "New World" [1996] and "Point of View" [2004]).

Cross-Curricular Connections:

Science

- Research the history of the telescope and microscope and how these inventions, which dramatically changed viewing perspectives, aided scientists in the study of humans and space.

Social Studies

- Research the advantages, disadvantages, and purposes of various map projections (Mercatur, Peters, Robinson, Winkel Tripel, etc.).

Related Children's Literature

Banyai, I. (1995). *Zoom*. New York: Puffin Books.

Banyai, I. (1998). *Re-Zoom*. New York: Penguin Young Readers Group.

Banyai, I. (2005). *Other side*. San Francisco: Chronicle Books.

Dickins, R. (2005). *The children's book of art: An introduction to famous paintings*. London: Usborne.

Ernst, L. (2004). *The turn-around, upside-down, alphabet book*. New York: Simon & Schuster Books for Young Readers.

Liao, J. (2006). *The sound of colors: A journey of the imagination*. New York: Little, Brown.

Mason, A. (1994). *Leonardo da Vinci: An introduction to the artist's life and work* (Barron's famous artist series). London: Aladdin Books.

Reynolds, P. (2003). *The dot*. Cambridge, MA: Candlewick Press.

Reynolds, P. (2004). *Ish*. Cambridge, MA: Candlewick Press.

Scieszka, J., & Smith, L. (2005). *Seen art?* New York: Viking Press.

Silverstein, S. (1996). *Falling up*. New York: HarperCollins.

Silverstein, S. (2004). *Where the sidewalk ends*. New York: HarperCollins.

Sis, P. (2000). *Madlenka*. New York: Scholastic.

Venezia, M. (1989). *Da Vinci* (Getting to know the world's greatest artists series). Chicago: Children's Press.

Wolfe, G. (2002). *Look! Zoom in on art*. New York: Oxford University Press.

Related Instructional Resources

Aigner-Clark, J. (2004). *Baby Einstein: The ABCs of art*. New York: Hyperion Books for Children.

Dickins, R. (2005). *The children's book of art: An introduction to famous paintings*. London: Usborne.

Evans, J., & Skelton, T. (2001). *How to teach art to children*. Monterey, CA: Evan-Moor.

Kohl, M., & Gainer, C. (1996). *MathArts: Exploring math through art for 3 to 6 year olds*. Beltsville, MD: Gryphon House.

Kohl, M., & Solga, K. (1996). *Discovering great artists: Hands-on art for children in the styles of the great masters*. Bellingham, WA: Bright Ring.

Krull, K. (1995). *Lives of the artists: Masterpieces, messes*. San Diego: Harcourt Brace.

Micklethwait, L. (1993). *A child's book of art: Great pictures: First words*. New York: Dorling Kindersley.

Press, J. (2001). *Around the world art & activities: Visiting the 7 continents through craft fun*. Charlotte, VT: Williamson.

Renshaw, A., & Ruggi, G. (2005). *The art book for children*. New York: Phaidon Press.

Smith, R. (1999). *DK art school: An introduction to perspective*. New York: DK Adult.

Williams, D. (1995). *Teaching mathematics through children's art*. Portsmouth, NH: Heinemann.

Related Websites

Major Modern and Contemporary Visual Artists
    http://www.the-artists.org/index.cfm

Map Projections
    http://www.btinternet.com/~se16/js/mapproj.htm
    http://math.rice.edu/~lanius/pres/map/mappro.html

Perspective
    http://mathforum.org/sum95/math_and/perspective/perspect.html
    http://www.mos.org/sln/Leonardo/ExploringLinearPerspective.html
    http://www.sanford-artedventures.com/create/tech_1pt_perspective.html
    http://studiochalkboard.evansville.edu/lp-intro.html
    http://www.dartmouth.edu/~matc/math5.geometry/unit11/unit11.html

Powers of Ten
    http://microcosm.web.cern.ch/microcosm/P10/english/welcome.html

Science, Optics, and You
    http://micro.magnet.fsu.edu/primer/java/scienceopticsu/powersof10/index.html

Teach Art—City Streets in One-Point Perspective Lesson Plan
    http://www.sanford-artedventures.com/teach/lp_1pointperspect_contents.html

Teach Art—Forms in Architecture Lesson Plan
    http://www.sanford-artedventures.com/teach/lp_forms_in_arch_contents.html

Probably Pistachio (2001)

by Stuart Murphy

HarperCollins, ISBN #0064467341

Miro: Earth and Sky (Art for Children Series) (1993)

by Claire-Helene Blanquet

Chelsea House, ISBN #0791028135

Joan Miro (Famous Artists Series) (1994)

by Nicholas Ross

Barron's Educational Series, ISBN #0812094271

Overview of Books: Readers will learn various words associated with probability (e.g., *for sure, always, never, sometimes, probably,* etc.) while following a young boy named Jack through his busy day in *Probably Pistachio*. In *Miro: Earth and Sky*, enjoy biographical facts and direct quotes from Miro interwoven into a story about a young girl whose teacher points out that her sleeping bag is decorated and patterned after a Miro painting. Thus, the class embarks on a journey into the life and works of Joan Miro. Ross's *Joan Miro* details a biography and includes images of the works of the Spanish surrealist painter and sculptor, Joan Miro, who is considered to be one of the most versatile masters of twentieth-century art.

Mathematical Concepts and Skills: likelihood, probability, randomness, sampling with replacement, prediction, law of large numbers

Visual Arts Concepts and Skills: line, shape, color, form, space, creating art (surrealist art), art history (work of Joan Miro)

Overview of Activities: Students predict the outcome of drawing colored marbles from a bag using sampling with replacement. Students also use, define, and discuss the meaning of various probability terms including *likely, unlikely, probable,* etc. Students then explore and learn about the life and artwork of Joan Miro, the Spanish surrealist who used a technique of random, imaginative drawing to create his artwork. Students create a Miro-like work of art, using his random drawing technique.

National Mathematics Standards (2000):	Students in grades 3 through 5 should "describe events as likely or unlikely and discuss the degree of likelihood using such words as *certain, equally likely,* and *impossible.*" They should "predict the probability of outcomes of simple experiments and test the predictions" and "understand that the measure of the likelihood of an event can be represented by a number from 0 to 1" (Data Analysis and Probability Standard) (p. 400).

National Visual Arts Standards (1994):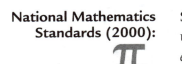

Students should understand and apply media, techniques, and processes (Content Standard 1) and "use different media, techniques, and processes to communicate ideas, experiences, and stories" (Achievement Standard c) (p. 34); choose and evaluate a range of subject matter, symbols, and ideas (Content Standard 3) and "select and use subject matter, symbols, and ideas to communicate meaning" (Achievement Standard b) (p. 34); make connections between visual arts and other disciplines (Content Standard 6) and "identify connections between the visual arts and other disciplines in the curriculum" (Achievement Standard b) (p. 35).

Materials:

images of Miro's *Constellations* works (e.g., *Harlequin's Carnival, Dutch Interior I, The Smile of Flaming Wings, Woman Encircled by the Flight of a Bird, For Emili Fernandez Miro, Woman and Bird in the Night, Wall of the Moon, Wall of the Sun,* etc.), colored marbles (or blocks), bag, Internet, thick black markers, oil paints (or another coloring medium), large white paper

Description of Activities:

1. Prior to class, fill a bag with seven blue marbles (or blocks) and three yellow marbles. (Use any two colors in this experiment.) Announce to the class that there are ten marbles in the bag, some of which are blue and some of which are yellow. Ask a few students to make a prediction as to how many marbles are blue and how many are yellow.

2. Introduce the terminology *random* and *sampling with replacement* by walking around the room, asking a student to draw one marble, at random, out of the bag, note its color, and then place it back in the bag (thus, sampling with replacement). Students should keep a running tally of what color is drawn each time. Carry out this experiment ten times. Students total their tallies, examine the data, and make a prediction as to how many of each colored marble are in the bag. Disclose how many of each colored marble is in the bag by dumping the bag onto a table. How accurate were their predictions? Are students surprised by the results?

3. Students discuss whether this experiment was fair; that is, did both colors have a fair chance of being drawn? Why or why not? How could we make this experiment fair? Students should offer that if there

are five blue and five yellow marbles in the bag, then both colors have a fair chance of being drawn at random. Encourage students to use percentages when describing the outcome possibilities (e.g., The blue marbles have a 50 percent chance of being drawn, and the yellow marbles also have a 50 percent chance of being drawn.). What was the probability of drawing a blue marble and a yellow marble in the initial experiment? (blue: 70 percent; yellow: 30 percent). Encourage students to see that the sum of the individual probabilities for any one event always equals 100 percent.

4. Ask students to describe events that would be very likely (e.g., If there are nine blue marbles and one yellow marble, it is *very likely* that I will draw a blue marble.), likely (e.g., If there are seven blue marbles and three yellow marbles, it is *likely* I will draw a blue marble), possible, probable, unlikely, impossible, etc.

5. Read *Probably Pistachio* in which students discover and hear other probability terms used in context (e.g., *probably, probably not, never, always,* etc.).

6. Place students in small groups and give each a bag with five blue marbles and five yellow marbles. Students sample with replacement ten times, recording what color marble was drawn at each trial (whether blue or yellow). Within their groups, did each color get drawn 50 percent of the time? If not, why might this have happened? Generate a discussion.

7. Sum all of the individual groups' data, creating one sum for the number of times a blue marble was drawn and one sum for the number of times a yellow marble was drawn. Did the percentage of times a blue (or yellow) marble was drawn come closer to equaling 50 percent? Why might a larger sample of data give us better results? Generate a discussion and introduce the Law of Large Numbers (also called Bernoulli's Law), which states that if an experiment is carried out a large number of times, the empirical (or experimental) probability of the event occurring tends toward the theoretical probability of the event occurring.

8. Share with students select passages about the life and artwork of Joan Miro from Blanquet's and Ross's books. Miro was a twentieth-century Spanish surrealist painter and sculptor. Many of his works (e.g., *Harlequin's Carnival, Dutch Interior I, The Smile of Flaming Wings,* etc.) have a whimsical and humorous quality, containing images of playfully distorted animal forms, twisted shapes, and odd geometric

constructions. Miro has been described as drawing by chance, a technique of random, imaginative draw, evident in his *Constellations* series. The talented artist also sculpted, worked in ceramics, and produced many mosaics and murals. Two of his most notable sculptures are two large ceramic murals entitled *Wall of the Moon* and *Wall of the Sun*, created for the UNESCO building in Paris. Share with students a variety of Miro's works. Facilitate a discussion about what features students find appealing (or unappealing) about his works.

9. Implement the activity described on page 19 in Ross's book where students create a Miro work by using his technique called drawing by chance. Provide students with thick black markers, oil paints (or another coloring medium), and large white paper. Using their markers, students close their eyes and make bold, random marks on their papers. Students open their eyes and, using their imaginations, look for and complete figures and shapes. Fill in the shapes using colored oil paints. Students then think of creative titles for their paintings, as did Miro.

10. Students share their artwork with the class. Students discuss whose artwork is most visually appealing and why and whose artwork was titled most creatively.

Assessment:
- Did students make reasonable predictions about the number of each of the colored marbles in the bag?

- Did students correctly tally and interpret the marble data?

- Did students use probability terms correctly when describing the outcomes of events?

- Did students create a piece of artwork in the spirit of Miro?

Activity Extensions:
- Visit the Marble Mania! website and explore an interactive tool that allows the user to explore randomness and probability by drawing larger numbers of marbles from a bag.

- Visit the Random Drawing Tool website in which an applet simulates someone randomly drawing numbered tickets from a box. The tool then displays the relative frequency of each ticket.

- Visit the Virtual Manipulatives—Spinners website and explore probability using a spinner with colored regions.

Cross-Curricular Connections:

Science

- Miro's most famous series of paintings was his *Constellations* series. Begin a unit on the universe and explore stars and constellations.

Social Studies

- Explore the geography and other demographics of the Catalonia region of Spain, where Joan Miro was born and lived most of his life.

Related Children's Literature

Axelrod, A. (2001). *Pigs at odds: Fun with math and games.* New York: Aladdin.

Blanquet, C. (1993). *Miro: Earth and sky* (Art for children series). New York: Chelsea House.

Linn, C. (1972). *Probability.* New York: Crowell.

Murphy, S. (2001). *Probably pistachio.* New York: HarperCollins.

Ross, N. (1994). *Joan Miro* (Famous artists series). Hauppauge, NY: Barron's Educational Series.

Srivastava, J. (1975). *Averages.* New York: Crowell.

Related Instructional Resources

Aigner-Clark, J. (2004). *Baby Einstein: The ABCs of art.* New York: Hyperion Books for Children.

Cushman, J. (1991). *Do you wanna bet? Your chance to find out about probability.* New York: Clarion Books.

Dickins, R. (2005). *The children's book of art: An introduction to famous paintings.* London: Usborne.

Evans, J., & Skelton, T. (2001). *How to teach art to children.* Monterey, CA: Evan-Moor.

Kohl, M., & Solga, K. (1996). *Discovering great artists: Hands-on art for children in the styles of the great masters.* Bellingham, WA: Bright Ring.

Krull, K. (1995). *Lives of the artists: Masterpieces, messes.* San Diego: Harcourt Brace.

Malet, R. (2003). *Joan Miro.* New York: Rizzoli.

Mink, J. (2000). *Miro.* Hohenzollernring, Germany: Taschen.

Renshaw, A., & Ruggi, G. (2005*). The art book for children.* New York: Phaidon Press.

Scieszka, J., & Smith, L. (2005). *Seen art?* New York: Viking Press.

Related Websites

Joan Miro

> http://www.artnet.com/artist/675008/joan-miro.html
> http://www.artcyclopedia.com/artists/miro_joan.html
> http://www.artelino.com/articles/joan_miro.asp
> http://www.enchantedlearning.com/artists/miro/
> http://www.halter.net/gallery/miro.html

Marble Mania!

> http://www.sciencenetlinks.com/interactives/marble/marblemania.html

Random Drawing Tool

> http://illuminations.nctm.org/ActivityDetail.aspx?id=67

Virtual Manipulatives—Spinners

> http://nlvm.usu.edu/en/nav/frames_asid_186_g_1_t_1.html?open=activities

Assessment Resources References

Bright, G., & Joyner, J. (1998). *Classroom assessment in mathematics*. Lanham, MD: University Press of America.

British Columbia Ministry of Education. (n.d.). *Handbook of assessment tools for process evaluation in mathematics*. Victoria, BC: The Ministry.

Bryant, D., & Driscoll, M. (1998). *Exploring classroom assessment in mathematics: A guide for professional development*. Reston, VA: NCTM.

Bush, W. (2001). *Mathematics assessment: Cases and discussion questions for grades K–5*. Reston, VA: NCTM.

Charles, R., Lester, F., & O'Daffer, P. (1987). *How to evaluate progress in problem solving*. Reston, VA: NCTM.

Clarke, D. (1997). *Constructive assessment in mathematics: Practical steps for classroom teachers*. Emeryville, CA: Key Curriculum Press.

Gawronski, J. (Ed.). (2005). *Mathematics assessment sampler: Grades 3–5*. Reston, VA: NCTM.

Kulm, G. (1994). *Mathematics assessment: What works in the classroom*. San Francisco: Jossey-Bass.

Madfes, T. (1999). *Learning from assessment: Tools for examining assessment through standards*. Reston, VA: NCTM.

Mathematical Sciences Education Board. (1994). *Measuring up: Prototypes for mathematics assessment*. Washington, DC: National Academy Press.

Montgomery, K. (2001). *Authentic assessment: A guide for elementary teachers*. New York: Addison Wesley Longman.

NCTM. (1995). *Assessment standards for school mathematics*. Reston, VA: NCTM.

Ott, J. (1994). *Alternate assessment in the mathematics classroom*. Columbus, OH: Glencoe/McGraw-Hill.

Pandey, T. (1991). *A sampler of mathematics assessment*. Sacramento: California Department of Education.

Schoenfeld, A. (1999). *Elementary grades assessment*. White Plains, NY: Dale Seymour.

Schoenfeld, A. (1999). *Middle grades assessment*. White Plains, NY: Dale Seymour.

Stenmark, J. (1989). *Assessment alternatives in mathematics: An overview of assessment techniques that promote learning*. Berkeley: University of California.

Stenmark, J. (Ed.) (1991). *Mathematics assessment: Myths, models, good questions, and practical suggestions*. Reston, VA: NCTM.

Stenmark, J., & Bush, W. (2001). *Mathematics assessment: A practical handbook for grades 3–5*. Reston, VA: NCTM.

Walch, J. (2003). *Assessment: Strategies for math*. Portland, ME: Walch.

Webb, N., & Coxford, A. (1993). *Assessment in the mathematics classroom*. Reston, VA: NCTM.

Children's Literature References

Adil, J. (2006). *Supply and demand.* Mankato, MN: Capstone Press.

Adler, D. (1991). *A picture book of Christopher Columbus.* New York: Scholastic.

Aird, H. (1986). *Henry Ford: Young man with ideas* (Childhood of famous Americans series). New York: Aladdin.

Aliki. (1963). *The story of Johnny Appleseed.* New York: Aladdin.

Aliki. (1995). *Mummies made in Egypt.* New York: HarperTrophy.

Anno, M. (1987). *Anno's sundial.* New York: Philomel Books.

Anno, M. (1999). *All in a day.* New York: Putnam.

Anno, M. (1999). *Anno's mysterious multiplying jar.* New York: Putnam.

Appel, J., & Guglielmo, A. (2006). *Feed Matisse's fish.* New York: Sterling.

Arnold, T. (2000). *Parts.* New York: Puffin Books.

Arnold, T. (2005). *More parts.* New York: Puffin Books.

Arnold, T. (2007). *Even more parts.* New York: Puffin Books.

Asch, F. (1994). *The earth and I.* New York: Scholastic.

Axelrod, A. (1997). *Pigs will be pigs: Fun with math and money.* New York: Aladdin Paperbacks.

Axelrod, A. (2001). *Pigs at odds: Fun with math and games.* New York: Aladdin.

Bang, M. (2005). *My light.* New York: Scholastic.

Banyai, I. (1995). *Zoom.* New York: Puffin Books.

Banyai, I. (1998). *Re-Zoom.* New York: Penguin Young Readers Group.

Banyai, I. (2005). *Other side.* San Francisco: Chronicle Books.

Barasch, L. (2005). *Ask Albert Einstein.* New York: Foster.

Bargallo, E. (2006). *My name is Picasso.* Hauppauge, NY: Barron's Educational Series.

Barner, B. (2002). *Stars! Stars! Stars!* San Francisco: Chronicle Books.

Barretta, G. (2006). *Now and Ben: The modern inventions of Ben Franklin.* New York: Holt.

Bateman, T. (1989). *Red, white, blue, and Uncle Who? The stories behind some of America's patriotic symbols.* New York: Holiday House.

Bell, N. (1982). *The book of where: Or how to be naturally geographic* (A brown paper schoolbook series). Boston: Little, Brown.

Bergen, D. (2004). *Life-size dinosaurs.* New York: Sterling.

Berger, M., & Berger, G. (1999). *Do stars have points? Questions and answers about stars and planets.* New York: Scholastic.

Birch, D. (1988). *The king's chessboard.* New York: Puffin Books.

Birmingham, D. (1991). *Look twice!* Norfolk, UK: Tarquin.

Birmingham, D. (1988). *M is for mirror.* Norfolk, UK: Tarquin.

Blanquet, C. (1993). *Miro: Earth and sky* (Art for children series). New York: Chelsea House.

Blood, C., & Link, M. (1990). *The goat in the rug.* New York: Aladdin.

Borden, L., & Kroeger, M. (2004). *Fly high! The story of Bessie Coleman.* New York: Aladdin Books.

Bouchard, D. (1999). *The dragon new year: A Chinese legend.* Atlanta: Peachtree.

Branley, F. (1981). *The sky is full of stars.* New York: HarperCollins.

Branley, F. (1987). *The moon seems to change.* New York: HarperCollins.

Branley, F. (1998). *The planets in our solar system.* New York: HarperCollins.

Branley, F. (1999). *Flash, crash, rumble, and roll.* New York: HarperCollins.

Branley, F. (2002). *The sun: Our nearest star.* New York: HarperCollins.

Brocklehurst, R. (2004). *Usborne children's picture atlas.* New York: Scholastic.

Brown, D. (2004). *Odd boy out: Young Albert Einstein.* Boston: Houghton Mifflin.

Brown, M. (1998). *I like stars.* New York: Golden Books.

Bruchac, H. (2001). *Heart of a chief.* New York: Puffin Books.

Bruchac, H. (2002). *Navajo long walk: Tragic story of a proud people's forced march from homeland.* Washington, DC: National Geographic Books.

Brumbeau, J. (2001). *The quiltmaker's gift.* New York: Scholastic.

Brumbeau, J. (2004). *The quiltmaker's journey.* New York: Orchard Books.

Buller, J., & Schade, S. (2005). *The first ladies* (Smart about series). New York: Grosset & Dunlap.

Buller, J., Schade, S., Cocca-Leffler, M., Holub, J., Kelley, T., & Regan, D. (2003). *Smart about the fifty states: A class report.* New York: Grosset & Dunlap.

Bunting, E. (1990). *How many days to America: A Thanksgiving story.* Boston: Houghton Mifflin.

Burns, M. (1994). *The greedy triangle.* New York: Scholastic.

Campbell, E. (2005). *Tangram magician.* Melbourne, FL: Blue Apple.

Chainan, M. (1998). *The chief's blanket.* Tiburon, CA: Kramer.

Charman, A. (2003). *I wonder why trees have leaves and other questions about plants.* Boston: Houghton Mifflin.

Cheney, L. (2002). *America: A patriotic primer.* New York: Simon & Schuster Books for Young Readers.

Cheney, L. (2003). *A is for Abigail: An almanac of amazing American women.* New York: Simon & Schuster Books for Young Readers.

Cheney, L. (2006). *Our fifty states: A family adventure across America.* New York: Simon & Schuster Books for Young Readers.

Chesanow, N. (1995). *Where do I live?* Hauppauge, NY: Barron's Educational Series.

Chinn, K. (1995). *Sam and the lucky money.* New York: Scholastic.

Chorao, K. (2001). *Shadow night.* New York: Dutton Children's Books.

Christelow, E. (2004). *Vote!* New York: Clarion Books.

Claybourne, A. (2006). *The shocking story of electricity.* Tulsa, OK: EDC.

Clements, A. (2006). *A million dots.* New York: Simon & Schuster Books for Young Readers.

Cole, J. (2000). *The magic school bus gets baked in a cake: A book about kitchen chemistry.* New York: Scholastic.

Crane, C. (2006). *D is for dragon: A China alphabet.* Chelsea, MI: Sleeping Bear Press.

Cronin, D. (2003). *Diary of a worm.* New York: Scholastic.

Cronin, D. (2004). *Duck for president.* New York: Simon & Schuster Books for Young Readers.

Cushman, J. (1991). *Do you wanna bet? Your chance to find out about probability.* New York: Clarion Books.

Cutts, D. (1998). *Thunder and lightning* (I can read about series). New York: Scholastic.

Davis, G. (2004). *Wackiest White House pets.* New York: Scholastic.

Davis, K. (2002). *Don't know much about the presidents.* New York: HarperCollins.

DeMauro, L. (2002). *Thomas Edison: A brilliant inventor* (Time for kids series). New York: HarperCollins.

Demi. (1997). *One grain of rice.* New York: Scholastic.

Demi. (2000). *Kites: Magic wishes that fly up to the sky.* New York: Dragonfly Books.

Demi. (2003). *Happy, happy Chinese New Year!* New York: Crown Books for Young Readers.

DeWitt, L. (1991). *What will the weather be?* New York: HarperCollins.

Dickins, R. (2005). *The children's book of art: An introduction to famous paintings.* London: Usborne.

Dodds, D. (1994). *The shape of things.* Cambridge, MA: Candlewick Press.

Dodds, D. (1999). *The great divide: A mathematical marathon.* Cambridge, MA: Candlewick Press.

Donovan, S. (2003). *Running for office: A look at political campaigns* (How government works series). Minneapolis: Lerner.

Dorros, A. (1990). *Feel the wind.* New York: HarperCollins.

Driscoll, M. (2004). *A child's introduction to the night sky.* New York: Black Dog & Leventhal.

Edmonds, W. (1994). *Big book of time.* New York: Readers Digest Kids.

Emberley, E. (1984). *Ed Emberley's picture pie: A circle drawing book.* Boston: Little, Brown.

Emberley, E. (2006). *Ed Emberley's picture pie 2: A drawing book and stencil.* Boston: Little, Brown.

Erickson, P. (1997). *Daily life in a covered wagon.* New York: Penguin Young Readers.

Ernst, L. (2004). *The turn-around, upside-down, alphabet book.* New York: Simon & Schuster Books for Young Readers.

Faerna, J. (1997). *Mondrian.* New York: Abrams.

Fifth-Grade Students of Holly Springs Elementary School, Pickens, S.C. (2000). *Perfect inventions = perfect world.* New York: Scholastic.

Fisher, L. (1997). *The gods and goddesses of ancient Egypt.* New York: Holiday House.

Flood, N. (2006). *The Navajo year, walk through many seasons.* Flagstaff, AZ: Salina Bookshelf.

Florian, D. (2001). *Lizards, frogs, and polliwogs.* Orlando, FL: Voyager Books.

Flournoy, V. (1985). *The patchwork quilt.* New York: Dial Books for Young Readers.

Folwer, A. (1992). *So that's how the moon changes shape!* New York: Scholastic.

Fradin, D. (2002). *Who was Ben Franklin?* New York: Penguin Young Readers.

Franco, B. (2003). *Super garage sale.* Vernon Hills, IL: ETA Cuisenaire.

Fraser, M. (1996). *Ten mile day: And the building of the Transcontinental Railroad.* New York: Holt.

Friedman, A. (1994). *A cloak for the dreamer.* New York: Scholastic.

Frith, M. (2005). *Who was Thomas Alva Edison?* New York: Penguin Young Readers.

Fritz, J. (1996). *What's the big idea, Ben Franklin?* New York: Penguin Young Readers.

Fritz, J. (1999). *You want women to vote, Lizzie Stanton?* New York: Putnam Juvenile.

Froman, R. (1975). *Angles are as easy as pie.* New York: Crowell.

Fuqua, N. (2004). *First pets: Presidential best friends.* New York: Scholastic.

Gag, W. (1996). *Millions of cats.* New York: Penguin Putnam.

Gallant, R. (1991). *The constellations: How they came to be.* New York: Four Winds Press.

Garrison, J., & Tubesing, A. (1996). *A million visions of peace: Wisdom from the Friends of Old Turtle.* New York: Scholastic.

Gelman, R. (2000). *Rice is life.* New York: Holt.

Gibbons, G. (1989). *Monarch butterfly.* New York: Scholastic.

Gibbons, G. (1995). *Planet Earth/Inside out.* New York: Morrow.

Gibbons, G. (1996). *The reasons for the seasons.* New York: Holiday House.

Gibbons, G. (1997). *The moon book.* New York: Holiday House.

Gibbons, G. (1999). *Stargazers.* New York: Holiday House.

Gibbons, G. (2004). *Mummies, pyramids, and pharaohs: A book about ancient Egypt.* New York: Little, Brown.

Gibbons, G. (2005). *Planets.* New York: Holiday House.

Gibbons, G. (2007). *The vegetables we eat.* New York: Holiday House.

Gifford, S. (2003). *Piece = part = portion.* Berkeley, CA: Tricycle Press.

Goldman, D. (2004). *Presidential losers.* Minneapolis: Lerner.

Goldsmith, M. (2001). *Galileo Galilei* (Scientists who made history series). New York: Raintree Steck-Vaughn.

Gordon, P., & Snow, R. (2004). *Kids learn America! Bringing geography to life with people, places & history.* Charlotte, VT: Williamson.

Grandfield, L. (2003). *America votes: How our president is elected.* Tonawanda, NY: Kids Can Press.

Greene, R. (1997). *When a line bends . . . A shape begins.* New York: Scholastic.

Grodin, E. (2004). *D is for democracy: A citizen's alphabet.* Chelsea, MI: Sleeping Bear Press.

Harper, C. (2001). *Imaginative inventions: The who, what, when, where, and why of roller skates, potato chips, marbles and pie (and more!).* Boston: Little, Brown.

Harris, N. (2004). *How big?* Oxfordshire, UK: Orpheus Books.

Higham, C. (2004). *Snowflakes for all seasons.* Layto, UT: Gibbs Smith.

Hirschmann, K. (2001). *Necco Sweethearts series: Math magic.* New York: Scholastic.

Hoban, T. (1986). *Shapes, shapes, shapes.* New York: Greenwillow Books.

Hoban, T. (2000). *Cubes, cones, cylinders, & spheres.* New York: Greenwillow Books.

Hoberman, M. (2000). *The seven silly eaters.* New York: Scholastic.

Hoose, P. (2001). *We were there, too! Young people in U.S. history.* New York: Farrar Straus Giroux.

Hoose, P. (2002). *It's our world, too!* New York: Farrar Straus Giroux.

Hulme, J. (2005). *Wild Fibonacci: Nature's secret code revealed.* Berkeley, CA: Tricycle Press.

Hutchins, P. (1986). *The doorbell rang.* New York: Greenwillow Books.

Jacobs, L. (1993). *Is somewhere always far away? Poems about places.* New York: Holt.

Jenkins, S. (1995). *Biggest, strongest, fastest.* Boston: Houghton Mifflin.

Jenkins, S. (1998). *Hottest, coldest, highest, deepest.* Boston: Houghton Mifflin.

Jenkins, S. (2004). *Actual size.* Boston: Houghton Mifflin.

Jenkins, S. (2005). *Prehistoric actual size.* Boston: Houghton Mifflin.

Jenkins, S. (2006). *Almost gone: The world's rarest animals.* New York: Scholastic.

Jenkins, S., & Page, R. (2003). *What do you do with a tail like this?* Boston: Houghton Mifflin.

Johnson, K., & O'Connor, J. (2002). *Henri Matisse: Drawing with scissors.* New York: Grosset & Dunlap.

Jolivet, J. (2002). *Zoo-ology.* Brookfield, CT: Roaring Brook Press.

Jolivet, J. (2005). *Almost everything.* Brookfield, CT: Roaring Brook Press.

Jonas, A. (1987). *Reflections.* New York: Greenwillow Books.

Keenan, S. (2004). *O, say can you see? America's symbols, landmarks, and important words.* New York: Scholastic.

Keller, L. (2002). *Scrambled states of America.* New York: Holt.

Kelley, T. (2002). *Pablo Picasso: Breaking all the rules* (Smart about art series). New York: Grosset & Dunlap.

Kerrod, R. (2002). *The book of constellations: Discover the secrets in the stars.* Hauppauge, NY: Barron's Educational Series.

Kincade, S. (1992). *Our time is now* (Young people changing the world). Upper Saddle River, NJ: Pearson Foundation.

Knowlton, J. (1985). *Maps and globes.* New York: HarperCollins.

Knowlton, J. (1988). *Geography from A to Z: A picture glossary.* New York: HarperCollins.

Kramer, S. (2004). *Who was Ferdinand Magellan?* (Who was . . . ? series). New York: Penguin Young Readers.

Krull, K. (2004). *A woman for president: The story of Victoria Woodhull.* New York: Walker Books for Young Readers.

Krupp, E. (1991). *Beyond the blue horizon: Myths and legends of the sun, moon, stars, and planets.* New York: HarperCollins.

Krupp, E., & Krupp, R. (1989). *The Big Dipper and you*. New York: Morrow.

Kupchella, R. (2004). *Girls can! Make it happen*. Golden Valley, MN: Tristan.

LaFontaine, B. (1998). *Great inventors and inventions* (100 things you should know about series). London: Dover.

Landau, E. (2003). *The president's work: A look at the executive branch* (How government works series). Minneapolis: Lerner.

Lasky, K. (1994). *The librarian who measured the earth*. Boston: Little, Brown.

Lasky, K. (1995). *The gates of the wind*. New York: Harcourt Children's Books.

Lay, K. (2004). *Crown me!* New York: Holiday House.

Leedy, L. (1997). *Measuring Penny*. New York: Holt.

Leedy, L. (2001). *The edible pyramid: Good eating everyday*. New York: Holiday House.

Leedy, L. (2003). *Mapping Penny's world*. New York: Holt.

Levy, D. (2003). *Stars and planets* (Discoveries series). New York: Barnes & Noble Books.

Lewis, B. (1992). *Kids with courage: True stories about young people making a difference*. Minneapolis: Free Spirit.

Lewis, B. (1998). *The kid's guide to social action: How to solve social problems you choose—and turn creative thinking into positive action*. Minneapolis: Free Spirit.

Lewis, J. (1998). *Doodle dandies: Poems that take shape*. New York: Aladdin.

Lewis, J. (2002). *A world of wonders: Geographic travels in verse and rhyme*. New York: Dial Books for Young Readers.

Liao, J. (2006). *The sound of colors: A journey of the imagination*. New York: Little, Brown.

Liatsos, S. (1999). *Poems to count on*. New York: Scholastic.

Linn, C. (1972). *Probability*. New York: Crowell.

Lionni, L. (1960). *Inch by inch*. New York: HarperCollins.

Ljungkvist, L. (2006). *Follow the line*. New York: Penguin.

Lomas Garza, C., Rohmer, H., Schecter, D., & Alarcon, F. X. (1999). *Magic windows/Ventanas mágicas*. San Francisco: Children's Book Press.

Losi, C. (1997). *The 512 ants on Sullivan Street*. New York: Scholastic.

Love, A., & Drake, J. (2004). *The kids' book of the night sky*. Tonawanda, NY: Kids Can Press.

Macaulay, D. (1982). *Pyramids*. Boston: Houghton Mifflin.

Maccarone, G. (1997). *Three pigs, one wolf, and seven magic shapes*. New York: Scholastic.

Mackey, L. (2004). *Money mama and the three little pigs*. Angoura Hills, CA: P4K.

Maestro, B. (1999). *The story of clocks and calendars*. New York: HarperCollins.

Maher, R. (2003). *Alice Yazzie's year*. Berkeley, CA: Tricycle Press.

Maltbie, P. (2005). *Picasso and Minou*. Watertown, MA: Charlesbridge.

Marsh, V. (1996). *Story puzzles: Tales in the tangram tradition*. Fort Atkinson, WI: Highsmith Press.

Martin, J. (1998). *Snowflake Bentley*. Boston: Houghton Mifflin.

Marzollo, J. (1994). *My first book of biographies: Great men and women every child should know*. New York: Scholastic.

Mason, A. (1994). *Leonardo da Vinci: An introduction to the artist's life and work* (Barron's famous artist series). London: Aladdin Books.

Mason, A. (1994). *Picasso: An introduction to the artist's life and work* (Barron's famous artist series). London: Aladdin Books.

Matthews, L. (1979). *Gator pie*. New York: Dodd, Mead.

Mayes, S. (2006). *Where does electricity come from?* Tulsa, OK: EDC.

McCallum, A. (2005). *Beanstalk: The measure of a giant*. Watertown, MA: Charlesbridge.

McCully, E. (1998). *The ballot box battle*. New York: Dragonfly Books.

McGovern, A. (1991). *If you sailed on the Mayflower in 1620*. New York: Scholastic.

The Metropolitan Museum of Art. (2004). *Museum 1 2 3*. New York: Little, Brown.

The Metropolitan Museum of Art. (2005). *Museum shapes*. New York: Little, Brown.

Micklethwait, L. (1993). *A child's book of art: Great pictures: First words*. New York: Dorling Kindersley.

Micklethwait, L. (1993). *I spy two eyes: Numbers in art*. New York: Greenwillow Books.

Micklethwait, L. (2004). *I spy shapes in art*. New York: Greenwillow Books.

Miles, M. (1985). *Annie and the old one*. Boston: Little, Brown.

Miller, D. (2003). *Arctic nights, arctic lights*. New York: Walker.

Milton, J. (1996). *Mummies* (All aboard reading series). New York: Grosset & Dunlap.

Mitton, J. (1998). *Zoo in the sky: A book of animal constellations*. Washington, DC: National Geographic Society.

Mitton, J. (2004). *Once upon a starry night: A book of constellations*. Washington, DC: National Geographic Society.

Morgan, R. (1999). *In the next three seconds*. New York: Puffin Books.

Morrissey, T. (2005). *My mom is a dragon*. San Francisco: ThingsAsian Press.

Moss, M. (2001). *Brave Harriet: The first woman to fly the English Channel*. San Diego: Silver Whistle.

Most, B. (1994). *How big were the dinosaurs?* Orlando, FL: Harcourt Brace.

Murphy, J. (2000). *Blizzard! The storm that changed America*. New York: Scholastic.

Murphy, S. (1996). *Give me half!* New York: HarperCollins.

Murphy, S. (1997). *Divide and ride*. New York: HarperCollins.

Murphy, S. (1998). *The penny pot*. New York: HarperCollins.

Murphy, S. (2000). *Let's fly a kite*. New York: HarperCollins.

Murphy, S. (2001). *Captain Invincible and the space shapes*. New York: HarperCollins.

Murphy, S. (2001). *Probably pistachio*. New York: HarperCollins.

Murphy, S. (2003). *Less than zero*. New York: HarperCollins.

Murphy, S. (2004). *Tally O'Malley*. New York: HarperCollins.

Myller, R. (1990). *How big is a foot?* New York: Dell Yearling.

Needham, K. (1993). *Why do people eat?* Tulsa, OK: EDC.

Neuschwander, C. (2003). *Sir Cumference and the sword in the cone: A Math Adventure*. Watertown, MA: Charlesbridge.

Neuschwander, C. (2005). *Mummy math: An adventure in geometry*. New York: Holt.

Nolan, H. (1995) *How much, how many, how far, how heavy, how long, how tall is 1000*. Tonawanda, NY: Kids Can Press.

O'Brien, P. (1999). *Gigantic! How big were the dinosaurs?* New York: Holt.

O'Neal, Z. (2001). *A long way to go: A story of women's right to vote* (Once upon America series). New York: Puffin Books.

Otto, C. (1996). *What color is camouflage?* New York: HarperCollins.

Oughton, J. (1996). *How the stars fell into the sky: A Navajo legend*. Boston: Houghton Mifflin.

Packard, E. (2000). *Big numbers: And pictures that show just how big they are!* Brookefield, CT: Millbrook Press.

Pallotta, J. (1999). *The Hershey's milk chocolate fractions book*. New York: Scholastic.

Pallotta, J. (2002). *Apple fractions*. New York: Scholastic.

Pallotta, J. (2003). *Hershey's kisses multiplication and division*. New York: Scholastic

Pallotta, J. (2006). *Snakes: Long, longer, longest*. New York: Scholastic.

Parker, S. (2005). *Electricity* (Eyewitness book series). New York: Dorling Kindersley.

Pearce, Q., & Fraser, M. (1991). *The stargazer's guide to the galaxy*. New York: RGA.

Pershing Accelerated School Students. (2002). *We dream of a world*. New York: Scholastic.

Pinczes, E. (1993). *One hundred hungry ants*. Boston: Houghton Mifflin.

Pinczes, E. (1995). *A remainder of one*. Boston: Houghton Mifflin.

Pinczes, E. (2001). *Inch worm and a half*. Boston: Houghton Mifflin.

Pluckrose, H. (1995). *Time*. New York: Scholastic.

Pomerantz, C. (1984). *The half birthday party*. New York: Clarion.

Prelutsky, J. (1984). *The new kid on the block*. New York: Scholastic.

Prelutsky, J. (1996). *A pizza the size of the sun*. New York: Scholastic.

Provensen, A. (1997). *The buck stops here: The president of the United States of America*. New York: Browndeer Press Paperbacks.

Rabe, T. (2001). *Oh, the things that you can do that are good for you! All about staying healthy*. New York: Random House.

Raboff, E. (1988). *Albrecht Durer*. New York: HarperCollins.

Reimer, L., & Reimer, W. (1995). *Mathematicians are people, too*. Palo Alto, CA: Dale Seymour.

Rey, H. A. (1980). *The stars: A new way to see them*. Boston: Houghton Mifflin.

Rey, H. A. (1982). *Find the constellations*. Boston: Houghton Mifflin.

Reynolds, P. (2003). *The dot*. Cambridge, MA: Candlewick Press.

Reynolds, P. (2004). *Ish*. Cambridge, MA: Candlewick Press.

Ridpath, I. (1988). *Star tales*. New York: Universe Books.

Ringgold, F. (1996). *Tar beach*. New York: Dragonfly Books.

Roca, N. (2002). *Boys and girls of the world: From one end to the other*. Hauppauge, NY: Barron's Educational Series.

Rockwell, A. (1998). *Our earth*. New York: Scholastic.

Rockwell, L. (1999). *Good enough to eat*. New York: Scholastic.

Roessel, M. (1993). *Kinaalda: A Navajo girl grows up*. Minneapolis: Lerner.

Roessel, M. (1995). *Songs from the loom: A Navajo girl learns to weave*. Minneapolis: Lerner.

Rosen, S. (1992). *How far is a star?* Minneapolis: Carolrhoda Books.

Ross, N. (1995). *Miro* (Famous artists series). Hauppauge, NY: Barron's Educational Series.

Royston, A. (2005). *Why do we need to eat?* Portsmouth, NH: Heinemann.

Roza, G. (2005). *An optical artist: Exploring patterns and symmetry*. New York: PowerKids Press.

Rubel, D. (1994). *Scholastic encyclopedia of the presidents and their times*. New York: Scholastic.

Ryan, P. (1999). *Amelia and Eleanor go for a ride*. New York: Scholastic.

Santella, A. (2003). *The Navajo* (True books: American Indian series). Chicago: Children's Press.

Sasaki, C. (2003). *The constellations: Stars and stories*. New York: Sterling.

Satterfield, K. (2005). *Benjamin Franklin: A man of many talents* (Time for kids series). New York: HarperCollins.

Saunders, H. (1988). *When are we ever gonna have to use this?* Palo Alto, CA: Dale Seymour.

Scarborough, K. (2001). *Pablo Picasso* (Artists in their times series). New York: Scholastic.

Schoberle, C. (1994). *Day lights, night lights*. New York: Simon & Schuster.

Schonberg, M. (2005). *I is for idea: An inventions alphabet*. Chelsea, MI: Sleeping Bear Press.

Schwartz, D. (1985). *How much is a million?* New York: Lothrop, Lee & Shepard.

Schwartz, D. (1989). *If you made a million*. New York: Lothrop, Lee & Shepard.

Schwartz, D. (1998). *G is for googol: A math alphabet book*. Berkeley, CA: Tricycle Press.

Schwartz, D. (1999). *If you hopped like a frog*. New York: Scholastic.

Schwartz, D. (1999). *On beyond a million.* New York: Random House.

Schwartz, D. (2003). *Millions to measure.* New York: HarperCollins.

Schwartz, D. (2005). *If dogs were dinosaurs.* New York: Scholastic.

Scieszka, J., & Smith, L. (1995). *Math curse.* New York: Penguin Books.

Scieszka, J., & Smith, L. (2004). *Science verse.* New York: Penguin Books.

Scieszka, J., & Smith, L. (2005). *Seen art?* New York: Viking Press.

Scillian, D. (2001). *A is for America: An American alphabet.* Chelsea, MI: Sleeping Bear Press.

Scillian, D. (2002). *One nation: America by the numbers.* Chelsea, MI: Sleeping Bear Press.

Scillian, D. (2003). *P is for passport.* Chelsea, MI: Sleeping Bear Press.

Sharmat, M. (1989). *Gregory, the terrible eater.* New York: Scholastic.

Shipton, J. (1999). *What If?* New York: Dial Books for Young Readers.

Silverstein, A., Silverstein, V., & Nunn, L. (2000). *Eat your vegetables! Drink your milk!* New York: Scholastic.

Silverstein, S. (1981). *A light in the attic.* New York: HarperCollins.

Silverstein, S. (1996). *Falling up.* New York: HarperCollins.

Silverstein, S. (2004). *Where the sidewalk ends.* New York: HarperCollins.

Simon, S. (2006). *Weather.* New York: HarperCollins.

Singer, M. (1991). *Nine o'clock lullaby.* New York: Scholastic.

Sipiera, P., & Sipiera, D. (1997). *Constellations.* Danbury, CT: Scholastic.

Sis, P. (1996). *Starry messenger.* New York: Farrar Straus Giroux.

Sis, P. (2000). *Madlenka.* New York: Scholastic.

Sis, P. (2004). *The train of states.* New York: Greenwillow Books.

Sitomer, M., & Sitomer, H. (1970). *What is symmetry?* New York: Crowell.

Smith, D. (2002). *If the world were a village: A book about the world's people.* Tonawanda, NY: Kids Can Press.

Smith, D. (2003). *Mapping the world by heart.* Watertown, MA: Snyder.

Smith, R., & Smith, M. (2005). *N is for our nation's capital: A Washington, DC, alphabet* (Discover America state by state alphabet series). Chelsea, MI: Sleeping Bear Press.

Sobel, S. (1999). *How elections work.* Hauppauge, NY: Barron's Educational Series.

Sobel, S. (1999). *How the U.S. government works.* Hauppauge, NY: Barron's Educational Series.

Spier, P. (2002). *People.* New York: Doubleday.

Srivastava, J. (1975). *Averages.* New York: Crowell.

St. George, J. (2002). *So you want to be an inventor?* New York: Penguin.

St. George, J. (2005). *So you want to be an explorer?* New York: Penguin.

Stephens, P. (2001). *Tessellations: The history and making of symmetrical design.* Aspen, CO: Crystal.

Stott, C. (2003). *I wonder why stars twinkle (and other questions about space).* New York: Kingfisher.

Sullivan, G. (1987) *Facts and fun about the presidents.* New York: Scholastic.

Supraner, R. (1997). *Weather* (I can read about series). New York: Scholastic.

Sutton, R. (2005). *Car* (Eyewitness books series). New York: Dorling Kindersley.

Sweeney, J. (1999). *Me and my place in space.* New York: Dragonfly Books.

Sweeney, J. (2001). *Me and the measure of things.* New York: Dragonfly Books.

Tang, G. (2003). *Math-terpieces: The art of problem solving.* New York: Scholastic.

Taylor, H. (1997). *Coyote places the stars.* New York: Aladdin.

Thimmesh, C. (2000). *Girls think of everything: Stories of ingenious inventions by women.* Boston: Houghton Mifflin.

Thimmesh, C. (2002). *The sky's the limit: Stories of discovery by women and girls.* Boston: Houghton Mifflin.

Thimmesh, C. (2004). *Madame President: The extraordinary, true, (and evolving) story of women in politics.* Boston: Houghton Mifflin.

Thompson, C. (1989). *Glow in the dark constellations: A field guide for young stargazers.* New York: Grosset & Dunlap.

Tompert, A. (1990). *Grandfather Tang's story: A tale told with tangrams.* New York: Dragonfly Books.

Turnbull, S. (2003). *Usborne beginners: Sun, moon and stars.* New York: Scholastic.

Turvey, P. (1994). *Inventions: Inventors and ingenious ideas* (Timelines series). London: Franklin Watts.

Twist, C. (2005). *Reptiles and amphibians dictionary: An A to Z of cold-blooded creatures.* New York: Andromeda Children's Books.

Vaughan, M. (1996). *The dancing dragon.* New York: Mondo.

Venezia, M. (1988). *Picasso* (Getting to know the world's greatest artists series). Chicago: Children's Press.

Venezia, M. (1989). *Da Vinci* (Getting to know the world's greatest artists series). Chicago: Children's Press.

Venezia, M. (1992). *Michelangelo* (Getting to know the world's greatest artists series). Chicago: Children's Press.

Venezia, M. (1993). *Georgia O'Keeffe* (Getting to know the world's greatest artists series). Chicago: Children's Press.

Venezia, M. (1997). *Henri Matisse* (Getting to know the world's greatest artists series). New York: Children's Press.

Venezia, M. (2001). *Roy Lichtenstein* (Getting to know the world's greatest artists series). New York: Children's Press.

Venezia, M. (2002). *Georges Seurat* (Getting to know the world's greatest artists series). New York: Children's Press.

Viorst, J. (1988). *Alexander, who used to be rich last Sunday.* New York: Aladdin Paperbacks.

Walker, L. (1994). *Roy Lichtenstein: The artist at work.* New York: Lodestar Books.

Waller, A. (1994). *Betsy Ross.* New York: Scholastic.

Walton, P. (2000). *The warlord's puzzle.* Gretna, LA: Pelican.

Wells, R. (1993). *Is a blue whale the biggest thing there is?* Morton Grove, IL: Whitman.

Wells, R. (1995). *What's smaller than a pygmy shrew?* Morton Grove, IL: Whitman.

Wells, R. (2000). *Can you count to a googol?* Morton Grove, IL: Whitman.

Wells, R. (2003). *How do you know what time it is?* Morton Grove, IL: Whitman.

Williams, R. (2001). *The coin counting book.* Watertown, MA: Charlesbridge.

Winter, J. (1998). *My name is Georgia.* Orlando, FL: Silver Whistle.

Wolfe, G. (2002). *Look! Zoom in on art.* New York: Oxford University Press.

Wood, R. (2003). *Great inventions* (Discoveries series). New York: Barnes & Noble Books.

Wulffson, D. (2001). *Kid who invented the trampoline: More surprising stories about inventions.* New York: Penguin Young Readers Group.

Wyatt, V. (2000). *Wacky plant cycles.* New York: Mondo.

Yolen, J. (1987). *The girl who loved the wind.* New York: HarperCollins.

Yolen, J. (1998). *The emperor and the kite.* New York: Putnam Books.

Zemach, M. (1993). *Three wishes: An old story.* New York: Farrar, Straus and Giroux.

Instructional Resources References

Recommended Book Series

100 Things You Should Know About Series (Barnes & Noble Books)

Artists in Their Times Series (Scholastic)

Barron's Famous Artist Series (Aladdin)

Childhood of Famous Americans Series (Aladdin)

Discover America State by State Alphabet Series (Sleeping Bear Press)

Discoveries Series (Barnes & Noble Books)

Don't Know Much About Series (HarperTrophy)

Eyewitness Books Series (Dorling Kindersley)

Eye Wonder Books Series (Dorling Kindersley)

Getting to Know the World's Greatest Artists Series (Children's Press)

Giants of Science Series (Penguin Young Readers)

History Maker Bio Series (Lerner)

How Government Works Series (Lerner)

Inventions That Shaped the World Series (Scholastic)

Inventor and Inventions Series (Benchmark Books)

Once Upon America Series (Puffin Books)

Scientists Who Made History Series (Raintree Steck-Vaughn)

Smart About Series (Grosset & Dunlap)

Smart About Art Series (Grosset & Dunlap)

Spend the Day In Series (Jossey-Bass)

Time for Kids Series (HarperCollins)

Timelines Series (Franklin Watts)

True Books: American Indian Series (Children's Press)

Who Was . . . ? Series (Penguin Young Readers)

Books

Aigner-Clark, J. (2004). *Baby Einstein: The ABCs of art*. New York: Hyperion Books for Children.

Aston, P. (2006). *Coloring book Kandinsky*. New York: Prestel.

Bando, I. (1995). *Geometry and fractions with tangrams*. Vernon Hills, IL: Learning Resources.

Bentley, W. (2000). *Snowflakes in photographs*. Mineola, NY: Dover Books.

Bentley, W., & Humphreys, W. (1962). *Snow crystals*. Mineola, NY: Dover Books.

Berger, M., & Berger, G. (1998). *Why don't haircuts hurt? Questions and answers about the human body*. New York: Scholastic.

Biesty, S. (2005). *Egypt in spectacular cross-section*. New York: Scholastic.

Bingham, C. & Lord, T. (2006). *Big book of transportation*. New York: Dorling Kindersley.

Brewer, D. (2004). *Inventions* (100 things you should know about series). New York: Barnes & Noble Books.

Brown, T. (1987). *Chinese New Year*. New York: Holt.

Burnie, D. (2000). *Light* (Eyewitness books series). New York: Dorling Kindersley.

Burnie, D. (2004). *Plant* (Eyewitness books series). London: Dorling Kindersley.

Casey, S. (2005). *Kids inventing! A handbook for young inventors*. San Francisco: Jossey-Bass.

Chan, H (2004). *Celebrating Chinese New Year: An activity book*. Cincinnati, OH: Asia for Kids.

Chartrand, M., Tirion, W., & Mechler, G. (1995). *National Audubon Society pocket guide to constellations of the northern skies*. New York: Knopf.

Cheney, L. (2005). *A time for freedom: What happened when in America*. New York: Simon & Schuster.

Conley, R. (2005). *The automobile* (Inventions that shaped the world series). New York: Scholastic.

Cribb, J. (2005). *Money* (Eyewitness books series). New York: Dorling Kindersley.

Dale Seymour Publications. (1991). *Tessellation winners: Escher-like original student art, the first contest.* Palo Alto, CA: Author.

Dale Seymour Publications. (1997). *Tessellation teaching masters.* Palo Alto, CA: Author.

D'Alusio, F. (1998). *Women in the material world.* San Francisco: Sierra Club Books.

Davis, K. (2004). *Don't know much about the 50 states* (Don't know much about series). New York: HarperTrophy.

Devrian Global Industries. (2006). *States activities book.* Union, NJ: Author.

Dickins, R. (2005). *The children's book of art: An introduction to famous paintings.* London: Usborne.

Dickinson, T. (1995). *Other worlds: A beginner's guide to planets and moons.* Tonawanda, NY: Firefly.

Dillon, S. (2003). *The Scholastic big book of holidays around the year.* New York: Scholastic.

Dineen, J. (1998). *Lift the lid on mummies: Unravel the mysteries of Egyptian tombs and make your own mummy!* (Lift the lid on series). Philadelphia: Running Press.

DK Publishing. (1998). *DK nature encyclopedia.* London: DK Children.

DK Publishing. (2005). *Food* (Eyewitness books series). New York: Author.

Driscoll, M. (2004). *A child's introduction to the night sky.* New York: Black Dog & Leventhal.

Egan, L. (1999). *Inventors and inventions.* New York: Scholastic.

Elfers, J., & Schuyt, M. (2000). *Tangrams: 1600 ancient Chinese puzzles.* New York: Barnes & Noble.

Escher, M. (2004). *M. C. Escher: The graphic work.* Hohenzollernring, Germany: Taschen.

Evans, J., & Skelton, T. (2001). *How to teach art to children.* Monterey, CA: Evan-Moor.

Farndon, J. (2002). *1000 facts on human body.* New York: Barnes & Noble Books.

Flack, J. (1989). *Inventing, inventions, inventing.* Portsmouth, NH: Libraries Unlimited.

Ford, B. E. (1990). *Tangrams: The magnificent seven piece puzzle.* Vallejo, CA: Tandora's Box Press.

Goodnow, J. (1994). *Math discoveries with tangrams.* Grand Rapids, MI: Ideal School Supply Company.

Gordon, P., & Snow, R. (2004). *Kids learn America! Bringing geography to life with people, places & history.* Charlotte, VT: Williamson.

Greenberg, D. (1999). *Funny & fabulous fraction stories.* New York: Scholastic.

Guerra, R. (2004). *The kite-making handbook.* Devon, UK: David & Charles.

Halpern, M. (2004). *Railroad fever: Building the Transcontinental Railroad 1830–1870.* Washington, DC: National Geographic Society.

Hare, T. (2005). *Animal fact file: Head-to-tail profiles of more than 90 mammals.* New York: Checkmark Books.

Harris, V. (1997). *Using multiethnic literature in the K–8 classroom.* Norwood, MA: Christopher-Gordon.

Hart, A., & Mantell, P. (1997). *Pyramids: 50 Hands-on activities to experience ancient Egypt.* Charlotte, VT: Williamson.

Hauser, J. (2004). *Little hands celebrate America: Learning about the USA through crafts & activities.* Charlotte, VT: Williamson.

Heap, C. (1996). *Big book of trains.* New York: Dorling Kindersley.

Heifetz, M., & Tirion, W. (2004). *A walk through the heavens: A guide to stars and constellations and their legends.* New York: Cambridge University Press.

Higham, C. (2004). *Snowflakes for all seasons.* Layto, UT: Gibbs Smith.

Holland, S. (2001). *Space* (Eye wonder series). New York: Dorling Kindersley.

Honan, L. (1999). *Spend the day in ancient Egypt: Projects and activities that bring the past to life* (Spend the day in series). New York: Jossey-Bass.

Honqxun, W. (1989). *Chinese kites: Traditional Chinese arts and culture.* San Francisco: China Books.

Hunt, L. (1971). *25 kites that fly*. Mineola, NY: Dover.

Jeffett, W., Miro, J., & Coyle, L. (2002). *The shape of color: Joan Miro's painted sculptures*. London: Scala.

Jones, L. (2003). *Kids around the world celebrate! The best feasts and festivals from many lands* (Kids around the world series). New York: Jossey-Bass.

Kassinger, R. (2002). *Build a better mousetrap: Make classic inventions, discover your problem-solving genius, and take the inventor's challenge*. Hoboken, NJ: Wiley.

Keilstrup, M. (1997). *Elegant designs for paper cutting*. Mineola, NY: Dover Books.

Kindersley, A., & Kindersley, B. (1997). *Children just like me! Celebrations*. New York: DK Children.

Kohl, M., & Solga, K. (1996). *Discovering great artists: Hands-on art for children in the styles of the great masters*. Bellingham, WA: Bright Ring.

Krull, K. (1993). *Lives of the musicians: Good times, bad times (and what the neighbors thought)*. San Diego: Harcourt.

Krull, K. (1995). *Lives of the artists: Masterpieces, messes*. San Diego: Harcourt Brace.

Lauw, D. (2001). *Electricity*. New York: Crabtree.

Levine, S., & Johnstone, L. (2003). *First science experiments: Wonderful weather*. New York: Sterling.

Levine, S., & Johnstone, L. (2005). *First science experiments: Nature, senses, weather, & machines*. New York: Sterling.

Levitt, I., & Marshall, R. (1992). *Star maps for beginners: 50th anniversary edition*. New York: Fireside.

Lewis, B. (1995). *The kid's guide to service projects: Over 500 service ideas for young people who want to make a difference*. Minneapolis: Free Spirit.

Lomas Garza, C. (1999). *Making magic windows: Creating papel picado/cut-paper art*. San Francisco: Children's Book Press.

Long, L. (2001). *Fabulous fractions: Games and activities that make math easy and fun*. Hoboken, NJ: Wiley.

Mack, L. (2004). *Weather* (Eye wonder series). New York: Dorling Kindersley.

Malet, R. (2003). *Joan Miro*. New York: Rizzoli.

Martschinke, J. (1997). *Tangrammables: A tangram activity book*. Vernon Hills, IL: Learning Resources.

Matthews, R. (2005). *Explorers* (Eyewitness books series). New York: Dorling Kindersley.

Menzel, P. (1995). *Material world: A global family portrait*. San Francisco: Sierra Club Books.

Micklethwait, L. (1993). *A child's book of art: Great pictures: First words*. New York: Dorling Kindersley.

Mink, J. (2000). *Miro*. Hohenzollernring, Germany: Taschen.

Mobley, C. (1994). *Navajo rugs and blankets: A coloring book*. Tucson, AZ: Rio Nuevo.

Mogard, S. (1992). *Windows to tangrams: Reproducible activities*. Covina, CA: American Teaching Aids.

Morrissey, T. (2006). *Hiss! Pop! Boom! Celebrating Chinese New Year*. San Francisco: ThingsAsian Press.

Murphy, F. (2002). *Our country*. New York: Scholastic Professional Books.

National Geographic Society. (2000). *National Geographic animal encyclopedia*. Hanover, PA: National Geographic Children's Books.

Oxlade, C. (1999). *Ships: A fascinating fact file and learn-it-yourself book* (Investigations series). London: Anness Publishing, Ltd.

Parsons, J. (2000). *Children's illustrated encyclopedia*. London: DK Children.

Pasachoff, J., & Percy, J. (Eds.). (2005). *Teaching and learning astronomy: Effective strategies for educators worldwide*. New York: Cambridge University Press.

Pelham, D. (2000). *Kites*. New York: Overlook TP.

Platt, R. (2003). *Hieroglyphics: The secrets of ancient Egyptian writing to unlock and discover* (Treasure chests series). Philadelphia, PA: Running Press Kids.

Press, J. (2001). *Around the world art & activities: Visiting the 7 continents through craft fun*. Charlotte, VT: Williamson.

Read, R. (1965). *Tangrams: 330 puzzles*. Mineola, NY: Dover.

Reed, B. L. (1987). *Easy-to-make decorative paper snowflakes.* Mineola, NY: Dover.

Renshaw, A., & Ruggi, G. (2005*). The art book for children.* New York: Phaidon Press.

Ryan, P. (1989). *Explorers and mapmakers.* New York: Lodestar Books.

Saunders, H. (1988). *When are we ever gonna have to use this?* Palo Alto, CA: Dale Seymour.

Schlosser, E., & Wilson, C. (2006). *Chew on this: Everything you don't want to know about fast food.* Boston: Houghton Mifflin.

Schwartz, D. (2001). *Q is for quark: A science alphabet.* Berkeley, CA: Ten Speed Press.

Scieszka, J., & Smith, L. (2005). *Seen art?* New York: Viking Press.

Shattschneider, D. (2005). *M. C. Escher: Visions of symmetry.* Petaluma, CA: Pomegranate.

Shattschneider, D., & Walker, W. (2005). *M. C. Escher kaleidocycles.* New York: Abrams.

Simmonds, N., Swartz, L., & Children's Museum, Boston. (2002). *Moonbeams, dumplings and dragon boats: A treasury of Chinese holiday tales, activities & recipes.* Fairbanks, AK: Gulliver Books.

Simon, S. (1992). *Our solar system, vol. 1.* New York: HarperCollins.

Simon, S. (1995). *The solar system: Facts and exploration.* New York: Holt.

Sipiera, P. (1991). *Globes* (A new true book series). Chicago: Children's Press.

Slapin, B., & Seale, D. (1992). *Through Indian eyes: The native experience in books for children.* Philadelphia: New Society Publishers.

Slocum, J., Botermans, J., Gebhardt, D., Ma, M., Ma, X., Raizer, H., Sonneveld, D., van Splunteren, C. (2003). *The tangram book.* New York: Sterling.

Smith, R. (1999). *DK art school: An introduction to perspective.* New York: DK Adult.

Sobel, D. (1995). *Longitude: The true story of a lone genius who solved the greatest scientific problem of his time.* New York: Walker.

Spilsbury, L. (2002). *Plant parts* (Life of plants series). Portsmouth, NH: Heinemann.

Stillinger, D. (2003). *Battery science: Make widgets that work and gadgets that go.* Palo Alto, CA: Klutz.

Taylor, B. (1993). *Maps and mapping* (Young discoveries series). New York: Kingfisher.

Twist, C. (2004). *Our solar system: A first introduction to space and the planets.* Hauppauge, NY: Barron's Educational Series.

Twist, C. (2005). *Reptiles and amphibians dictionary: An A to Z of cold-blooded creatures.* New York: Scholastic.

Unwin, M. (1993). *Science with plants* (Science activities series). Tulsa, OK: EDC.

VanCleave, J. (2004). *Scientists through the ages.* Hoboken, NJ: Wiley.

VanCleave, J. (2006). *Energy for every kid.* Hoboken, NJ: Wiley.

Ward, R. (2004). K–8 preservice teachers' journey into the global village: Exploring real-world data using children's literature and technology. *Arizona Reading Journal, 31*(1), 43–47.

Wilkinson, P. (1995). *Transportation* (Ideas that changed the world series). New York: Chelsea House.

Williams, D. (1995). *Teaching mathematics through children's art.* Portsmouth, NH: Heinemann.

Research References

Arhar, J. (1997). The effects of interdisciplinary teaming on students and teachers. In J. L. Irvin (Ed.), *What current research says to the middle level practitioner* (pp. 49–56). Columbus, OH: National Middle School Association.

Avery, C., & Avery, K. (2001). Kids teaching kids. *Journal of Adolescent & Adult Literacy, 44*(5), 434–435.

Bailey, L. (2000). Integrated curriculum: What parents tell us about their children's experience. *The Educational Forum, 64*(3), 236–242.

Basista, B., & Mathews, S. (2002). Integrated science and mathematics professional development programs. *School Science and Mathematics, 102*(7), 359–370.

Beane, J. (1993). *The middle school curriculum: From rhetoric to reality* (2nd ed.). Columbus, OH: National Middle School Association.

Beane, J. (1995). Curriculum integration and the disciplines of knowledge. *Phi Delta Kappan, 76*(8), 616–622.

Beane, J. (1997). *Curriculum integration: Designing the core of democratic education.* New York: Teachers College Press.

Bickley-Green, C. (1995). Math and art curriculum integration: A post-modern foundation. *Studies in Art Education, 37*(1), 6–18.

Bransford, J., Catterall, J., Deasy, R., Goren, P., Harman, A., Herbert, D., Levine, F., Seidel, S., & Sroufe, G. (2004). *The arts and education: New opportunities for research.* Washington, DC: Arts Education Partnership.

Bruner, J. (1977). *The process of education.* Cambridge, MA: Harvard University Press.

Burns, M. (1995). *Math and literature (K–3), vol. 1.* Sausalito, CA: Math Solutions.

Burns, M., & Sheffield, S. (2004). *Math and literature.* Sausalito, CA: Math Solutions.

Butzow, C., & Butzow, J. (2006). *The world of work through children's literature: An integrated approach.* Greenwood Village, CO: Teacher Ideas Press.

Capraro, R. M., & Capraro, M. M. (2006). Are you really going to read us a story? Learning geometry through children's mathematics literature. *Reading Psychology, 27*(1), 21–36.

Carr, K., Buchanan, D., Wentz, J., Weiss, M., & Brant, K. (2001). Not just for the primary grades: A bibliography of picture books for secondary content teachers. *Journal of Adolescent & Adult Literacy, 45*(2), 146–153.

Caskey, M. (2001). A lingering question for middle school: What is the fate of integrated curriculum? *Childhood Education 78*(2), 97–99.

Caskey, M. M., & Johnston, J. H. (1996). Hard work ahead: Authentic curriculum under construction. *Schools in the Middle, 6*(2), 11–18.

Cobb, P. (2000). The importance of a situated view of learning to the design of research and instruction. In J. Boaler (Ed.), *Multiple perspectives on mathematics teaching and learning.* Westport, CT: Greenwood.

Cornett, C. (2003). *Creating meaning through literature and the arts.* Upper Saddle River, NJ: Merrill/Prentice-Hall.

Davies, M. A. (1992). Are interdisciplinary units worthwhile? Ask students. In J. Lounsbury (Ed.), *Connecting the curriculum through interdisciplinary instruction.* Columbus, OH: National Middle School Association.

Deasy, R. J. (Ed.). (2002). *Critical links: Learning in the arts and student academic and social development.* Washington, DC: Arts Education Partnership.

Dewey, J. (1924). *Democracy and education: An introduction to the philosophy of education.* New York: Macmillan.

Dewey, J. (1933). *How we think.* Chicago: Regnery.

Donoghue, M. (2001). *Using literature activities to teach content areas to emergent readers.* Needham Heights, MA: Allyn & Bacon.

Drake, S. (1998). *Creating integrated curriculum: Proven ways to increase student learning.* Thousand Oaks, CA: Corwin Press.

Drake, S., & Burns, R. (2004). *Meeting standards through integrated curriculum.* Alexandria, VA: Association for Supervision and Curriculum Development.

Draper, R. (2002). School mathematics reform, constructivism, and literacy: A case for literacy instruction in the reform-oriented math classroom. *Journal of Adolescent & Adult Literacy, 45*(6), 520–529.

Efland, A. (2002). *Art and cognition: Integrating the visual arts in the curriculum.* New York: Teachers College Press.

Eisner, E. (1998). Does experience in the arts boost academic achievement? *Arts Education, 51*(1), 5–15.

Eisner, E. (2004). *The arts and the creation of mind.* New Haven, CT: Yale University Press.

Fiske, E. B. (Ed.). (1999). *Champions of change: The impact of the arts on learning.* Washington, DC: Arts Education Partnership.

Fredericks, A. (1991). *Social studies through children's literature: An integrated approach.* Greenwood Village, CO: Teacher Ideas Press.

Fredericks, A. (2000). *More social studies through children's literature: An integrated approach.* Greenwood Village, CO: Teacher Ideas Press.

Gallavan, N. (2001). Four lessons that integrate math and social studies. *Social Studies and the Young Learner, 13*(3), 25–28.

Gardner, H., (1997). A primer of multiple intelligences. *NEA Today, 15*(7), 17.

Gelineau, R. (2003). *Integrating arts across the elementary school curriculum.* Belmont, CA: Thomson Wadsworth.

Hellwig, S. Monroe, E. E., & Jacobs, J. S. (2000). Making informed choices: Selecting children's trade books for mathematics instruction. *Teaching Children Mathematics, 7,* 138–143.

Howey, K. (1996). Designing coherent and effective teacher education programs. In J. Sikula, T. J. Buttery, & E. Guyton (Eds.), *Handbook of research on teacher education* (2nd ed., pp. 143–170). New York: Simon & Schuster.

Hunsader, P. (2004). Mathematics trade books: Establishing their value and assessing their quality. *The Reading Teacher, 7*(57), 618–629.

International Reading Association (IRA) (2006). Excellent reading teachers: A position statement of the International Reading Association. In R. D. Robinson (Ed.), *Issues and Innovations in Literacy Education* (pp. 19–24). Newark, DE: Author.

Jacobs, H. (1989). The interdisciplinary concept model: A step-by-step approach for developing integrated units of study. In H. H. Jacobs (Ed.), *Interdisciplinary curriculum: Design and implementation* (pp. 53–65). Alexandria, VA: Association for Supervision and Curriculum Development.

Jensen, E. (2001). *Arts with the brain in mind.* Alexandria, VA: Association for Supervision and Curriculum Development.

Johnson, N., & Giorgis, C. (2001). Interacting with the curriculum. *The Reading Teacher, 55*(2), 204–213.

Kaser, S. (2001). Searching the heavens with children's literature: A design for teaching science. *Language Arts, 78*(4), 348–356.

Kim, M., Andrews, R., & Carr, D. (2004). Traditional versus integrated preservice teacher education curriculum. *Journal of Teacher Education, 55*(4), 341–356.

Kleiman, G. (1991). Mathematics across the curriculum. *Educational Leadership, 49*(2), 48–51.

Leitze, A. R. (1997). Connecting process problem solving to children's literature. *Teaching Children Mathematics, 3,* 398–405.

Leu, D. J., Castek, J., Henry, L. A., Coiro, J., & McMullan, M. (2004). The lessons that children teach us: Integrating children's literature and the new literacies of the internet. *The Reading Teacher, 57*(5), 496–503.

MacGregor, M., & Price, E. (1999). An exploration of aspects of language proficiency and algebra learning. *Journal for Research in Mathematics Education, 30,* 449–467.

Martinez, M., & McGee, L. (2000). Children's literature and reading instruction: Past, present, and future. *Reading Research Quarterly, 35*(1), 54–169.

McCoy, M. (2003, Spring/Summer). Language, math, social studies, and...worms? *Integrating the Early Childhood Curriculum, 2,* 3–8.

McDonald, N., & Fisher, D. (2006). *Teaching literacy through the arts.* New York: Guilford Press.

Meinbach, A., Fredericks, A., & Rothlein, L. (2000). *The complete guide to thematic units: Creating the integrated curriculum.* Norwood, MA: Christopher Gordon.

Monroe, E., & Livingston, N. (2002). It figures: Language and mathematics add up through children's literature. *The Dragon Lode, 20*(2), 37–41.

Moss, B. (2003). *Exploring the literature of fact: Children's nonfiction trade books in the elementary classroom.* New York: Guilford Press.

Moyer, P. (2000). Communicating mathematically: Children's literature as a natural connection. *The Reading Teacher, 54,* 246–255.

Muller, D., & Ward, R. (2007). Art and algebra? Middle school students discover algebra in Calder mobiles. *Mathematics School, 36*(3), 15–21.

Music Educators National Conference (MENC). (1994). *National standards for arts education.* Reston, VA: Author.

National Association for Core Curriculum. (2000). *A bibliography of research on the effectiveness of block-time, core, and interdisciplinary team teaching programs.* Kent, OH: Author.

National Council for the Social Studies (NCSS). (1994). *Curriculum standards for the social studies.* Silver Spring, MD: Author.

National Council of Teachers of English (NCTE) and International Reading Association (IRA). (1996). *Standards for the English language arts.* Urbana, IL: NCTE.

National Council of Teachers of Mathematics (NCTM). (1989). *Curriculum and evaluation standards for school mathematics.* Reston, VA: Author.

National Council of Teachers of Mathematics (NCTM). (2000). *Principles and standards for school mathematics.* Reston, VA: Author.

National Middle School Association (NMSA). (1995). *This we believe: Developmentally responsive middle level schools.* Columbus, OH: Author.

National Research Council (NRC). (1996). *National science education standards.* Washington, DC: National Academy Press.

Perkins, D. (1989). Selecting fertile themes for integrated learning. In H. H. Jacobs (Ed.), *Interdisciplinary curriculum: Design and implementation* (pp. 67–76). Alexandria, VA: Association for Supervision and Curriculum Development.

Phillips, P., & Bickley-Green, C. (1998). Integrating art and mathematics. *Principal, 77*(4), 46–49.

Putnam, R., & Borko, H. (2000). What do new views of knowledge and thinking have to say about research on teacher learning? *Educational Researcher, 29*(1), 4–15.

Rose, M. (2000). Lessons: Social Studies/Math Millennium mastery. *Instructor, 109*(5), 14.

Roth, W., & McGinn, M. (1998). Knowing, researching, and reporting science education: Lessons from science and technology studies. *Journal of Research in Science Teaching, 35*(2), 213–235.

Schiro, M. (1997). *Integrating children's literature and mathematics in the classroom: Children as meaning makers, problem solvers, and literary critics.* New York: Teachers College Press.

Schwartz, S., & Pollishuke, M. (2005). Planning an integrated curriculum. In K. Revington (Ed.), *Creating the dynamic classroom: A handbook for teachers* (pp. 44–69). Toronto: Pearson Education Canada.

Scripp, L. (2002). An overview of research on music and learning. In R. J. Deasy (Ed.), *Critical links: Learning in the arts and student academic and social development.* Washington, DC: Arts Education Partnership.

Thompson, D., & Holyoke, K. (2000, Summer). Using children's literature to link mathematics and social studies: A multicultural exploration with bread. *Trends & Issues: The Publication of the Florida Council for the Social Studies, 12,* 22–24.

Vars, G. (1996). Effects of interdisciplinary curriculum and instruction. In P. S. Hlebowitsh &

W. G. Wraga (Eds.), *Annual review of research for school leaders* (pp. 147–164). Reston, VA: National Association of Secondary School Principals and Scholastic Publishing.

Vars, G. (1997). Effects of integrative curriculum and instruction. In J. E. Irvin (Ed.), *What current research says to the middle level practitioner* (pp. 179–186). Columbus, OH: National Middle School Association.

Vars, G., & Beane, J. (2000). Integrative curriculum in a standards-based world. ERIC Digest. (ERIC Document Reproduction Service No. ED 441618) [Online]. Available: www.ed.gov/databases/ERIC_Digests/ ed441618.html

Walling, D. (2005). *Visual knowing: Connecting art and ideas across the curriculum.* Thousand Oaks, CA: Corwin Press.

Ward, R. (2003). How much is a billion? A lot more than you think! *Arizona Reading Journal, 30*(1), 27–29.

Ward, R. (2004a). K–8 preservice teachers author a mathematical piece of children's literature. *The California Reader, 38*(1), 24–30.

Ward, R. (2004b). K–8 preservice teachers' journey into the global village: Exploring real-world data using children's literature and technology. *Arizona Reading Journal, 31*(1), 43–47.

Ward, R. (2004c). Looking for math in all the right places. *The California Reader, 38*(2), 58–65.

Ward, R. (2005). Using children's literature to inspire K–8 preservice teachers' future mathematics pedagogy. *The Reading Teacher, 59*(2), 132–143.

Ward, R. (2006a, Spring). Modeling effective pedagogical strategies for teaching mathematics. *The Charter Schools Resource Journal,* 1–9.

Ward, R. (2006b, January). One if by land; *three* if by sea? *Mathematics Teaching, 194,* 20–21.

Ward, R., & Muller, D. (2006, September). Algebra and art. *Mathematics Teaching, 198,* 22–26.

Watts, S. (2004, Summer). Arts-infused summer school. *New Horizons for Learning Online Journal, 10*(3), Retrieved March 12, 2007 from http://www.newhorizons.org/strategies/arts/watts2.htm

Whitin, D., & Whitin, P. (1996). Fostering metaphorical thinking through children's literature. In P. C. Elliott (Ed.), *Communication in mathematics K–12 and beyond, 1996 yearbook of the National Council of Teachers of Mathematics* (pp. 60–65). Reston, VA: National Council of Teachers of Mathematics.

Whitin, D., & Whitin, P. (2004). *New visions for linking literature and mathematics.* Urbana, IL: National Council of Teachers of English.

Whitin, D., & Wilde, S. (1992). *Read any good math lately?* Portsmouth, NH: Heinemann.

Whitin, D., & Wilde, S. (1995). *It's the story that counts.* Portsmouth, NH: Heinemann.

Wortham, S. (1996). Bringing it all together. In S. C. Wortham (Ed.), *The integrated classroom: The assessment-curriculum link in early childhood education* (pp. 326–346). Englewood Cliffs, NJ: Prentice-Hall.

Young, J. (2001). Why are we reading a book during math time? How mathematics and literature relate. *The Dragon Lode, 19*(2), 13–18.

Appendix
Assessment Tools and Rubrics

As described in the introduction to this book, this appendix includes several assessment tools and rubrics (see below) that a teacher might employ as a means to better assess students as they engage in the literature-based activities. Other helpful assessment resources are included in the "Assessment Resources References" section.

Observation Log (to observe students on a rolling basis engaged in an individual or group activity) p. 214

Observation Log (to observe students working individually or in a group) p. 215

Observation Log (to observe students working in a group) p. 216

Analytic Scoring Scale (to assess students working individually or in a group) p. 217

Inventory of Student's Mathematical Disposition (to assess a student's mathematical disposition working individually) p. 218

Mathematical Disposition Checklist (to assess a student's mathematical disposition working in a group) p. 219

Observation Log (to be completed by students working in a group activity) p. 220

Group Assessment (to be completed by students working in a group activity) p. 221

Collaborative Report (to be completed by both the student and teacher) p. 222

Sample Writing Prompts (to assess students' mathematical thinking and learning experiences) p. 223

Observation Log

Name: _____

Date	Activity	Observed Behavior

Comments:

Observation Log

Name: _____

Activity: _____

Date: _____

Objectives or Goals	Observed Behavior	Comments

Observation Log

Name: _____

Date	Activity	Participation in Tasks 0: Little or none 1: Engaged 2: Fully engaged	Participation in Discussions 0: Little or none 1: Engaged 2: Fully engaged	Collaboration with Team 0: Little or none 1: Average 2: Above average	Comments

Analytic Scoring Scale

Understanding the problem

0: Complete misunderstanding of the problem

1: Part of the problem misunderstood or misinterpreted

2: Complete understanding of the problem

Planning a solution

0: No attempt, or totally inappropriate plan

1: Partially correct plan based on part of the problem being interpreted correctly

2: Plan could have led to a correct solution if implemented properly

Getting an answer

0: No answer, or wrong answer based on an inappropriate plan

1: Copying error; computational error; partial answer for a problem with multiple answers

2: Correct answer and correct label for the answer

(Source: Charles, Lester, & O'Daffer, 1987)

Inventory of Student's Mathematical Disposition

Name: _____

	Date	Comments
Confident in using mathematics		
Flexible in doing mathematics		
Perseveres at mathematical tasks		
Shows curiosity in doing mathematics		
Reflects on own thinking		
Values applications of mathematics		
Appreciates role of mathematics		

(Derived from Stenmark, 1991, p. 34)

Mathematical Disposition Checklist

	Student 1	Student 2	Student 3	Student 4
Confidence • Initiates questions • Is sure answers will be found • Helps others with problems • Other:				
Flexibility • Solves problems in more than one way • Changes opinion when given a convincing argument • Other:				
Perseverance				
Curiosity				
Reflective				
Appreciation for mathematics				

(Derived from Stenmark, 1991, p. 34)

Observation Log

Group members: _____

Activity title: _____

Name	Assigned Task	Task Completed? (Y or N)	Comments

Group Assessment

Group members: _____

Activity title: _____

Did your group . . .	☺	☺	☹
Listen			
Talk about the Task			
Cooperate			
Finish the Task			

What went well? _____

_____

_____

What would you do differently? _____

_____

_____

(Derived from Stenmark, 1991, p. 34)

Collaborative Report

Student Name: _____ Date: _____

Teacher Name: _____ Date: _____

Scale: 2 – Mastered fully   1 – Partial mastery   0 – Did not master

Criterion or Task	Student Rating	Teacher Rating

Student's comments: _____

_____

Teacher's comments: _____

_____

Sample Writing Prompts

- In your own words, explain the meaning of . . .

- The most important thing I learned in math class today (or this week) is . . .

- The most important thing to understand about *polygons* is . . .
  (*Note:* change *polygons* to the concept explored)

- I discovered that . . .

- Explain your reasoning about . . .

- I know my solution is correct because . . .

- I feel confident about my solution because . . .

- I am still uncertain about . . .

- Describe any instances during which you became stuck and how you became "unstuck" while solving the problem.

- Describe a real-world experience/connection to the mathematical concept you learned about today.

- Write a letter to a classmate who did not attend class today so that he or she will understand what you learned about.

- Draw a picture or diagram showing how the concepts you learned about today are connected.

(Derived from Stenmark, 1991, p. 34)

Index